European Regulation of Medical Devices and Pharmaceuticals

Nupur Chowdhury

European Regulation of Medical Devices and Pharmaceuticals

Regulatee Expectations of Legal Certainty

Springer

Nupur Chowdhury
Department of Public Administration
School of Management and Governance
University of Twente
Enschede
The Netherlands

Previous versions of Chapters 2, 5 and 8 have been published in the following journals: Chowdhury/Wessel, 'Conceptualizing Multilevel Regulation in the EU: A Legal Translation of Multilevel Governance?' (2012) 18 European Law Journal 335–357; Chowdhury, 'Common Market but divergent regulatory practices: Exploring European regulation and the effect on regulatory uncertainty in the marketing authorization of medical products', (2013) 35 Journal of European Integration, 635–652.; Chowdhury, 'Limits to the legal deliberation of science questions: A case study of borderline medical products in Europe', (2012) 14 Pharmaceuticals Policy and Law 157–175.

ISBN 978-3-319-35321-0 ISBN 978-3-319-04594-8 (eBook)
DOI 10.1007/978-3-319-04594-8
Springer Cham Heidelberg New York Dordrecht London

Softcover reprint of the hardcover 1st edition 2014

Printed on acid-free paper

Springer is part of Springer Science+Business Media (www.springer.com)

Summary

One of the primary functions of law is to ensure that the legal structure governing all social relations is predictable, coherent, consistent, and applicable. All these characteristics of law taken together are referred to as legal certainty. In traditional approaches to legal certainty, law is regarded as a hierarchic system of rules characterized by stability, clarity, uniformity, calculable enforcement, publicity, and predictability. However, the current reality is that national legal systems no longer operate in isolation, but within a multilevel legal order, wherein norms created at both the international and the regional level are directly applicable to national legal systems. Also norm creation is no longer the exclusive prerogative of public officials of the state: private actors have an increasing influence on norm creation as well. Social scientists have referred to this phenomenon of interacting and overlapping competences as multilevel governance. Only recently have legal scholars focused attention on the increasing interconnectedness (and therefore the concomitant loss of primacy of national legal orders) between the global, European, and national regulatory spheres through the concept of multilevel regulation.

In this project I use multilevel regulation as a term to characterize a regulatory space in which the process of rule making, rule application, and rule adjudication (regulatory life cycle) is dispersed across more than one administrative or territorial level amongst several different actors, both public and private. I draw on the concept of a regulatory space, using it as a framing device to differentiate between specific aspects of policy fields. The relationship between actors in such a space is non-hierarchical. Lack of central ordering of the regulatory life cycle within this regulatory space is the most important feature of such a space.

The implications of multilevel regulation for legal certainty have attracted limited attention from scholars. The demand for legal certainty in regulatory practice is still a puzzle. I explore the idea of legal certainty in terms of perception and expectations of regulatees in the context of medical products. By medical products I mean pharmaceuticals and medical devices which can be differentiated as two regulatory spaces and therefore form two case studies. As an exploratory project, this book is necessarily stepping into new territory in terms of investigating legal certainty first in terms of regulatee perceptions and expectations and second, because it studies this in the context of multilevel regulation.

Acknowledgments

This book is based on the Ph.D. thesis that was developed at the Law and Regulation Group, Department of Public Administration, School of Management and Governance, University of Twente and defended on September 6, 2013. First I wish to thank both my promoters Barbel Dorbeck-Jung and Ramses Wessel. I am honored and grateful to have had you both to guide me in this journey. Barbel, you have been extremely patient, caring, and always helpful in providing me with complete access to you for discussions on any matter. I appreciate both Bernard's and your hospitality in welcoming me to your home and generally making me feel welcome in the faculty. I am also happy that I got to develop my skills in empirical methodology primarily due to your encouragement. Ramses, thank you for your support and your critical comments on the book—they have contributed significantly in shaping my ideas. I also thoroughly enjoyed the opportunity to work with you on a critical theoretical aspect of the book.

I would also like to thank all my teachers, Mrs. Samuels (who unfortunately has left us but continues to inspire us), Miss K. Avari and Miss Ahmed from Pratt Memorial School; and Prof. Rina Kashyap and Prof. Nivedita Menon from Lady Shri Ram College. I also wish to thank Prof. M.P. Singh for always being there to encourage and motivate us to be good human beings first and then legal academics.

My time at the faculty would not have been half as much fun, without the company of Sabine Hoogstad, Martin Holterman, Evisa Kica, Maurits Sanders, and Aline Reichow. I reached Enschede by train on 28 February 2009 and did not know anybody in this city. But I leave with the gift of friendship and wonderful memories. I am also indebted to Ria and Manon for providing invaluable help on matters that were even beyond their call of duty. I also had an opportunity to collaborate with all other faculty members of the LEGS group, thanks to Michiel Heldeweg. This was a wonderful opportunity for me and thank you for giving me this opportunity. I would also like to thank Prof. Ruiter, Dr. Carlie Geerdink, Dr. Shawn Donnelly, Dr. Pieter-Jan Klok, and Prof. Kees Aarts for taking out time to advise me on key points in the development of my research.

There were a number of external resource persons who have extended help and support and therefore played a critical role in the completion of this book.

First I would like to thank Dr. Robert Geertsma for participating in the pilot study and providing me with great insight into the working of the medical device expert group under the European Commission. Thank you also for suggesting Erik Vollebregt as a potential resource person for this project. Thank you Erik for your extraordinary gesture of taking me as an intern at Axon Lawyers to get an inside perspective on regulatory problems surrounding borderline products. I would also like to thank all the interviewees who participated in the case studies. Most have requested anonymity, and therefore I cannot name them. Without their participation, this book would not have been written. I would also like to appreciate the help extended by Dr. Ingo Rohfling in reviewing and commenting on the methodology of this book.

Thank you all for your generosity and friendship. Lastly I would like to thank my family, Ma, Sharat, Dipics, and Bhaiti, without whose support and guidance this journey would not have been completed. This book is dedicated to our daughter Rahini whose cooperation was critical in the final days of writing of the book. I am also thankful to Prof. C. Raj Kumar, Jindal Global Law School, for giving me an opportunity to teach law students, and also the library staff for providing me with quiet space in the final days of the completion of this book. Finally I am grateful to Anke Seyfried and Julia Pelikan from Springer for working with me in finalizing the manuscript.

Enschede, Netherlands — Nupur Chowdhury
31 October 2013

Abbreviations

AIMDD	Active Implantable Medical Device Directive
ANU	Australian National University
Bfarm	Federal Institute for Drugs and Medical Devices
CAT	Committee for Advanced Therapies
CEN	European Committee for Standardization
CHMP	Committee for Medicinal Products for Human Use
CP	Centralized Process
DCP	Decentralized Process
DG SANCO	Director General for Health and Consumers
DIA	Drug Information Association
ECJ	European Court of Justice
ESO	European Standardization Organizations
EU	European Union
EUI	European University Institute
FSC	Forest Stewardship Council
GAL	Global Administrative Law
GHTF	Global Harmonization Task Force
ICANN	Internet Corporation for Assigned Names and Numbers
ICAO	International Civil Aviation Organization
ICH	International Conference on Harmonisation of Technical Requirements for Registration of Pharmaceuticals for Human Use
IMDRF	International Medical Device Regulators Forum
IVDDD	In Vitro Diagnostic Device Directive
MDD	Medical Device Directive
MDEG	Medical Device Expert Group
MHRA	Medicines and Healthcare products Regulatory Agency
MRP	Mutual Recognition Process
NCAs	National Competent Authorities
SME	Small and Medium Scale Enterprises
USFDA	United States Food and Drugs Agency

Contents

Chapter 1
Introduction

1.1 Introduction to the Problem

> In an internal market of 32 participating countries that are subject to constant scientific and technological progress, important differences in interpreting and applying the rules have emerged, thus undermining the legislation's main objectives – the safety of devices and their free circulation in the internal market. Moreover, there are regulatory gaps or uncertainties with regard to certain products. The regulatory system has also suffered from a lack of transparency and shortcomings in its implementation, in particular in the fields of market surveillance, vigilance and functioning of notified bodies.[1]

This preceding quote was made in the context of a proposal for amending the current legislative framework that regulates the market authorization of medical devices in Europe. It highlights the problems of having multiple administrative levels which may not be operating within a well laid out chain of command that is characteristic of national legal orders. It is a good illustration of how national legal orders are no longer self-contained, clearly demarcated hierarchical systems of legal rules that operate within well-defined national boundaries but are increasingly enmeshed within regional, international and global legal regimes. Simply put, legal rules are generated at multiple administrative levels—and multilevel regulation[2] seems to have become the norm rather than the exception in the world today.

The idea of national legal orders operating within sovereign nation states sustained the foundational division between monistic and dualistic systems of

[1] See Communication from the Commission to the European Parliament, the Council, the European Economic and Social Committee and the Committee of Regions, 26 September 2012, Doc. Ref. COM (2012) 540 final.

[2] The term was first discussed by way of descriptive examples from the legal arena in Wessel and Wouters (2008), pp. 9–47. This is a critical theoretical concept that has been developed by me in Chap. 2.

N. Chowdhury, *European Regulation of Medical Devices and Pharmaceuticals*,
DOI 10.1007/978-3-319-04594-8_1, © Springer International Publishing Switzerland 2014

laws.[3] Globalization has undermined the autonomy of such national legal orders.[4] The nature and scope of these changes can be categorized as horizontal and vertical—which by no means are separate and each, seem to feed off the other.

Horizontally, the prime development has been the growing participation of private actors in the development of public legal rules.[5] In some senses the participation of private actors was present earlier—however they operated within the well-defined formats of delegation and accountability mechanisms.[6] The last few decades have seen an exponential growth in the role and function of private actors—viz. private standardization bodies (e.g. ISO, IEC, FSC and ITU[7]); epistemic communities,[8] professional associations, international organizations[9] and non-governmental organizations in rule-making, rule-application and rule-adjudication activities[10] with reference to public rules. A large variety and a great number of private actors are directly involved in these activities—which were previously the exclusive domain of public actors.[11] Public actors increasingly cooperate, compete and in some cases share regulatory authority[12] with a range of private actors specifically in areas of rule-making and rule-application activities.[13] The incentive for participation of private actors in such activities is fairly obvious, in terms of benefitting from the play of rules. What explains the increasing reliance of public officials on these private actors? These public officials are increasingly confronted by technical expertise deficits. These deficits are prone to arise especially in areas of technology regulation wherein rulemaking requires

---

[3] See for instance for an excellent discussion of Carl Schmitt idea's on this subject, Zarmanian (2006), pp. 41–67.

[4] Ulrich (2010), pp. 1–49.

[5] Chesterman and Fisher (2009).

[6] Aman (2002), pp. 1687–1716.

[7] Although the ITU is an intergovernmental body—it has extensive participation of private experts.

[8] See Haas (1992), pp. 1–35; and Jansen and Roquas (2002).

[9] Here I refer to regulatory activities that go beyond that which is clearly delegated by the member states of the international organizations; and which include soft law that international organizations are increasingly developing in their specific fields of operation. See for instance, Barnett and Finnemore (2004). By one account, the number of international organizations has risen from 37 in 1909 to approximately 1,536 in 2011. Jeffrey (2012), pp. 99–127.

[10] I use these three phases to refer to the activities concerning the formation of these public rules; application of these public rules by public officials and adjudication in the case of conflict between differing interpretations as to the meaning of these public rules. Taken together they constitute the life-cycle of regulations. See for similar usage; Zaring (2008), pp. 563–611 and Camacho-Romisher (2000), pp. 569–601.

[11] Marie Diller (2011), pp. 481–536.

[12] Dezaley (1996) at 84.

[13] See amongst others; Slawotsky (2012), pp. 79–90; Hollis (2002), pp. 235–255; and Meidinger (2006), pp. 47–87.

technical standards that require specific domain knowledge[14] that may not be readily available within generalized public bureaucracies and amongst regulators.[15]

Developments vertically allude to the structure of the rule-making, rule application and rule adjudication activities that have transformed from predominantly hierarchical to decentralized modes of governance. This trend is aligned to the growing involvement of technical experts and is in fact a function of their involvement. Let me explain. National legal orders are structured to operate in a top down hierarchical fashion wherein all regulatory functions are distributed amongst authorities who may delegate it to functionaries lower down the order in terms of execution. In case of any jurisdictional conflicts or those regarding interpretation of rules—there are clear conflict rules that come into operation and such conflicts are usually referred to an another authority higher up in the chain of command. This is in stark contrast to decentralized modes where regulatory authority is heterarchically arranged and where mandates may overlap in the absence of clearly laid down jurisdictions and conflict rules.[16] The involvement of technical experts from the private sector results in the development of decentralized governance structures and the construction of new professional regulatory cultures. Professional associations of doctors, accountants, lawyers, scientists, managers and economists—in many ways constitute a new *cadre class*[17] that participate in regulatory activities. Their participation has become necessary because of the complexity of social life—differentiated into spheres of logic and action.[18]

This is reflected in the division of the legal order into specialized sub-fields. International law is of course characterized by a lack of central ordering—but this specialization—has become more pronounced by the production of norms by private actors either through formal delegation[19] or in other cases according the norms generated by them *ex post* recognition.[20] Within international law, this has led to fears of fragmentation in absence of clear rules of conflict given the

[14] de Chazournes (2012), pp. 479–481.

[15] Turner (2008) at 160.

[16] Heterarchy is a term used to characterize different forms of horizontal and vertical relations between the regulation regimes where mixed and that horizontal structures dominate. For instance the standardization of safety requirements related to products, which is primarily provided on the basis of cooperation between private and public actors. In this example, hierarchic legislation plays only a role when it comes to the incorporation of private standardization into law. See Teubner (1997a) and Kooiman (2003).

[17] I use this phrase 'cadre class' deliberately to allude to Max Weber's use of the term to predict increasing differentiation of social spheres and therefore the trend towards specialization.

[18] Van Der Pijl (1998).

[19] For instance the Technical Barriers to Trade Agreement recognizes the ISO as a valid source of international standards and therefore create a presumption of conformity with the Agreement in case of member states taking measures that concern public health and safety.

[20] For instance the *New Approach* Directives in the European Union recognize international standards that are formulated by the European standard organizations as 'harmonized standards' that carry a presumption of conformity. E.g. Council Directive 93/42/EEC of 14 June 1993 concerning medical devices (OJ L 169, 12.7.1993, p. 1).

non-hierarchical setting.[21] This notion of fragmentation through 'expertization'[22] primarily illustrates the idea that the unity of the legal order[23] will be undermined and thereby the certainty, predictability, coherence and consistency of the legal relations. In other words this would result in regulatory gaps and uncertainty and thereby challenge legal certainty.[24]

The other important and perhaps expected consequence of such developments that have animated legal theorists is the issue of legitimacy and accountability deficits.[25] Law derives its authority from the *ex ante* democratic legitimacy that empowers rule makers to make rules. Moreover accountability of public actors is ensured through numerous *ex post* administrative rules that govern public decision-making. Both these aspects are however structurally unavailable for private actors that participate in regulatory activities.

In the following sub-section, I discuss the major theoretical expositions that have taken cognizance of these horizontal and vertical developments and have sought to address them by devising, formulating and creating new theoretical concepts and reshaping some old concepts. The objective here is to provide an overview of the response from legal theorists to these developments. Keeping in mind that there are primarily two theoretical implications posed by these developments—that of a challenge to legal certainty and to legitimacy and accountability—this would also allow me to clearly identify the quality and depth of attention paid to each of these two problem areas. And, thus I hope to clearly underscore the relevance and the *raison de etre* for writing this book.

1.2 Theoretical Landscape of Legal Responses

How have legal theorists reacted to these developments? These developments have questioned our conventional understanding[26] of the nature of law, the functions of law and the fundamental characteristics of the legal order. I will focus attention on

---

[21] Koskenniemi and Leino (2002), pp. 553–579; Koskenniemi (2007), pp. 1–30.

[22] Koskenniemi (2009), pp. 7–19. Teubner and Fischer-Lescano (2004), pp. 999–1046.

[23] An interesting European research project is the COST Action on 'Fragmentation as Expertization: Rethinking the Fragmentation and Constitutionalization of International Law.' The project leaders contend that "The specific legal regime co-determines the framing of the questions posed to experts, the ways to assess scientific outputs and the manner in which scientific insights are translated into legal and political decision-making. The increasing technocratization and legalization of politics is accompanied by an increasing diversification in the production, assessment and application of (legal) knowledge." See project webpage: http://www.il-cf.eu/index.php?option=com_content&view=article&id=20&Itemid=24 (last accessed 4 March 2013).

[24] Werner (2007), pp. 17–30.

[25] See for both a theoretical analysis and a descriptive overview of such developments; Pauwelyn et al. (2012) and Berman et al. (2012).

[26] By conventional understanding—I refer to the legal positivist view of law that have focussed on the internal structural dimension of what law is and thus what the legal order looks like. Starting

two sets of approaches that have engaged directly with these developments. The first set, represents a search for unity in the face of these developments—and in the process reaffirms the idea of a coherent and consistent (if not hierarchic) legal order. International constitutionalism and 'global administrative law' (GAL) are two such approaches. The second set approaches include legal pluralism and systems theory—that are based on the presumption that society is characterized by multiple systems of social ordering—and law is just one of many concomitant systems. I have chosen to focus attention on these two sets of approaches; viz. international constitutionalism, GAL, legal pluralism and systems theory; precisely because all of them have seek to explore, explicate and develop theoretical concepts to address these developments. Together therefore they provide a valuable foundation to my own explorations into legal certainty in the context of these developments.

1.2.1 International Constitutionalism and Global Administrative Law

Scholars advocating International constitutionalism have underlined the need for a system of horizontal values that could bring some unity and coherence in the face of fragmentation. Both procedural values such as fairness and justice as well as expanding on the more substantive values of *jus cogens* have been suggested as a meta rule for ensuring if not convergence at least co-existence of closed international and autonomous legal orders (e.g. World Trade Organization).[27] Others have also taken this opportunity to also look inwards as to the ideas of constitutive power and legality[28] and the continued problem of sovereign boundaries as an impediment to the pursuit of global justice[29] and also in evolving a constitutional consensus in specific international legal regimes; given that sectoral fragmentation is also another aspect of international law.[30] Development of non-statist 'legal'[31]

with Austin's theory of law as the command of a sovereign, which were backed by the threat of sanction; to Kelsen's pure theory of law which traced all legal rules to a *grundnorm* that sat atop of a hierarchy of all lower legal norms; to Hart's distinction between primary and secondary norms and the idea that law is not followed because of the threat of coercive sanction but because of an internal sense of obligation. It is the study of the internal structure of the legal order that distinguishes theorists in the legal positivist tradition from theorists like legal pluralists that look at law from an external perspective. See Austin and Rumble (1995); Kelsen (1967); Raz (1979) at 122–145; and Hart (1961).

[27] See Walker (2002), pp. 317–359; Dunoff and Trachtman (2009); Klabbers (2004), pp. 31–58; and de Wet (2006), pp. 611–632.

[28] Dyzenhaus (2012), pp. 229–260.

[29] Follesdal (2012), pp. 261–277.

[30] Heller et al. (2012), pp. 278–312; and Jillions (2012), pp. 429–454. Havercroft (2012), pp. 120–140.

[31] I use the term 'legal' to refer to some form of private ordering of value systems—that reflect the interests and objectives of actors structuring and operating these regimes.

regimes such as *lex mercatoria*,[32] internet regulation by ICANN[33] and global supply chain management by multinational corporations have also exacerbated this process of fragmentation and non-communication that is anathema to the developments of meta rules.[34] One important characteristic that defines studies on international constitutionalism is the preponderance of international legal orders that are linked to statist initiatives as differentiated from transnational governance regimes that are beyond the nation state. Studies of international constitutionalism have therefore been coloured by statist impulses that are necessarily aligned to the notion of a sovereign nation state. This has also been evident in the cross currents of opinion that discuss this bias within international constitutionalism.

In an edited collection of articles in their book[35]—*Ruling the World*—scholars Jeff Dunoff and Joel Trachtman view international constitutionalism in purely instrumental and minimalistic terms, as that which influences the production of international law. Thus international constitutionalism is an internal process and imperative of international legal orders and regulatory regimes that should be judged in its own terms—as either enabling or impeding the pursuit of global public goods. On the other hand, Neil Walker is far more critical of the usage of the term 'international constitutionalism.' He discusses how the term is embedded within liberal democratic political theory discourses of the nation state. And therefore the usage of the term necessarily alludes to the values that are enshrined—rule of law, democratic deliberation and protection of rights—and which act as limitations on the powers of the state. Thus, within the international domain the adoption of the term is not value free but value laden. He evocatively poses the question: 'can the rise of a new constitutionalism be an answer to the decline of the old constitutionalism?'[36] The argument forwarded here is that given that domestic constitutionalism tied to nation state seems to be increasingly challenged by international processes and actors involved in law-making activities that are beyond the nation state—does international constitutionalism's—search for the identification of global public values (most famously enshrined through *jus cogens* principles)—seek to replace domestic constitutions within nation states? The presumption here is that international constitutionalism is not a benign theoretical tool—but a decidedly political enterprise—that seeks to push the adoption of a certain kind of liberal political values—which may be used to restrict the power of states to pursue their own national policies.[37]

The GAL project, on the other hand focuses on non-statist developments—developments that are fuelled by private actors.[38] Taking off from an administrative

---

[32] Michaels (2007), pp. 447–468.

[33] See Goldsmith (2000); and Mayer (2000), pp. 149–169.

[34] Abbott and Snidal (2009).

[35] See Dunoff and Trachtman (2009).

[36] See Walker (2009).

[37] Walker (2011), pp. 369–385 and Walker (2008), pp. 519–543.

[38] For an interesting comparison of the two approaches see Ming-Sung (2013), pp. 437–468.

law paradigm, specific attention is paid to augmenting the legitimacy and accountability of these international processes. The emphasis is on identifying and developing mechanisms for improving deliberative processes within regulatory spaces[39] populated by both private and public actors within international organizations. Unlike in the case of international constitutionalism, GAL scholars have made efforts in recording instances of GAL through case studies and attention has now shifted to the 'internal side of law'—procedural aspects in identifying common concerns that processes producing GAL need to address. This is in marked contrast with constitutionalism where attention is more on the external dimension of legitimacy of law—through a higher political text.[40]

GAL scholars do not differentiate between distinct levels or even types of regulation i.e. private and public, local, national, international.[41] Instead they subsume all regulation under the moniker, 'administration' that is taking place in the global administrative space. This global regulatory space is populated by a gamut of actors that have little in common in terms of institutional structures and functions except that they operate within this space. This includes international institutions, regulatory networks and domestic administrators that operate within regional/international legal frameworks.[42] The sheer variety of actors includes entities that are private, public and also private–public partnerships with hybrid governance structures. Governance is mostly decentralized and not controlled by a single entity and therefore although there is possibility for collaboration it may at times also lead to duplication, concurrence and competition. More interestingly GAL scholars also underline the fact that not all actors functioning within this regulatory space are 'willing participants'—they give the example of domestic courts who are frequently confronted with legal disputes and issues—that are primarily triggered by ruptures within this global regulatory space and therefore much beyond the remit and jurisdiction of domestic courts.[43]

The major focus of GAL scholars has been to first map the scale, dimension and features of the phenomenon and then more importantly to explore and evaluate legal mechanisms, regulatory principles and sectoral practices that affect or directly address the accountability and thereby legitimacy[44] of these processes. Thus issues like transparency and public participation in decision-making, rationality and legality and review of decision making have been at the heart of GAL discussions. The first wave of studies on GAL adopted a case study approach of explicating the

[39] The term 'space' as used in the context of GAL is similar to the theoretical construct of 'regulatory space' as developed by Hancher and Moran. See Hancher and Moran (1989) at 271–299. This is a key concept used in this book; see footnote 70 in this chapter for a brief description of the concept and how it is used in this book.

[40] Ladeur (2009).

[41] Kingsbury et al. (2005), pp. 15–62.

[42] See for instance; Zaring (1998), pp. 292–297; Kalypso and Shaffer (2005), pp. 263–317.

[43] Lang (2008).

[44] For an interesting discussion of the theoretical implications of choosing different accountability mechanisms and whether legal accountability serves as an alternative to democratic accountability, see Stewart (2008).

phenomenon and the search for commonality and unity between the instances and was therefore decidedly inductive in its orientation.[45] However recently there has been a move towards building a better theoretical understanding of GAL. One such promising effort[46] has been made by Benedict Kingsbury by elucidating the criterion of 'publicness'.[47] The concept of 'publicness' is used here to convey the understanding that law-making is addressed towards the *public* and therefore should fulfil the aspiration of being applicable and of use to the public. Kingsbury argues that increasingly one is able to discern a commitment to 'publicness' by actors in the field of GAL. In the form of a direct or indirect commitment or even as aspiration to fulfil some demands of legality, rationality, proportionality, rule of law and recognition of certain basic human rights. This imperative is what characterizes GAL actors.[48]

1.2.2 Legal Pluralism and Systems Theory

The second sets of responses are those that advocate the idea of legal pluralism.[49] Legal pluralism is based on the premise that state law is not the only source of legal norms. Legal norms may also be sourced from other systems of social orderings viz. religion, culture, community, etc.[50] Once we move away from the shadow of a "legal order" or even "legal orders"—parallelism of normative value systems seem intuitively attractive and even acceptable in the context of international law.[51] However this does not mean the abandonment of a search for order. Order is sought to be maintained not through an established hierarchy of norms—but via a system of conflict rules that allow for interaction between the normative orders and resolution in cases of conflict.[52] An approach which is similar to the conflict of law rules that

---

[45] See Cavalieri et al. (2012).

[46] Other efforts include; Krisch (2009a); and De Burca (2008), pp. 101–158.

[47] Kingsbury (2009), pp. 23–57. See also von Bogdandy et al. (2010).

[48] Another important conceptualization of these processes has been the project on 'Informal International Law Making' (see Pauwelyn et al. 2012 and Berman et al. 2012). Informality of these processes has been captured through the aspects of output, processes and actors involved. Reasons for proliferation of such processes are also discussed. Most pertinently, the authors argue that lack of democratic legitimacy in such processes can be countered by procedural meta norms—referred to as 'thick stakeholder consensus' that act as review mechanisms for actors, processes and output. They suggest that as a benchmark this could be normatively superior to "thin state consent" which is the fundamental validation for international law.

[49] Studies on legal pluralism were developed to explore non-legal normative systems that may operate alongside law in the context of nation states. However the same conceptual framework has been applied in the context of international context.

[50] See Merry (1988), pp. 869–901; Moore (1973), pp. 719–746; and Griffiths (1986), pp. 15–29.

[51] Zumbansen (2010), pp. 141–189.

[52] Berman (2007), pp. 1155–1237; Burke-White (2004), pp. 963–979; Twining (2009), pp. 473–518.

operate within private international law. Private international law has also served as an inspiration for applying the conceptual framework of interlegality[53] to transnational governance as an arena for productive normative contestation.[54] The goal of such approaches has been to unearth evidence of concomitant normative systems and explore ways in which these systems interact and communicate.

The systems theory of law, argues that modern society is divided into functionally differentiated sub systems—viz. law, religion, politics, economics.[55] Law as a separate system of social ordering—is characterized by a distinct binary code (legal/illegal) and a conditional program. Each social ordering also develops its own specialized communication systems. These systems exists concurrently and are open to influence by each other—so they share a heteronomous relationship and communicate with each other through what is referred to as 'structural coupling'.[56] Thus there has been an expansion of private and 'unofficial' legal orders that cater to specific sectors—the internet, sports organizations, private investment, and commercial transactions—and generate norms within functionally self-sustaining normative orders. Gunter Teubner has further developed this theory by proposing for social constitutionalism as a normative corollary to greater differentiation and rationalization in world society.[57] The process of juridification of autonomous institutional spheres will result in different civic constitutions.[58]

However the use of term 'constitutionalism' has been criticized by Nico Krisch, who while agreeing with Teubner on the greater differentiation within society (refers to it as 'post national society')—highlights the weakness of idea constitutionalism itself—the idea of an overarching framework with ultimate authority.[59] Underlining the strength of a pluralist order in terms of adaptability, space of contestation and the checks and balances between different legal systems—he hopes that self-legislating equals can order the political space through deliberative processes that would ensure a balance between inclusiveness and particularity.[60] The problem though, that continues to haunt legal pluralism as well as systems theory discourses, is the criteria to differentiate normative systems or legal orders—lack of a demarcation criteria means that all social norms are recognized as potential legal norms—i.e. they operate and exists in a stand-alone system of normative ordering. This seeks to explain as much as it confounds.

---

[53] de Sousa Santos (1987), pp. 279–302. de Sousa Santos (2002).

[54] Wai (2008), pp. 107–128. Also see Michaels (2005), pp. 1209–1259.

[55] Luhmann (1977), pp. 29–53. Luhmann (1985, 2004) and Teubner (1993).

[56] Structural coupling in this regard is referred to as 'zones of contact' in specific instances through which autopoietic systems may communicate and interact with each other. See Nobles and Schiff (2012), pp. 265–269.

[57] See Teubner (2002) at 311.

[58] Teubner (2004), pp. 3–28.

[59] Here it is important to point out—that Teubner's idea of social constitutionalism refers to the process of reification of values within normative orders in society. Therefore society would be many such constitutions operating concomitantly. This is different from Krisch's idea of constitutionalism to mean one overarching framework of values that governs society.

[60] Krisch (2009b, 2012).

The essential difference between legal theorists working within the theoretical frameworks of legal pluralism and systems theory from those working with categories such as international constitutionalism and GAL, is the primary presumption from whence both start. Whereas the former allows (and is therefore comfortable with) for multiple sets of normative orderings and the ruptures therewith and is content to explore some form of rudimentary conflict rules to enable communication and interaction between seemingly closed normative orders; the latter is keen on developing meta rules—be that in the form of substantive meta rules (e.g. *jus cogens*) or procedural safeguards (viz. 'publicness' criteria) to address accountability deficits.

1.2.3 Spotlight on an Under-Researched Issue

As I have mentioned in the concluding sentence in Sect. 1.2, together these two sets of approaches provide valuable foundations to my own explorations on legal certainty. This includes the appreciation of the pluralist nature of such processes. Thus apart from the fact that these processes fall outside the formal legal order—there is little commonality in the institutional structure, processes and the nature of actors involved. Further the review of these approaches makes it apparent that aligning with the dichotomy of international and national legal orders is of limited purchase and it makes far more sense to study these processes in the context of domain/issue specific 'regulatory spaces'. Thus the unity of legal orders reflect an academic aspiration rather than an approximation of reality.

As I have explained at the end of Sect. 1.1, there are primarily two theoretical implications of the horizontal and vertical developments that are shaping the world—issue of legal certainty; and that of legitimacy and accountability. In the following paragraph I briefly explicate these two implications.

Legal positivists explain legal certainty—in terms of predictability, certainty, coherence and consistency of the legal relations in society—this is ensured through a hierarchical system of normative ordering—characteristic of national legal orders.[61] The idea of hierarchy encapsulates the possibility of identifying always a higher rule in case of norm conflict or reference to an authority with powers to give conclusive rulings on such conflicts and thereby ensuring juridical unity of the legal order and reducing (if not eliminating) uncertainty and ensuring legal certainty. Globalization has challenged the sanctity of national legal orders.[62] Although structurally domestic legal orders continue to exist, they increasingly interact and respond to other specialized normative orders that focus on specific sectors. These normative orders function alongside and interact with national legal orders (and in some cases may penetrate them) and heterarchy rather than hierarchy seems to be a more apt description of the nature of the relationship between these

---

[61] Pino (1999), pp. 513–536; and Christiano and Sciaraffa (2003), pp. 487–512.

[62] See Mac Cormick (1999) and de Witte (2003).

normative orders.[63] Multiplicity of normative orders and the nature of relationship being heterarchical would be expected to result in norm confusion and conflict and thereby challenge and potentially undermine legal certainty.

The involvement of non-state actors or private actors pose a separate but related problem. Admittedly their involvement in rule-making, rule application and rule adjudication activities[64] is not new. Whereas earlier these activities were conducted within well laid out frameworks of delegation and supervision by public authorities; increasingly we find non-state actors involved through direct action in these activities within specialized regimes. The involvement of private actors and the norms generated by them gain acceptability because in many cases, these actors constitute technical expert networks, professional associations and epistemic communities which dominate access to technical knowledge that is fundamental to establishing regulatory control. This is specifically the case in areas where products and processes regulated are highly varied and driven by technological changes—domain knowledge then becomes imperative in designing and implementing regulatory controls. Thus for instance, technical knowledge or expertise constitutes a separate and legitimate basis for participating in rule making, rule application and rule adjudication activities[65]—differentiated from the logic that public rules should be made by public authorities—that are delegated with this responsibility by elected legislatures. In the context of EU law, *the New Approach* directives[66] only lay down general legal principles—and actual standards for guiding compliance are produced by private standardization bodies (e.g. CEN) which operate under the separate institutional framework of the ISO.

These standards are ex post recognized as legal rules (referred to as harmonized standards) that carry the presumption of conformity with the general legal principles. However this 'recognition' only addresses the legitimacy of these rules in a limited fashion. The primary issue here is how to ensure private actors involved in public regulation activities—rule making, rule application and rule adjudication—are held accountable to certain public interest principles? Increasing specialization of goods and services have necessitated reliance on domain knowledge for ensuring regulatory control—this domain knowledge is accessed through private actors that function outside the frameworks of review that govern public officials (administrative law) and this raises intrinsic questions of accountability of these private actors and therefore the legitimacy of the norms generated by them.

As is evident from our discussion in the two preceding sections; scholars working within GAL; have chosen to focus attention on procedural frameworks that address accountability deficits that are characteristic of such non-statist

[63] Teubner (1989, 1997b).

[64] See Zaring (2008), pp. 563–611; Camacho-Romisher (2000), pp. 569–601. Also Scott et al. (2011).

[65] See footnote 20.

[66] European Commission (2000). New Approach Directives cover a wide variety of products—including chemicals, construction products, cosmetics, machinery, medical devices, personal protection equipment and toys. List available on the website: http://www.newapproach.org/Directives/DirectiveList.asp.

processes that involve rule making, rule application and rule adjudication. They contend that non-state actors involved in public regulation are keenly aware of the need to address perceptions of accountability deficit that undermine the legitimacy of their activities. International constitutionalism scholars have built on debates of fragmentation in the context of international legal regimes by advancing the argument that individual international legal orders should be assessed on the basis of whether they advance or limit the achievement of global public goods and this would be a mechanism for assessing ex post legitimacy of these legal orders. Thus they support the application of *jus cogens* principles as a benchmark for assessing legitimacy of these legal orders.

Scholars working on transnational legal pluralism and systems theory do not have to show fidelity to the idea of a legal order and have therefore focussed attention on explicating the process of communication; interaction and penetration between normative systems of ordering that characterise the world today. The idea of conflict rules or other background conditions that allow for interaction between these legal orders are of particular interest to these scholars. Thus the aim has been to investigate how conflict is avoided or circumvented between these concomitant systems of normative orderings rather than to aspire for legal certainty in terms of consistency, clarity and predictability.

From this short theoretical overview it is evident that scholars have given greater attention to the theoretical implication of accountability and legitimacy resulting from these horizontal and vertical developments rather than on legal certainty. Part of the reason is the strong structural presumption that operates amongst legal positivists—that of a hierarchical legal order that is structured towards ensuring legal certainty—is no longer valid in absolute terms. As is evident from our discussion of the horizontal and vertical developments—there is a multiplicity of legal orders; both statist and non-statist operate concomitantly and seem to be sharing a heterarchical rather than a hierarchical relationship—and this seems to beg the obvious conclusion that legal certainty is therefore necessarily challenged in this context. Therefore there are strong reasons to assess what seems like an obvious conclusion. This has not been done.

This book seeks to address this discrepancy of attention that legal certainty has received in the hands of legal scholars that have theorized on the current horizontal and vertical developments. There has been a wealth of research on the 'principle' of legal certainty from the perspective of legal positivism.[67] However limited research has been conducted on the empirical understanding of the value and application of legal certainty from a regulatee perspective. This book is an attempt to partially redress this imbalance. As an exploratory study, the emphasis is on developing a conceptual framework of multilevel regulation and in identifying the dimensions of legal certainty as perceived and expected by regulatees. In that sense, this is a *sui generis* study on a research problem that has not been framed or analyzed in this manner. However it is important to underline, that the research does not aim to establish a causal relationship between multilevel regulation and legal certainty.

---

[67] See Chap. 3 for the detailed discussion of this issue.

Any attempt to investigate causality can only ensue after conceptualization and theorization of the horizontal and vertical developments discussed above. Accordingly this study is an attempt to explore these developments through the conceptualization of "multilevel regulation" and the dimensions of legal certainty (as experienced by regulatees) in such a context.

In the following section (Sect. 1.3) I outline the heuristic device—'multilevel regulation'[68] in the context of perspectives on legal certainty (also as a counterpoint to a hierarchic legal order) adopted here to best capture the horizontal and vertical developments that are shaping the world and investigations its implications for legal certainty in terms of expectations and perceptions of actors. This is an important step in the specification of the research problem which I address in this book. I also discuss my choice of medical products regulation in Europe as a case study for undertaking my empirical investigations. In the last and final section (Sect. 1.4) I discuss the primary research question that this book seeks to address and the various chapter outlines.

1.3 Multilevel Regulation and Legal Certainty

In this project I use multilevel regulation[69] as a term to characterize a regulatory space[70] in which the process of rule making, rule application and rule adjudication (that forms the regulatory life cycle)[71] is dispersed across more

[68] The first structured analysis of the concept of multilevel regulation was developed in the book: Føllesdal et al. (2008) at 9–47. Also see Chowdhury and Wessel (2012), pp. 335–357.

[69] I use the term regulation as defined by Black; 'intentional attempts to control or order people or state of affairs (albeit mindful of the unintended consequences of those intentions)'. See Black (2002). This definition departs critically from that as proposed by Philip Selznick—'the sustained and focused control exercised by a public authority over activities valued by the community', which only includes reference to controls exercised by public authority. This definition is too limiting, for the purposes of this book—because private actors also exercise control over specific public interest functions. Therefore for the purposes of this book, I choose to use Black's definition of regulation—as it is broader and therefore captures new kinds of regulatory actors and new forms of regulation. See Selznick (1985) at 363.

[70] See Hancher and Moran (1989). The term 'regulatory space' has been used as referred to by Hancher and Moran within regulatory theory—in that regulation involves a mixture of private and public characteristics that involve dynamic relationships between and within organizations and actors who may come together to occupy a shared space that is characterised by a number of regulatory issues subject to public decision-making. While they have developed the term to characterize national level regulatory processes, herein I use it in a limited sense to denote the nature of norms (hard and soft norms), process of norm creation, enforcement and adjudication and also the various public private actors involved in this process within a specific regulatory sectors that may be integrated vertically across international, regional, national and sub-national levels.

[71] Rule making refers to activities related to the formulation or the drawing up of standards or obligations that directly aim to guide or shape public behavior. Rule application follows subsequent to rule making and refers to the imposition of the rules by actors which are specifically tasked with this function. They oversee public behavior that is supposed to be guided by these rules

than one administrative or territorial level amongst several different actors, both public and private. It is important to point out that my reference to 'regulation' instead of 'law' is deliberate. The term 'regulation' allows me to capture those rules which may not fall within the black letter of 'law' but is nevertheless developed with the objective of control or shaping of public behaviour.[72] Thus activities of non-state actors involved in rule making, rule application and rule adjudication are also investigated.

I draw on the concept of a regulatory space, using it as a framing device to differentiate between specific aspects of policy fields. The relationship between actors in such a space is heterarchical and may be independent of each other. Lack of central ordering of the regulatory life cycle within this regulatory space is the most important feature of such a space. Thus, as a heuristic device 'multilevel regulation', stands in opposition to a hierarchical legal order which is characterized by juridical unity (as was the case of most national sovereign legal orders during the pre-globalization era). If it was hierarchy of rules that ensured legal certainty (as is assumed by legal positivists)—then this creates the expectation (indeed for legal positivists this is a foregone conclusion) that loss of that hierarchy should undermine or challenge legal certainty in such regulatory spaces as those characterized by multilevel regulation. Multilevel regulation, therefore, undermines the thesis of centrality of national law, which is a basic assumption of the traditional concept of legal certainty.[73] This has led scholars to question the value and relevance of legal certainty within such multilevel regulatory spaces.[74] However, the widespread espousals of 'legal certainty' within legislation[75] and in the European public policy debates[76] belie such a conclusion.

(this is based on similar definitions forwarded by Baldwin, Cave and Lodge; see Baldwin et al. 2012 at 227). Rule adjudication refers to the provision of authoritative interpretation of the rules and may be required if there exists competing interpretations of the rules.

[72] This decision to use the term 'regulation' and not 'law' in order to capture a greater number of social processes—is in some ways inspired by the typology (repressive, autonomous and responsive law) developed Philippe Nonet and Philip Selznick in which they study law as a sociopolitical phenomenon. See Nonet and Selznick (1978).

[73] Dorbeck-Jung (2009), pp. 258–289.

[74] Scheuerman (1999) at 243–266.

[75] Recital 7 of Directive 2004/27/EC of the European Parliament and of the Council of 31 March 2004, amending Directive 2001/83/EC on the Community code relating to medicinal products for human use. OJ. L. 136. Also Recital 28 of Regulation (EC) No. 726/2004 of the European Parliament and of the Council of 31 March 2004, laying down Community procedures for the authorisation and supervision of medicinal products for human and veterinary use and establishing a European Medicines Agency. O.J. L. 136.

[76] Press Release on 9 March 2007, Companies researching and developing treatments for rare diseases welcome draft Commission guideline providing legal certainty on market exclusivity for Orphan Medicines. Brussels. Press Release on 26 January 2007, COCIR contribution to the consultation initiated by DG SANCO regarding community action on health services. CISCO IBSG, Engagement Snapshot, 'Creating legal certainty for e-health across the European Union', 2008. CPME/2009/003 EN, 'CPME Statement on the proposal for a directive on the application of patient's rights in cross-border healthcare.' December 2008 COFACE 2009.

I make two critical methodological choices—first, I distance myself from the logical positivist presumption that legal certainty can only be ensured within a hierarchically structured legal order. Thus it is possible for legal certainty to be ensured by other structural or procedural mechanisms. Second, I choose to explore the idea of legal certainty in terms of expectations and perceptions of social actors and in terms of their ideas on calculability of law.[77] Calculability of law is intrinsic to the idea of law as an aspect of social system that allows members of society to be involved in exchange of goods and services. The crux of legal certainty is the idea of calculability of social relations that ensures predictability of legal consequences in undertaking (or abstaining from) an action.

I investigate the idea of legal certainty in terms of regulatory expectations and perceptions of regulatees that function in different regulatory spaces. If one were to presume calculability of law is *sine qua non* to all social action—then the value of legal certainty to social actors (in this specific case regulatees) cannot be underestimated. Given that regulatory spaces may have over time become more multilevel in nature—how has that impacted perceptions and expectations of regulatees? How have regulatees pursued and accessed legal certainty within such regulatory spaces? How does law ensure calculability?[78] How important is calculability and predictability in society? Are social actors willing to trade-off calculability for some other values? What are the mechanisms adopted by regulatees to pursue and access legal certainty in such regulatory spaces? My focus therefore is on investigating the practice of law in society rather than on legal theory—and thus I adopt a Weberian socio-legal lens that focuses attention on the reasons behind social acceptability and enforceability of legal norms in practice.[79]

These questions allude to the research problem that is explored through two case studies of European regulation. I choose these two regulatory spaces within European regulation—marketing authorization of medical devices and marketing authorization of pharmaceutical—and they form the basis of two case studies. The primary motive for case selection was that *prima facie* these two regulatory spaces seem to be structured hierarchically (pharmaceuticals) and heterarchically (medical devices) and therefore together they provide a suitable contrast for further investigation on multilevelness of these regulatory spaces.[80] Thus these regulatory spaces may differ in terms of regulatee perception and expectations of legal certainty.[81]

---

[77] Another reason for undertaking an empirical investigation of actor perceptions and expectations of legal certainty is because there is a predominance of studies on the legal principle of legal certainty and very few on the idea of legal certainty from a socio-legal perspective. See Chap. 3 for a detailed discussion on this point.

[78] Max Weber's notion of law and his idea of legal certainty—that was developed with the view of ensuring calculability for economic actors.

[79] See for a good overview, Swedberg (2006), pp. 61–81; and Deflem (2008).

[80] The reasons for case selection are addressed in greater detail in Chap. 3.

[81] An argument for these case studies being the 'most likely case' (medical devices) and 'least likely case' (pharmaceuticals) may also be made in terms of the likelihood that multilevel regulation will impact legal certainty.

Different levels of multilevelness may provide a richer variety of insights into the practice of legal certainty. These two regulatory spaces are also interesting because both are currently in the cusp of fundamental changes in the regulatory framework.[82] This lends additional currency to the book—as it would help explore the regulatee perceptions of these fundamental changes. Empirical understanding of the value of legal certainty—including preferred mechanisms for accessing legal certainty by regulatees especially in times of fundamental change—may contribute insights that can help delineate regulatee positions on policy debates in both these regulatory spaces.

1.4 Research Question and Chapter Outline

Thus the primary research question which I will address in this book is as follows:

- *How do regulatees pursue legal certainty in the context of the multilevel European medical product regulation*?

In order to address the primary research question—the first step would be to develop and explicate the theoretical concept of multilevel regulation. This is imperative so as to describe and capture both the horizontal and vertical developments that have been discussed in Sect. 1.1. The development of this concept would in terms of forming a set of criteria that would be the basis for differentiating between regulatory spaces.[83] Thus the first sub-research question is as follows:

- *What are the criteria for establishing multilevelness of a regulatory space*?

The other critical concept is that of legal certainty. Given that this is a socio-legal study; and the focus is to explore the regulatee perspectives of legal certainty; I need to develop some idea about the constitutive elements of the concept of legal certainty. These elements can then be used as reference points while constructing the questionnaire which will be used in the interviews with regulatees. Thus the second sub-research question is as follows:

---

[82] For instance in the case of medical devices; the European Commission has proposed two new Regulations to replace the medical device and the *in vitro* diagnostic medical device Directives that have been applicable in the EU for over the last 20 years. See footnote 1 in this chapter. The European Commission is currently undertaking public consultations on ATMP (Advanced Therapy Medicinal Product) and Paediatric medicinal products. See http://ec.europa.eu/health/documents/new_en.htm.

[83] Although I eschew the idea that a regulatory space is either multilevel or not—so it is not a binary concepts; this is an exploratory study and only the first step in the exploration of the concept of multilevel regulation—I will not be making any claims for establishing or identifying degrees of multilevelness. My limited claim is that multilevel regulation is opposite to a hierarchical legal order and there is a continuum between them—and therefore regulatory spaces can be more or less multilevel in nature—although I am not in a position to propose an effective measurement for assessment of levels.

- *What are the constitutive elements of the concept of legal certainty*?

Following from this the next step would be to undertake an assessment of these two regulatory spaces—that comprise European medical product regulation—in terms of establishing their place in the continuum and gauging the multilevelness prevalent in both these regulatory spaces. Here I will use the criteria developed earlier (Chap. 2) to make this assessment. This assessment would also be the basis for differentiating between these two regulatory spaces. This description of multilevelness is according to the formal regulatory structure. Subsequently regulatees in the interviews will be confronted with this analysis. The purpose is to assess the de facto perspective or 'in practice' perceptions of multilevelness. This is critical to understanding how regulatees pursue legal certainty within these regulatory spaces—which although may be formally characterised by multilevelness may be perceived quite differently by regulatees and consequently how they pursue legal certainty will also be determined by their perception. Thus the third and fourth sub-research questions are as follows:

- *Is the European medical product regulation multilevel in nature*?
- *What are the regulatee perceptions of multilevelness of regulatory spaces*?

Finally the primary aim of this book is to explore regulatee perspectives and expectations with regard to legal certainty in the context of multilevel regulation and to delineate the manner in which regulatees pursue legal certainty. This refers to their outlook on legal certainty. The term expectations includes the value imbued on legal certainty by regulatees and the mechanisms privileged by regulatees in pursuit of that value and consequently their preference for the regulatory structure that can ensure legal certainty for them. Thus the fifth sub-research question is as follows:

- *What are regulatee perceptions and expectations with regard to legal certainty*?

Taken together these five research questions will allow me to answer the primary research question. All the five sub-research questions are addressed individually in the chapters of this book. The progress of the book can be marked out in separate steps. First, is to conceptualize multilevel regulation. Second, evaluate the concept of legal certainty and identify certain dimensions that have becomes the basis for constructing the qualitative case study. Third, develop a clear methodology for the two case studies and explain the methodological choices made. The fourth step was to conduct the case studies—through document analysis and field interviews of regulatees. The fifth step is to analyze, collate and present the results of the two case studies. This finally leads to the conclusion which answers the primary research question.

Chapter 2 addresses the first sub research question—"*What are the criteria for establishing multilevelness of a regulatory space*?" I begin with the idea of regulation and then explore neighboring concepts like "multilevel governance" as valuable in grasping certain aspects of theorizing which seek to address social activities that are administered by not one but at several levels. I develop and explain the different dimensions of the concept of multilevel regulation. This leads me to establish specific criteria for gauging multilevelness of a regulatory space.

Chapter 3 addresses the second sub-research question—"*What are the constitutive elements of the concept of legal certainty*?" This chapter provides a literature review of the "principle of legal certainty" thus highlighting the paucity of studies on empirical aspects of legal certainty. It builds the case for focusing attention on the perspective of regulatees by contextualizing Max Weber's idea of law and legal certainty—that was developed with the view of ensuring calculability for economic actors. Further I also study ECJ case law[84] in order to identify a set of notions that capture litigant (this would include both regulators and regulatees) expectations of legal certainty in the context of European litigation. These notions are referred to in the questionnaire which I use for conducting the interviews with regulatees.

Chapter 4 clarifies the methodological aspects of this research and the choices made at each step of the book. Both concepts of "multilevel regulation" and "legal certainty" have been used here in a novel manner—and therefore the need to explain the nature of these concepts. As mentioned earlier, given that this is an exploratory study the focus is on conceptualization rather that establishing causality. Regulatee perspectives and expectations are mapped through interviews and document analysis. Recruitment of manufacturers is critical to the process since the focus is on regulatees. Aspects critical to the construction of the two case studies—research methods and the recruitment and sampling strategy are explained. Lastly checks and balances adopted for ensuring the qualitative validity of the data are discussed.

Chapter 5 discusses the structure and findings of the pilot study that was conducted leading up to the two case studies. The medical product sector is characterized by a regulatory patchwork of European and national laws and guidelines operating concurrently with each other. Each of these sectors are characterized by different levels of regulatory uncertainty that may undermine the effectiveness of the regulatory framework. How have European regulation shaped individual product sectors? How has that impacted regulatory uncertainty in that sector? What has been the impact of regulatory compliance? Drawing on documentary research and fieldwork interviews this pilot study conducted in Netherlands, finds that ATMPs and medical device sectors exhibit high level of regulatory uncertainty. Although the sources of uncertainty vary across each of the sectors, in some instances when regulatory uncertainty has reached unmanageable levels, measures have been taken by regulators to address it. Regulatees themselves have developed a complex compliance strategy that allows them to tolerate and in certain circumstances even circumvent regulatory uncertainty. These findings were the basis for developing the case studies, in terms of identifying pathways of analysis within the literature review and also helped in the formulation of the questionnaires.

Chapters 6 and 7 presents the research results of the two case studies and both follow the same structure. Sub-research questions 3, 4 and 5—*Is the European*

[84] I choose to focus on ECJ case law because both the case studies are on European regulatory spaces.

medical product regulation multilevel in nature? What are the regulatee perceptions of multilevelness of regulatory spaces? What are the regulatee perceptions and expectations with regard to legal certainty?—are addressed in the context of the two case studies. In both these chapters; I begin with a history of the two regulatory spaces in order to identify the benchmarks on how regulations developed in these two regulatory spaces and provide the context for the subsequent discussion. This is followed by my descriptive mapping of both these regulatory spaces in terms of multilevelness. In the next section regulatees are confronted with the results of this formal review of multilevelness and asked to comment on it—do they agree with the findings or do they have a different perception. This allows us to understand how these two regulatory spaces are perceived and whether the academic review corresponds to regulatee perceptions. This is critical because empirical notions may depart from academic presumptions about how the regulatory spaces are structured. Thus the utility of the concept of 'multilevel regulation' in empirical studies is also investigated. Subsequently I analyze regulatee expectations of legal certainty; followed by the primary findings of both these case studies.

Chapter 8 can be best described as an excursus in terms of the primary research question. Thus it does not stand as a fully formed case study along with the other two case studies—given that the same research questions were not investigated in the context of borderline products. However I use the word case study here to represent an investigation of regulatory uncertainty within borderline products given that they are a sub-category of medical products that frequently defy regulatory product categorization. Due to this reason, regulatory uncertainty is endemic to this product category. Regulatory gaps causing regulatory uncertainty and the institutional challenges of addressing this uncertainty are discussed in this chapter specifically with reference to case law. Given that the ECJ is the final authority on the interpretation of EU law, this chapter discusses the jurisprudence on this issue that has been developed by the ECJ and the national courts.

Chapter 9 is the concluding chapter. It reviews and reflects on the findings of the two case studies (and also the pilot and borderline products study) in the context of the primary research question. It is important to reiterate that the empirical findings are obviously limited by the scale of the case studies. However the value of this book can be defended on the grounds that it develops and operationalizes the conceptual model of multilevel regulation. Multilevel regulation builds on neighboring concepts like multilevel governance and is a useful in benchmarking regulatory spaces. This in way overcomes the traditional deficits of working with the notion of a national legal order. Further regulatee perspectives on legal certainty in the context of operation of public law has been an under researched area. This book is then treading new ground in assessing the value of legal certainty for regulatees, especially in the context of the changing dynamics of the way in which regulation is being conducted. It highlights the reflexivity with which regulatees have been able to pursue legal certainty within these changing dynamics.

Lastly two annexures are appended to the book. Annexure I and II are the questionnaires for the two case studies on medical devices and pharmaceutical products respectively.

References

Abbott KW, Snidal D (2009) The governance triangle: regulatory standards, institutions, and the shadow of the state. In: Mattli W, Woods N (eds) The politics of global regulation. Princeton University Press, New Jersey

Aman AC (2002) Globalization, democracy and the need for a new administrative law symposium on new forms of governance: ceding public power to private actors. UCLA Law Rev 49: 1687–1716

Austin J, Rumble W (ed) (1995) The province of jurisprudence determined (1832). Cambridge University Press, Cambridge, U.K

Baldwin R, Cave M, Lodge M (ed) (2012) Understanding regulation. Oxford University Press, Oxford U.K

Barnett M, Finnemore M (2004) Rules for the world: international organizations in global politics. Cornell University Press, New York

Berman A, Duquet S, Pauwelyn J, Wessel R, Wouters J (eds) (2012) Informal international lawmaking: case studies. Torkel Opsahl Academic Publisher, Oslo

Black J (2002) Critical reflections on regulation. CARR Discussion Paper Series 4, The London School of Economics and Political Science

Burke-White WW (2004) International legal pluralism. Mich J Int Law 25:963–979

Camacho-Romisher L (2000) The regulatory life cycle and regulatory concerns for the utilities of the Northern Mariana Islands. Nat Resour J 40:569–601

Cavalieri E, Carotti B, Casini L, MacDonald E, Cassese S (eds) (2012) Global administrative law: the casebook, 3rd edn. Institute for International Law and Justice, New York

Chesterman S, Fisher A (eds) (2009) Private security, public order: the outsourcing of public services and its limits. Oxford University Press, Oxford, U.K

Chowdhury N, Wessel RA (2012) Conceptualizing multilevel regulation in the EU: a legal translation of multilevel governance? Eur Law J 18:335–357

Christiano T, Sciaraffa S (2003) Legal positivism and the nature of legal obligation. Law Philos 22:487–512

De Burca G (2008) Developing democracy beyond the state. Columbia J Transnational Law 46: 101–158

de Chazournes LB (2012) Introduction: courts and tribunals and the treatment of scientific issues. J Int Dispute Settlement 3:479–481

de Sousa Santos B (1987) Law: a map of misreading. Towards a postmodern conception of law. J Law Soc 14:279–302

de Sousa Santos B (2002) Towards a new legal common sense, 2nd edn. LexisNexis Butterworths, London, U.K

de Wet E (2006) The emergence of international and regional value systems as a manifestation of an international constitutional order. Leiden J Int Law 19:611–632

de Witte B (2003) Do not mention the word: sovereignty in two Europhile countries. In Walker N (ed) Sovereignty in transition. Hart, Oxford, U.K

Deflem M (2008) Sociology of law: visions of a scholarly tradition. Cambridge University Press

Dezaley Y (1996) Between the state, law and the market: the social and professional stakes in the construction and definition of a regulatory arena. In: Bratton WW et al (eds) International regulatory competition and coordination. Clarendon, Oxford, U.K., p 84

Dorbeck-Jung BR (2009) Global trade: changes in the conceptualisation of legal certainty. In: Gessner V (ed) Contractual certainty in international trade. Hart, Oxford, pp 258–289

Dunoff J, Trachtman JP (2009) A functional approach to international constitutionalization. In: Dunoff J, Trachtman JP (eds) Ruling the world? Constitutionalism, international law, and global governance. Cambridge University Press, New York

Dyzenhaus D (2012) Constitutionalism in an old key: legality and constituent power. Global Constitutionalism 1:229–260

European Commission (2000) Guide to the implementation of directives based on the new approach and the global approach. European Communities

Follesdal A (2012) Global distributive justice? State boundaries as a normative problem. Global Constitutionalism 1:261–277

Føllesdal A, Wessel RA, Wouters J (eds) (2008) Multilevel regulation and the EU: the interplay between global, European and national normative processes. Martinus Nijhoff, Leiden, pp 9–47

Goldsmith J (2000) The internet, conflicts of regulation and international harmonization. In: Engel C (ed) Governance of global networks in the light of differing local values. Nomos, Baden-Baden

Griffiths J (1986) What is legal pluralism? J Legal Pluralism 24:15–29

Haas PM (1992) Introduction: epistemic communities and international policy coordination. Int Organ 46:1–35

Hancher L, Moran M (1989) Organising regulatory space. In: Hancher L, Moran M (eds) Capitalism, culture and economic regulation. Oxford University Press, Oxford, U.K., pp 271–299

Hart HLA (1961) The concept of law. Oxford University Press, Oxford, U.K

Havercroft J (2012) Was Westphalia 'all that'? Hobbes, Bellarmine and the norm of non-intervention. Global Constitutionalism 1:120–140

Heller R, Kahl M, Pisoiu D (2012) The 'dark' side of normative argumentation – the case of counterterrorism policy. Global Constitutionalism 1:278–312

Hollis DB (2002) Private actors in public international law: Amicus Curiae and the case for the retention of state sovereignty. Boston College Int Comp Law Rev 25:235–255

Jansen K, Roquas E (2002) Absentee expertise: international epistemic communities and biotechnology regulation in Latin America. Paper presented at the conference on science and citizenship in a global context: challenges from new technologies, Institute of Development Studies, Brighton, 12–13 December 2002

Jeffrey DL (2012) Is sovereign equality obsolete? Understanding twenty-first century international organizations. Netherlands Yearbook Int Law 43:99–127

Jillions A (2012) Commanding the commons: constitutional enforcement and the law of the sea. Global Constitutionalism 1:429–454

Kalypso N, Shaffer G (2005) Transnational mutual recognition regimes: governance without global government. Law Contemp Probl 68:263–317

Kelsen H (1967) Pure theory of law (trans: Knight M). University of California Press, California

Kingsbury B (2009) The concept of 'Law' in global administrative law. Eur J Int Law 20:23–57

Kingsbury B, Krisch N, Stewart R (2005) The emergence of global administrative law. Law Contemp Probl 68:15–62

Klabbers J (2004) Constitutionalism lite. Int Organ Law Rev 1:31–58

Kooiman J (2003) Governing as governance. Sage, London

Koskenniemi M (2007) The fate of public international law: between technique and politics. Modern Law Rev 70:1–30

Koskenniemi M (2009) The politics of international law. Twenty years later. Eur J Int Law 20:7–19

Koskenniemi M, Leino P (2002) Fragmentation of international law? Postmodern anxieties. Leiden J Int Law 15:553–579

Krisch N (2009a) Global administrative law and the constitutional ambition. LSE Law, Society and Economy Working Papers, London School of Economics and Political Science

Krisch N (2009b) Case for pluralism in postnational law. LSE Law, Society and Economy Working Papers, London School of Economics and Political Science

Krisch N (2012) Beyond constitutionalism: the pluralist structure of postnational law. Oxford University Press, Oxford, U.K

Ladeur K-H (2009) The emergence of global administrative law and transnational regulation. International Law and Justice Working Papers, New York University School of Law

Lang A (2008) Global administrative law in domestic courts: holding global administrative law bodies accountable. International Law and Justice Working Papers, New York University School of Law
Luhmann N (1977) Differentiation of society. Can J Sociol 2:29–53
Luhmann N (1985) A sociological theory of law. Routledge, Oxford, U.K
Luhmann N (2004) Law as a social system. Oxford University Press, Oxford, U.K
Mac Cormick N (1999) Questioning sovereignty. Oxford University Press, Oxford, U.K
Marie Diller J (2011) Private standardization in public international lawmaking. Mich J Int Law 33:481–536
Mayer FC (2000) Europe and the internet: the old world and the new medium. Eur J Int Law 11:149–169
Meidinger E (2006) The administrative law of global private–public regulation: the case of forestry. Eur J Int Law 17:47–87
Merry SE (1988) Legal pluralism. Law Soc Rev 22:869–901
Michaels R (2005) The re-statement of non-state law: the state, choice of law and the challenge of global legal pluralism. Wayne Law Rev 51:1209–1259
Michaels R (2007) The true Lex Mercatoria: law beyond the state. Indiana J Global Legal Stud 14:447–468
Ming-Sung K (2013) On the constitutional question in global governance: global administrative law and the conflicts-law approach in comparison. Global Constitutionalism 2:437–468
Moore SF (1973) Law and social change: the semi-autonomous social field as an appropriate subject of study. Law Soc Rev 7:719–746
Nobles R, Schiff D (2012) Using systems theory to study legal pluralism: what could be gained? Law Soc Rev 46:265–269
Nonet P, Selznick P (1978) Law & society in transition: toward responsive law. Transaction Publishers, New York
Pauwelyn J, Wessel R, Wouters J (eds) (2012) Informal international law-making. Oxford University Press, Oxford, U.K
Pino G (1999) The place of legal positivism in contemporary constitutional states. Law Philos 18513–536
Raz J (1979) Kelsen's theory of the basic norm. In: Raz J (ed) The authority of law: essays on law and morality. Clarendon Press, Oxford, U.K., pp 122–145
Scheuerman WE (1999) Globalization and the fate of law. In: Dyzenhaus D (ed) Recrafting the rule of law. Hart, Oxford, U.K., pp 243–266
Schiff Berman P (2007) Global legal pluralism. Southern Calif Law Rev 80:1155–1237
Scott C, Cafaggi F, Senden L (eds) (2011) The challenge of transnational private regulation: conceptual and constitutional debates. Wiley-Blackwell, New Jersey
Selznick P (1985) Focusing organizational research on regulation. In: Noll R (ed) Regulatory policy and the social sciences. University of California Press, California, p 363
Slawotsky J (2012) The global corporation as international law actor. Virginia J Int Law 52:79–90
Stewart R (2008) Accountability, participation, and the problem of disregard in global regulatory governance. International Legal Theory Colloquium, New York University Law School. http://iilj.org/courses/2008IILJCColloquium.asp
Swedberg R (2006) Max Weber's contribution to the economic sociology of law. Annu Rev Law Soc Sci 2:61–81
Teubner G (1989) How the law thinks: towards a constructivist epistemology of law. Working Paper no. 89/393. European University Institute
Teubner G (1993) Law as an autopoietic system. Blackwell, Oxford, U.K
Teubner G (ed) (1997a) Global law without a state. Aldershot, Dartmouth
Teubner G (1997b) Global Bukowina: legal pluralism in world society. In: Teubner G (ed) Global law without a state. Dartmouth Publishing Group, Dartmouth
Teubner G (2002) Hybrid laws: constitutionalizing private governance networks. In: Kagan R, Winston K (eds) Legality and community. Berkeley Public Policy Press, Berkeley, p 311

Teubner G (2004) Societal constitutionalism: alternatives to state-centered constitutional theory? In: Joerges C, Sand I-J, Teubner G (eds) Constitutionalism and transnational governance. Hart Publishing, Portland, Oregon, pp 3–28

Teubner G, Fischer-Lescano A (2004) Regime-collisions: the vain search for legal unity in the fragmentation of global law. Mich J Int Law 25:999–1046

Turner S (2008) Expertise and the process of policy making: the EU's new model of legitimacy. In: Eliason S (ed) Building civil society and democracy in New Europe. Cambridge Scholars Publishing, Cambridge, p 160

Twining W (2009) Normative and legal pluralism: a global perspective. Duke J Comp Int Law 20:473–518

Ulrich S (2010) Legal order in a global world – the development of a fragmented system of national, international and private norms. In: von Armin B, Wolfrum R (eds) Max Planck Yearbook of United Nations Law, vol 14. Brill, Leiden, pp 1–49

Van Der Pijl K (1998) Transnational classes and international relations. Routledge, London/ New York

von Bogdandy A, Dann P, Goldmann M (2010) Developing the publicness of public international law: towards a legal framework for global governance activities. In: von Bogdandy A, Wolfrum R, von Bernstorff J, Dann P, Goldmann M (eds) The exercise of public authority by international institutions: advancing international institutional law. Springer, Heidelberg

Wai R (2008) The interlegality of private international law. Law Contemp Probl 71:107–128

Walker N (2002) The idea of constitutional pluralism. Mod Law Rev 65:317–359

Walker N (2008) Taking constitutionalism beyond the state. Polit Stud 56:519–543

Walker N (2009) Reframing EU constitutionalism. Blog of the European Journal of International Law. http://www.ejiltalk.org/reframing-eu-constitutionalism/

Walker N (2011) Reconciling Mac Cormick: constitutional pluralism and the unity of practical reason. Ratio Juris 24:369–85

Werner W (2007) Constitutionalisation, fragmentation, politicisation: the Constitutionalisation of international law as a Janus-faced phenomenon. Griffen's View 8:17–30

Wessel RA, Wouters J (2008) The phenomenon of multilevel regulation. In: Wessel RA, Wouters J (eds) Multilevel regulation and the EU: the interplay between global, European and national normative processes. Martinus Nijhoff, Leiden, pp 9–47

Zaring D (1998) International law by other means: the twilight existence of international financial regulatory organizations. Texas Int Law J 33:292–297

Zaring D (2008) Rulemaking and adjudication in international law. Columbia J Transnational Law 46:563–611

Zarmanian T (2006) Carl Schmitt and the problem of legal order: from domestic to international. Leiden J Int Law 19:41–67

Zumbansen P (2010) Transnational legal pluralism. Transnational Legal Theory 10:141–189

Chapter 2
Conceptualizing Multilevel Regulation

2.1 Introduction

This chapter addresses the first sub-research question: *What are the criteria for establishing multilevelness of a regulatory space?* This chapter discusses the genesis of the term multilevel regulation—in terms of how it builds and departs from the neighboring concept of 'multilevel governance.' More pertinently it identifies key features of this concept and ultimately a set of criteria that will allow us to apply the concept to understand current developments in regulatory spaces. This is a necessary first step to describe and capture both the horizontal and vertical developments that have been discussed in Sect. 1.1.

Since more than three decades, regulation has emerged as an exciting area of social science research, drawing primary from the disciplines of economics, political science and law.[1] In the US, the 1960s and 1970s witnessed an explosion of regulatory research flowing from the new structures of health safety and environment regulation.[2] The setting up of a number of independent institutions (agencies)—saw the shift away from control through bureaucracy to technocrats operating through independent federal regulatory commissions. Typically these commissions subsumed the powers of rule making, monitoring and enforcement and sanctioning.[3] Scholars focused at the level of the agency on aspects like architecture, institutional setting and rule specificity.[4] Across the Atlantic, in the UK, legislatures retained rule making authority and delegation was limited to enforcement or sanctioning operations that were given to central bodies such as the Health and Safety Executive or utilities regulators (viz. electricity and railways). It underlines the importance of regulatory cultures in the design of

[1] Noll (1995).

[2] See Wilson (1980), Bardach and Kagan (1982), and Ostrom (1990).

[3] Selznick (1985), p. 363. See on the history of regulation, Rabin (1994).

[4] See Breyer (1982); Peltzman (1989), pp. 1–59; and Diver (1983), pp. 65–109.

N. Chowdhury, *European Regulation of Medical Devices and Pharmaceuticals*,
DOI 10.1007/978-3-319-04594-8_2,

institutions and choice of enforcement tools.[5] The French school of regulation theory in the seventies[6] chose to focus on the conflictual dynamics of capitalist markets embedded in an understanding of the different phases of capitalist development and types of capitalist formation. Since the early nineties with increasing Europeanization, studies on regulation within the political entity of the European Union have also emerged.[7] Diffusion of regulatory authority to supranational bodies, private institutions and their undermining of modes of democratic control and legislative accountability are themes that have been explored.[8]

Current research has focused on several aspects of regulatory theory. The research team at ANU led by Professor Braithwaite has concentrated on the challenges of regulatory enforcement, in their graduated scale of enforcement paradigm and the pioneering study on responsive regulation.[9] Responsive regulation does not suggest a certain regulatory type; it supports the opening up of discursive spaces, wherein regulators can consider a range of outcomes taking into consideration the specific characteristics of the regulated industry. Specific regulatory interventions for networked industries like energy, electricity and telecommunications has been explored by researchers at the EUI.[10] A more systemic perspective on risk as the central organizing principle underlying regulation; has been adopted by others in explaining the varieties of enforced self-regulation and risk management practiced at the firm level and how that connects to the systemic level as steered by public regulators.[11]

Both policymakers and academic scholars from law and politics have come to accept the fact that the process of regulation has undergone a significant change over the last two decades. It has gone from being a limited political activity of the State—that of managing the market to secure public interest goals—to that of a more open-ended process through which an independent public (technocratic) authority interacts with a host of public and private actors (regulatees) in norm formation, norm application and norm adjudication within a specific public policy area.[12] This de-coupling

---

[5] Meidinger (1987), pp. 355–386.

[6] Aglietta (1979). Also, Brenner and Glick (1991), pp. 45–119. Lipietz (1986), pp. 13–32. Boyer (1990).

[7] See Majone (1994), pp. 77–101; Majone (1997), pp. 139–167; Vogel (2003), pp. 557–580; and Coen and Doyle (2000), pp. 83–106.

[8] Schepel (2005) at 407. Teubner (1997), pp. 145–169.

[9] See Ayres and Braithwaite (1992), Gunningham and Grabosky (1998), and Braithwaite (2002).

[10] See for instance, Bauknecht (2011) and Bickenbach (2000).

[11] See the Centre for Analysis of Risk and Regulation (CARR) at the London School of Economics. See for instance, Benzer (2011) and Etienne (2010).

[12] This would include both hard and soft norms. Hard norms have a binding effect which is missing in soft norms. In other words, hard norms penalize non-compliance (legal penalties), whereas there are no penal sanctions attached to soft norms. However there may well be other kinds of sanctions—such as social sanctions—that may be attached to soft norms. Scholars like Linda Senden and Francis Snyder have argued that soft norms may be as 'binding' as hard norms (see Senden 2004 and Snyder 1993). Here I refer to 'bindingness' in terms of legal penalties that is liable to be imposed for non-compliance.

of the state from its regulatory activities has been widely analyzed and commented by political scientists.[13] Scott most famously termed it as the "rise of the post-regulatory State".[14] This process has been characterized as open-ended, since both the rationale and the manner in which regulation is conducted, has increasingly come to resemble a negotiated outcome resulting from the interaction between multiple actors.

This phenomenon has now come to characterize regulation in a number of policy sectors[15] in most countries and (given the nature and distribution of political authority in Europe) those in Europe in particular. As mentioned above, one of the rationales that have acted as a catalyst for cooperation of international regulation has been the probability of negative externalities that could result from activities carried out within national boundaries. The objective of free trade has also been a key driver of regional and international regulation efforts that focus on harmonization in standard setting. Similar rationales have also driven efforts for the 'Europeanization' of public policy issues in Europe.[16] This trend refers to the extending mandate of European institutions to cover hitherto national public policy areas. With this, more and more sectoral regulation has seen the emergence and active participation of both private and public actors operating at the European level. Regulatory mandates reflecting the shared competences between the Member States and the European Commission have made a direct impact in opening up the regulatory space[17] to include a wide variety of actors operating at multiple administrative levels. Another important driver fuelling this expansion of the regulatory space (to include actors operating at multiple levels) has been the regulatory expertise deficits that have emerged in high technology areas.

Depending on the nature of the public policy field, these actors may include a range of public and private actors not only operating nationally but also at the sub-national, European and even international levels. Certain kinds of public policy issues, viz. environment, have enormous potential for negative externalities are ideal candidates for regional and international regulation. Others like specific aspects of health systems (pharmaceuticals and service delivery) are increasingly subject to EU regulation due to the freedom of movement provisions in the EU Treaties.[18] The actors that play a critical role in the regulatory process (design,

[13] De-coupling refers to the distancing of the State from its functions as a regulator (including that of norm formation, norm enforcement and norm adjudication). Julia Black refers to this as a process of de-centering. Black (2001), pp. 103–147.

[14] Scott (2004). See also Loughlin and Scott (1997). See generally, Majone (1996); McGowan and Seabright (1995), Moran (2002), pp. 391–413.

[15] This is especially true for those sectors—environment, finance, and health policy—where negative externalities are enormous and regional and global regulatory initiatives are well developed.

[16] Lenschow (2006) at 55–71; Princen (2007), pp. 21–38; Dimitrakopoulis and Richardson (2004) at 335–356.

[17] Here I use the concept of 'regulatory space' as developed by Hancher and Moran (1989), pp. 271–299. See also footnotes 39 and 70 in Chap. 1.

[18] Articles 18, 39, 43, 28 and 49 of the Treaty on the Functioning of the European Union (TFEU).

implementation and enforcement of norms) may therefore be drawn from more than one administrative level (sub-national, European and international)—and this phenomenon is referred to as multilevel regulation. Multilevel regulation essentially refers to the nature of regulatory activity in a specific sector/on a specific issue—and by definition it involves a range of actors, who may be operating at different administrative levels—but come together to interact and negotiate both substantive and procedural norms that regulate all activities in that sector. I understand "regulation" in a broad sense here, referring to the setting of rules, standards or principles that govern conduct by public and/or private actors. Whereas "rules" are the most constraining and rigid, "standards" leave a greater range of choice or discretion, while "principles" is still more flexible, leaving scope to balance a number of (policy) considerations.[19] However, it is important to note that the interaction between norms[20] may occur within well drawn out institutionalized settings and through formalized processes or could be more informal in nature and therefore prone to inequitable outcomes for the regulatory actors and may also result in compromise or even negation of public interest. Thus, a relatively new phenomenon emerged: *informal* international regulation or law-making. The type of rules these bodies produce is 'informal' in the sense that they deviate from traditional law-making in relation to three aspects: *output*, *process* or the *actors involved*.[21] Hence, Pauwelyn defined informal international law-making as: "Cross-border cooperation between public authorities, with or without the participation of private actors and/or international organizations, in a forum other than a traditional international organization (process informality), and/or as between actors other than traditional diplomatic actors (such as regulators or agencies) (actor informality), and/or which does not result in a formal treaty or legally enforceable commitment (output informality)."[22]

I develop a concept of multilevel regulation that captures several developments within the general process and functioning of regulatory regimes[23] in Europe.[24] First, is the move away from the state as the primary actor within the regulatory process, to that of a more fluid regulatory space that is populated by both private and public actors that play critical roles in the design, enforcement and adjudication of norms. Second, these actors may be drawn from different administrative

---

[19] See Wessel and Wouters (2008), pp. 9–47. See for my understanding of the term 'regulation' footnote 71 in Chap. 1.

[20] By norms I mean rules that constitute, recognize or facilitate the achievement of certain public values by laying down prescriptive forms of public behavior.

[21] See Pauwelyn et al. (2012).

[22] Pauwelyn et al. (2012), p. 4.

[23] Refer to the definition of "regulatory regime"—'A regulatory regime is a system of control which may comprise many actors, but within which it is possible to identify standards of some kind, ways of detecting deviation from the standards, and mechanisms for correcting such deviations' given by Hood et al. (2001).

[24] For instance, an argument supporting the EU as a multilevel polity; see; Benz (2007); Brownsword and Somsen (2009), pp. 1–73.

levels—i.e. it may include international organizations, European regulators, national industry associations, multi-national companies, competent authorities of member states, private standardization organizations, to name just a few. Together these actors may constitute the regulatory space for a specific sector—medical products for instance. Third, the regulatory space may or may not be reflected in the formal legal framework that governs that sector. In other words the regulatory space may be populated with actors that do not have formal legal roles but who nevertheless play a critical role in the regulatory process. Thus norm formation, norm application and norm adjudication may happen at different administrative/governance levels with little or no reference to each other and more critically without reference to the formal legal systems that are in place nationally and at the European level. The danger of regulatory overlap and dissonance as an outcome of lack of cohesiveness and fragmentation may lead to regulatory uncertainty and may in the process undermine legal certainty in a regulatory space that is characterized by such multi-levelness.

Here it is important to note that I do differentiate between regulatory uncertainty and legal certainty. Regulatory uncertainty as a term is used widely in management studies and also in public regulation.[25] Whereas there may be pockets within the regulatory space that may be characterized by regulatory uncertainty, legal certainty is a feature of the regulatory space at the macro level. Thus although regulatory spaces may witness regulatory uncertainty this may not necessarily lead to a challenge of legal certainty.

The concept of regulatory space is primarily used here as a framing device or an analytical tool[26] to carry out a mapping of relevant actors, the distribution of resources and competences between them, and the process of interactions between them. Regulatory space also allows for flexibility in the delimitation of a regulatory sector/regime in terms of the specific aspects[27] to be studied. Thus for instance, it is possible to distinguish—intellectual property regulation of pharmaceutical products as a separate regulatory space—from that of product safety regulation of pharmaceutical products. This allows researchers to undertake an in-depth study of a specific aspect of the regulatory regime. Concentrating on different kinds of regulatory competence enables us to identify a range of actors that inhabit the regulatory space. On the basis of their actions within the entire regulatory lifecycle, it is possible to identify the relative importance of the actors in terms of regulators

[25] Brennan and Schwartz (1982), pp. 506–521. Levinson (2012).

[26] Similar applications of this concept in socio-legal studies include, Kaye and Gibbons (2008), pp. 111–130; and Faulkner (2012), pp. 165–184. For discussions reflecting on the idea of 'space' in the context of regulation; See Butler (2009), pp. 313–332; and Blandy and Sibley (2010), pp. 275–284.

[27] By aspects I refer to different public interest objectives that may govern different parts of the process or product that is sought to be regulated. Thus the purpose (public interest objectives) for regulating pricing and reimbursement of pharmaceuticals is different from regulating the marketing authorization of pharmaceuticals. Thus marketing authorization and reimbursement are two specific aspects—which may be constituted by two different regulatory spaces.

(who are involved in rule formulation), regulatees (who are receivers of rules and may also be involved in rule application) and other stakeholders (who may be indirectly affected by rule application or implementation of rules by regulatees or may play a reactive role in terms of following the rules). This is admittedly a simplification; it is of course possible that some of the actors could also play multiple roles. However it is necessary to underline that by drawing attention to the diversity of (and unequal in terms of regulatory resources) actors inhabiting this space, the concept provides us with a theoretical avenue for a better analysis of functions and capacities of actors. I use the concept of regulatory space as against policy spaces,[28] regimes[29] or sites of governance[30] because; I want to focus on a specific aspect within a policy field/space (in our case marketing authorization of medical devices). I find the other three alternatives to be broader and more loosely defined in terms of the relationship between the constituent units. Within a regulatory space, the constituents are actors and they are the primary drivers of regulatory actions.

Ultimately, multilevel regulation allows me to highlight a regulatory space that is operating vertically. Hence there are regulatory actors, functioning at different administrative levels—who are not in hierarchical relationship with each other, but who may take cognizance of each other. Globalization has reconfigured most regulatory spaces in a vertical fashion, wherein national legal systems function as another administrative level rather than a separate legal system. It highlights the explicit or indirect relationships between the different actors within a specific regulatory space and how this affects rule making, rule application and rule adjudication activities. The central presumption of a legal systems approach to regulation is that higher level structures shape lower level entities. I explicitly abandon this presumption for the possibility of regulatory actors being motivated not only by their location within that administrative level but also by their membership of specific networks which may operate at other administrative levels (an obvious example being the CEN as a member of the ISO network also has rule making authority under the *New Approach* regulatory sectors). Thus a specific regulatory space that may concomitantly exist as an enclave across several independent but interconnected legal systems.

Robert Ahdieh's vision of intersystemic regulation[31] is a current legal reality and his attempts to interpret interactions between multiple regulatory authorities as hierarchic, dialogic or 'dialectical regulation' forms an inspiration for multilevel regulation. Paul Schiff Berman built on Ahdieh's research, to also include non-state actors. He has argued for the need to study plural law making communities and by implication, the deterritorialization of legal effects.[32] Francis Snyder, in his work

[28] Wallace et al. (2010).

[29] Krasner (1982), pp. 185–205.

[30] Snyder (2001), p. 251.

[31] Ahdieh (2006), p. 863.

[32] Schiff Berman (2006), p. 929.

on sites of governance for understanding global legal pluralism[33] resulting from globalization, also seems to challenge the territorial obsession that the legal systems approach has always propounded. Do the 'levels' in multilevel regulation represent this obsession with territoriality? The answer has to be in the negative, since the locus of the national state is not given primacy. I believe that regulatory spaces represent more useful units of analysis. I locate actors involved in rule making, rule application or rule adjudication activities at the various *administrative levels*. Our manner of using levels does not give primacy to one administrative level over another but is more of a descriptive tag to capture the location of different regulatory actors. In that sense, the concept is not a normative project but simply a descriptive tool to capture current regulatory processes.

The chapter proceeds in four steps. In Sect. 2.2, I investigate the literature on the use of the neighboring concept of multilevel governance highlighting the different disciplines and policy studies that have used the concept of multi-level governance to capture a wide variety of governance developments within Europe. Given that multi-level regulation and multi-level governance has been used interchangeably within such studies,[34] it is important to explore whether at the conceptual level there are certain similarities or whether the two can be separated and its implication for evolving a conceptual definition of multi-level regulation. In Sect. 2.3, I propose a definition of multilevel regulation and discuss the key features which such a definition should capture. Given the multi-dimensional and largely fluid nature of social science concepts that capture phenomena as evolving in reality—the family resemblance structure is more appropriate than the essentialist structure of necessary and sufficient condition. I also investigate how legal scholars have responded to these debates on regulation. And, assess those on legal pluralism to highlight the ways in which multilevel regulation builds on them. In Sect. 2.4, I make some concluding remarks.

2.2 Multilevel Governance as an Inspiration for Multilevel Regulation

Current usage of the term "multilevel governance" seems to be widespread and prolific amongst both political scientists as well as policymakers. However, there are significant differences between multilevel governance as a descriptive concept developed to theorize decision-making within European policy processes and multilevel governance as a policy goal underlying the European integration project. Although the currency of these two conceptions have in some senses fed off each other, it is important to study them separately, given that each have different

[33] Snyder (2010), p. 407.

[34] European styles or approaches to regulation as being distinctive and reflecting the distinctive politico-institutional structures of European Union, See Hancher and Moran (1989), pp. 271–299.

functions and therefore differ in their substantive implications. My focus here is on excavating the contours of the descriptive concept to then investigate whether it is possible to whittle down (in a rather reductionist manner) certain core features of the concept. Nevertheless the political foundations of this concept have to a large extent also molded (and to some extent have limited) the applicability of this concept; the debate on whether this concept primarily characterizes a European political phenomenon is still open. I will revisit this issue in the following paragraphs.

Most accept Gary Marks' study of European structural policymaking in the early 1990s as one of the first expositions of the concept of multilevel governance.[35] The initial definition was therefore necessarily broad and referred to multilevel governance as:

> a system of continuous negotiation among nested governments at several territorial tiers – supranational, national, regional, and local – as a result of a broad process of institutional creation and decisional allocation.

Subsequently this definition was refined further by Marks and Hooghe in 2003; as implying "reallocation of authority upwards, downwards and sideways from central states."[36] Others like Kohler-Koch and Rittberger have also highlighted the role of private actors in these governance arrangements and the interdependence between them and other actors.[37] Shared decision-making by actors operating across different administrative levels have been split into horizontal and vertical multilevel governance. The former highlights the shift in responsibility within governance arrangements from government actors to a host of private actors (non-profit and others).[38] While the latter refers to governance shifts away from the nation state to other administrative levels (sub-national, regional and international).[39] Multilevel governance processes simultaneously make accessible, European governance arrangements to a wide range of actors operating at different levels and thereby making it more complex and therefore difficult to map.

Marks and Hooghe tried to address this problem by distinguishing between Type I and Type II versions of multilevel governance. They contend that Type I resembles federal arrangements and intergovernmental arrangements and are characteristic of general purpose jurisdictions, where functions are bundled and there are multiple (but limited) levels of government within a system-wide architecture. The Type II version is characterized by functionally specific jurisdictions, operating at different territorial levels in a flexible manner. They gave the example of such kind of arrangements operating at the local level in Switzerland (where *Zweckverbände* operate as goal oriented jurisdictions). They also underline that such governance

---

[35] Marks (1993) at 391–410.

[36] Hooghe and Marks (2001, 2003).

[37] Kohler-Koch and Rittberger (2006), pp. 27–49.

[38] Eckerberg and Joas (2004), pp. 405–412.

[39] Watson et al. (2004).

arrangements have also been variously referred to in scholarship as polycentric governance,[40] and FOCJ (functional, overlapping, and competing jurisdictions).[41]

Various scholars have attempted to define the concept of multilevel governance. Phillipe Schmitter defined it:

> As an arrangement for making binding decisions that engages a multiplicity of politically independent but otherwise interdependent actors – private and public – at different levels of territorial aggregation in more or less continuous negotiation/deliberation/implementation, and that does not assign exclusive policy competence or assert a stable hierarchy of political authority to any of these levels.[42]

This definition highlights the nature of engagement of multiple actors within such arrangements. The nature of engagement is not passive but active and also substantive in terms of shaping and steering decision making. Peters and Pierre's study zeroes in on a set of descriptions of multilevel governance: (1) it is governance (as opposed to government); (2) "refers to particular kinds of relationships between several institutional levels" not hierarchically ordered but more contextually defined; (3) "denotes a negotiated order rather than an order defined by formalized legal frameworks", and, (4) "frequently conceived of as a political game."[43] This again underlines the highly flexible nature of such arrangements and their decoupling from the statist administrative arrangements.

Bach and Flinders stress that there is no one definition of multilevel governance (henceforth MLG) that enjoys consensus across academic disciplines.[44]

Although the development of MLG as a concept is closely connected with the European political integration process, there have been several studies that have explored specific sectors like environmental policy. One such excellent empirical study was by Walti, in which she investigated whether MLG structures affect environmental policy in industrialized countries. The study used two theoretical strands: functional federalism; which underlines the efficiency enhancement capabilities of decentralized governance, and the actor related theory of federalism that stresses the potential for fragmentation and multiple veto points in such a system.[45] The study concluded that "multilevel structures do play a role in environmental policy, albeit often an indirect one: to the extent that multilevel governance variables have a direct impact on environmental performance, their effect appears to be positive."[46] This would seem to suggest that regulatory structures and distribution of competences ensuring subsidiarity will have a positive[47] impact in sectors wherein regulatory actions are influenced greatly by local factors.

---

[40] The foremost proponents being Vincent and Elinor Ostrom; Ostrom (1999) at 52–74. Also see Andersson and Ostrom (2008), pp. 71–93.

[41] Frey and Eichenberger (1999).

[42] Schmitter (2004), pp. 45–74.

[43] Peters and Pierre (2004).

[44] Bache and Flinders (2004).

[45] Walti (2004), pp. 599–634.

[46] Walti (2004), p. 624.

[47] Positive in this context refers to effectiveness in terms of achieving the policy objectives.

If I were to provide for a tightly bound concept of multilevel governance (for instance like Pattoni's list of features) then it would seem that MLG could be used to characterize any policy field within or outside the EU that displays those particular features—and this policy field can operate at the national, European, or international level. Indeed this seems to be the presumption in studies of specific policy fields like energy efficiency,[48] environment,[49] food safety,[50] and even development aid[51]; in the context of MLG. Part of the reason why there is a lack of consensus relates to the wide range of definitions of MLG which scholars[52] have worked with leading to what Sartori termed as "conceptual stretching".[53]

Other perspectives on European governance have also come from within the legal discipline. One of the earlier examples of this investigation was Markus Jachtenfuchs work on European governance,[54] in which he made the plea to refocus attention on the effects of globalization and functional differentiation instead of addressing exclusively the question whether the national member states will be replaced or overtaken by the European polity. In that sense the European governance was reconceived as dynamic arena through the nation states negotiated the pressures of globalization and functional differentiation as propounded in the systems theory.[55] Another key focus driving studies of European regulation has been the issue of democratic legitimacy of the European Union.[56] The shift from law-based to nodal (network based) governance within the EU—by focusing on such processes as the OMC (open method of coordination) has been highlighted.[57] Legitimacy deficits could also be addressed via multilevel control.[58] Others have sought to reveal the negative implications of having multilevel governance within the European Union as a normative project,[59] where the *demos* is sought to be replaced with expertise and technical knowledge that form the basis of new public management. Scholars like Charles F. Sabel and Jonathan Zeitlin have characterized European regulatory processes as "new architecture of experimental

[48] International Energy Agency (2009).

[49] Paraskevopoulos (2006).

[50] Bernauer and Caduff (2004).

[51] Patrick et al. (2005).

[52] See Gualini (2004). Stubbs (2005), pp. 66–87.

[53] Sartori (1994).

[54] Jachtenfuchs (1995), pp. 115–133.

[55] In systems theory, sub-systems based on functionality develop self-logic to a degree to which they become immune to external influence and become self-referential in action. Here the state is not seen as the primary basis for social organization—as the political arena is just one of the many arenas of functional differentiation. And, therefore reflection and not hierarchy becomes the new medium of governance. See Teubner (1987) at 3–48.

[56] Carter and Scott (1998), pp. 429–445.

[57] Radaelli (2003); Kersbergen and Waarden (2004), p. 143. More generally see de Burca and Scott (2006).

[58] Scott (2008), p. 59.

[59] Shore (2011), pp. 287–303.

governance" highlighting a set of distinct features of European governance like framework goals that are set jointly by member states and European institutions, autonomy to local bodies within member states to device strategies and mechanisms to implement those rules and also to participate in a peer review process that regularly reviews their performance. They refer to this as direct deliberative polyarchy (DDP); and argue that it does promote new forms of democratic accountability which is not akin to representative democracy.

I do not use multilevel regulation as a normative concept and in that sense it does not resemble multilevel regulation as it has been developed by European policymakers. Multilevel regulation is developed as a frame of reference to capture developments that are vertically linked across administrative or territorial levels within a specific regulatory space. Therefore, two important assumptions underlying this concept are first; regulatory actions—like rule making, rule application and rule adjudication is dispersed vertically across administrative levels. And, in that sense I eschew the horizontality of networks and sites of governance. Second, multilevel regulation also assumes a dispersion of authority amongst public and private actors. These actors may be acting cooperatively or in competition with one other. In the following section I draw a distinction between regulation and governance in order to also highlight the differences between multilevel governance and multilevel regulation. Looking at multilevel regulation as a legal translation of multilevel governance would be a simplification and, that which has limited descriptive power.

2.3 Defining Multilevel Regulation

2.3.1 How Is Multilevel Regulation Different from Multilevel Governance?

It may not come as a surprise that the difference between the concept of multilevel regulation and multilevel governance primarily lies in the distinction between what is known as "governance" and "regulation" in academic literature. As a heuristic category, *governance* refers to the shift in nature and process of policymaking within the modern nation state, in which, the government is in a relationship of negotiation and cooperation with private actors, in setting up and implementing binding rules which may be implemented beyond the realm of the nation state, and also in the form of societal self-regulation.[60] In reductionist terms, one of the most important contexts of the usage of the term 'governance' has been in the delivery of public goods and services, in the post privatization era[61]—in which the state is

60 Mayntz (1998).

61 Atkinson and Coleman (1992), pp. 154–180.

transformed into a gate-keeper ensuring that public goods are distributed in a fair and effective manner. And, on the other hand *regulation* refers to the control of private behavior by public agencies to ensure that public interest is not violated within specific fields of delivery of goods and services.[62] This control is achieved via a body of administrative rules. The term is also used in the context of self-controlling behavior by private entities—self-regulation. As is apparent from the exposition of these two ideal type concepts, 'regulation' brings with it more of a statist[63] implication than 'governance'. Scholars have also argued that regulation is a smaller species of action within the broader field called governance, based on their functionality.[64] The purpose of regulation is limited—to that of steering private action with the aim of achieving a public good/goal. Therefore, multilevel governance refers to a range of policymaking activities both within and outside the nation state. Multilevel regulation on the other hand refers to the dispersed nature of rule making, rule application and rule adjudication activities across different administrative levels both within and beyond the nation state.

It is clear from the above that the primary point of difference between multilevel governance and multilevel regulation is the nature of outcome of such processes. Since multilevel regulation is closely connected with state centric processes the process of regulation has a direct or indirect (for instance self-regulation is often initiated in the shadow of formal legal requirements)[65] reference to formal legal processes either at the national, European or international levels. In any case, the outcome of such a process will have an effect in terms of influencing or shaping the legal relationship[66] between the producers and enforcers,[67] and the followers of such norms and also the regulatory behavior of individual actors[68] operating within the sector. This is not contingent on the nature of the norms—hard or soft norms[69]—this holds true for both kinds of rules. Given that multilevel regulation shares a referential relationship with law, the entire range of activities covering the regulatory lifecycle[70] is reflected within multilevel regulation. Thus multilevel regulation includes the process of making, application and adjudication of regulatory rules. To reiterate an earlier point, the key point of difference between multilevel regulation and multilevel governance is that the question of regulatory

---

[62] Scott (2001a), pp. 301–316.

[63] Laffont (1994), pp. 507–37.

[64] Governance is about providing, distributing and regulating; See Braithwaite et al. (2007), pp. 1–7.

[65] Heritier and Eckert (2008), pp. 113–138.

[66] In making this argument I may be accused by what John Griffith referred to as "the ideology of legal centralism"—exclusive focus on state law. We do not focus on only state law—but only rules that intend o create some regulatory effect—in terms of shaping behaviour.

[67] Grabosky (1995), pp. 347–69.

[68] See for a discussion of factors that influences regulatee behaviour towards compliance. Hopkins (1994), pp. 431–443.

[69] For a discussion on hard and soft norms see footnote 12 in this chapter.

[70] See footnote 10 and 71 in Chap. 1 for my understanding of the term 'regulatory lifecycle'.

effect of the activities. Given that Multilevel regulation will cover only such activities which would directly or indirectly have a regulatory effect—the scope of activities are much narrower than those which are covered under the concept of multilevel governance. Therefore, only those activities which directly or indirectly affect the regulatory behavior of the regulator or the regulatees are included within the definition of multilevel regulation.

2.3.2 Towards a Definition of Multilevel Regulation: An Analysis of Key Features

Multilevel Regulation is a term used to characterize a regulatory space, in which the process of rule making, rule application and rule adjudication[71] is dispersed across more than one administrative or territorial level amongst several different actors, both public and private. The relationship between the actors is non-hierarchical and may be independent of each other. Lack of central ordering of the regulatory lifecycle within this regulatory space is the primary feature of multilevel regulation.

In order to understand the substantive import of the above definition of Multilevel regulation, it is important to clarify some of the aspects of this description. First, I have defined Multilevel regulation as feature of a regulatory space. Herein I draw on the concept of regulatory space developed by Hancher and Moran. The primary theoretical assumption underlying this concept is the de-centering of the process of regulation from the state apparatus, and in which the state or public actors are just one of many regulatory actors (who are widely varied in nature and size) that interact with another to produce certain regulatory effects within the space. Thus formal legal authority is just one of many sources of regulatory power. Monopoly over technical expertise can be another resource.[72] The presence of different sources of regulatory power, also leads to an uneven distribution of that power amongst the various actors. Regulatory power in this context refers to the ability of influencing and shaping substantive and procedural rules that govern regulatory outcomes within the specific regulatory space. The process of interaction between these regulatory actors is through both formal and through informal networks—which as Scott put it is characterized by "negotiated interdependence and bargaining".[73] This concept has, however, been criticized by Black,[74] because it considers too many variables that may lead to obfuscation rather than illumination of the reality. I think this criticism would stand when the concept is used in an isolated manner. However, as an analytical tool it is just a useful first order framing device that allows us to focus on certain specific aspects of the regulatory regime

[71] Therefore we extend it to the entire regulatory lifecycle, See Hood et al. (2001).

[72] Ruiter and Wessel (2012).

[73] Scott (2001b), pp. 329–353.

[74] Black (2001), pp. 103–107.

and the micro-level dynamics within that regime, and enables us to identify certain regulatory trends and contextualize macro-level developments that may be an outcome of such micro-dynamics.

Other characteristics include, the distribution of these rule making, rule implementation and rule application activities across a diverse number of actors operating at different levels. The idea is to draw attention to two aspects. First that the regulatory process can be split into these three aspects: rule making, rule application and rule adjudication. Second, rules in this context mean both substantive and procedural norms that may or may not have legal sanction. Thus, it will also include private industry standardization codes that may be followed by a number of manufacturers and receive informal recognition by enforcement agencies and therefore indirect sanction under law. Thus the nature of rules—whether they are soft or hard law[75]—is not relevant, to their identity—as long as they influence and shape regulatory behavior of the actors operating within that regulatory space. Another aspect of this definition is that the sources of these rules and the actors that take part in the processes of rule-making, rule application and rule adjudication could operate at different administrative or territorial levels. I have used the words administrative *or* territorial to convey sub-national levels as well as regional or international levels. In this case, within national states, regional authorities may be administratively constructed—for instance like sub-national entities (e.g. Notified Bodies that oversees application of medical devices regulation within EU member states[76]), and outside nation states, regional players—viz. European Union and internationally, organizations like the United Nations operate—may play important roles within a regulatory space.

It is important to note that the relationship between the actors involved within the regulatory space, are necessarily non-hierarchical in nature. This is so because the actors are not self-identified members operating within a well-defined and well-ordered regulatory system—which is based on legal rules. In this case I specifically use the concept of regulatory space because it allows us the flexibility to focus on a specific aspect of the system that is not operating within a defined institutional system of rules—with clear hierarchy of order wherein each actors has been given a specific task within the system and operate in full knowledge of that competence. In this case the actors operating within the regime may not have the formal authority to act and therefore cannot be said to be in any hierarchical or even a well-defined relationship with other actors. The relationship between the actors is not defined by an ordered system of legal rules, but is contingent on their control of resources and in that sense it could well be a competitive or a collaborative relationship between actors at different points within the regulatory process and is therefore inherently pluralistic in nature. Another implication of such a construction is that there is a possibility that each of these actors could operate in dissonance with each other. In other words the lack of hierarchy and therefore the absence of any presumption of central ordering means that the actors playing identical and even similar functions

[75] Meaning of hard and soft norms has been discussed earlier. See footnote 12 in this chapter.

[76] Scott (2002), pp. 56–76.

could operate concomitantly and independently of (and therefore also at crossroads with) each other. In fact within specific regulatory sectors, it is a two way process, wherein national regulators participate in European and transnational regulatory networks that make rules for the domestic markets.[77]

The primary hook on which this construct of a regulatory space operates is how it responds to the question of delimitation. In other words, how do you limit the boundaries of a regulatory space and how do you therefore distinguish one regulatory space from another? The primary issue of difference between two regulatory spaces is the objective or subject of regulation. Thus the regulatory space for pharmaceutical pricing is different from marketing authorization of pharmaceuticals. This, to an extent, helps to distinguish between two analogous but different regulatory spaces. Another mode of delimiting a regulatory space is in terms of the legal rules that construct or operationalize that regulatory space. Certain rules will be of primary importance and others will only regulate certain minor or residual aspects of the regulatory space. Of course this does not preclude a certain degree of overlap between two regulatory spaces. Hancher and Moran chose to focus on the 'range of issues' that define or are *sui generis* to that regulatory space. This is similar to the object/subject of regulation argument which we referred to earlier. The underlying assumption is that each regulatory space can be differentiated in terms of the range of issues that is specific to it.

2.3.3 Multilevel Regulation: Response from Legal Scholars

Globalization and its impact on the role of law has been an important arena of legal research that has provided the impetus to re-engage with the idea of legal pluralism. The acceptance that there are co-existing normative orders that challenge state led law making in several areas has been explored by lawyers[78] and other researchers from social sciences and anthropology.[79] Pluralists have sought to record and analyze spaces characterized by multiplicity of norms functioning in the absence of a meta-norm and of complex overlapping institutional norm production authorities. Francis Snyder's idea of global legal pluralism includes two aspects; the structural and the relational. The former, relates to the several sites that may be structurally different—comprising of legal institutions, binding norms and dispute resolution processes. And the latter, refers to the diversity of relation types between these sites, ranging from autonomy to independence.[80] Braithwaite and Drahos have argued that increasingly in a number of policy areas, transnational private

[77] See footnotes 39 and 70 in Chap. 1 for a discussion on regulatory space.

[78] Maitland (1898), p. 13.

[79] Berman (2006); Ullmann (2010); Engle Merry (1991), p. 889. Engle Merry (1997), p. 247. Burke-White (2004), pp. 963–979.

[80] Snyder (2010), p. 407.

regulation is being adopted by nations (referring to them as rule-takers rather than rule makers).[81] They identify policy areas such as environment and financial security, where global regulation has driven down standards. And, contrast it to general economic regulation. 'Structural coupling' is the term suggested by Larry Catá Backer, to refer to what is taking place between private governance systems and public governance systems transnationally leading to a 'coordinated meta governance'.[82]

The global administrative law project[83] led the movement by highlighting the enormous growth of trans-governmental regulation across a diverse number of sectors—banking and financial regulation, environmental protection, public health and safety, labor standards, humanitarian issues and consequently the upward delegation of regulatory decision making authority. This growing integration of hitherto national policy sectors with global regulatory processes is a reality in a number of policy sectors and poses a challenge to the national structure of constitutional checks and balances which were built to safeguard and legitimize such decision-making processes. Within European studies, legal scholars like Pernice and De Witte have developed the multilevel constitutionalism as a framework to describe the uniquely *sui generis* relationship between two supreme legal institutions functioning nationally and regionally.[84] Lastly, as mentioned earlier Berman's approach to globalization is first to accept the existence of hybrid legal spaces, where the actor is regulated by multiple normative frames. This may result in conflict, although this, he contends, should not be seen as a negative. This pushes the utility of legal pluralism from just being a descriptive concept to one that can provide important clues to the design of institutional structures and mechanisms that allow for a sort of peaceful co-existence of normative structures.[85]

In the second place, scholars have argued for a multilevel regulatory regime in the case of specific policy issues such as climate change, which requires a multilevel and multi-actor approach.[86] The primary aspects of this phenomenon being of interest to legal scholars, is the multiplication of formal and informal fora wherein regulation formation is taking place. There is a great diversity in the nature of fora—and that also includes those that focus on developing technical regulations within a specific context—for instance the ICAO on aircraft engine emissions.[87] It is necessary to underline that over the past decade there has been have been a spurt

[81] Braithwaite and Drahos (2000). Another example being the entire area of international standardization led by ISO; See Schepel (2005).

[82] Please note this usage is distinct and entirely unconnected to as used by Gunther Teubner. Backer (2011).

[83] Kingsbury et al. (2005), pp. 15–62.

[84] Pernice (1998); Pernice (1999), pp. 703–750.

[85] Schiff Berman (2007), pp. 1155–1237.

[86] Kern (2010). Rabe (2007), pp. 423–444.

[87] Annex 16—Environmental Protection, Volume II—Aircraft Engine Emissions to the Convention on International Civil Aviation, Ninth Edition, 2006. http://www.icao.int/icaonet/dcs/7300_cons.pdf (accessed June 10 2010).

in the activity of technical forums set up internationally to develop technical norms (some perhaps soft). Most of these forums operate under the aegis of one or the other intergovernmental body—i.e. they draw substantial amount of legitimacy for their activity by being associated with them. However, they are usually independent in terms of their own membership and functions from these intergovernmental bodies. Their basic claim to the legitimacy of their activity and therefore for the norms they are generating—is via their technical expertise. The production of norms therefore has been dispersed across a number of forums which may be only tenuously linked to intergovernmental organizations.[88] This means that constitutional checks which were practiced within such organizations are not in force and therefore may not inhibit norms being produced in such non-governmental forums. This is possibly the primary legal puzzle which scholars have to address in this context: how to ensure that international norms are constitutionally valid.[89]

2.4 Conclusion

My aim here was to understand the several meanings and the contexts in which the concept of multilevel regulation has emerged in order to isolate a set of criteria to define multilevelness of a regulatory space. In this endeavor, I first concentrate, on providing a brief historical overview of the development of the concept of multilevel governance. Although these two concepts have sometimes been used interchangeably by scholars, I have argued that they are distinct from each other. The point of difference between multilevel regulation and multilevel governance is the question of regulatory effect of the activities. While multilevel regulation will cover only such activities which directly or indirectly have a legal effect—the scope of activities are much narrower than those which are covered under the multilevel governance concept. Therefore, only those activities which directly or indirectly affect the regulatory behavior of the regulator or the regulatees are included within the definition of multilevel regulation. I have also argued that the European context within which the concept evolved does not primarily limit the application of the concept to study European regulatory activities. Given the definition that was presented in this paper, it is possible to have regulatory spaces characterised by multilevel regulation in other countries/regions as well.

I have also sought to develop multilevel regulation as a characteristic of a regulatory space, which would allow for a wider and more specific usage of the concept. Indeed that has been one of the hallmarks of its present usage where it has been used to illustrate specific international processes that can also be subsumed under different and other competing labels such as the 'post-regulatory state.' I have also developed the concept with the assumption that the multilevelness of a

[88] Chiti and Wessel (2011).

[89] Weil (1983), pp. 413–442; Falk (1988), p. 137; and Chinkin (1989), pp. 850–866.

regulatory space may vary over time (depending on the nature of the regulatory process or the shift of competences from the national to the EU level), and therefore a regulatory space can be characterized by high or low multilevelness. In that sense, a negative concept of multilevel regulation would refer to hierarchical bound public regulation of a regulatory space within nation states, wherein there is a clear difference between a regulator and a regulatee, and all regulatory activity can be traced inside the chain of public actors aligned together within the government and functionally responsible to one single public actors within the state.

With the continuing blurring of boundaries between legal orders, the notion of multilevel regulation may be helpful in explaining newer forms of regulation, which in many regulatory spaces are increasingly in the hands of a variety of actors at different levels of governance. Accepting and defining this phenomenon is the first step, but more importantly, the possible consequences open a new research agenda in which many of the foundations of legal science (concerning the sources of law, the rule of law and the binding nature of norms) requires re-assessment.

The primary objective of this chapter was to address the first sub-research question—"*What are the criteria for establishing multilevelness of a regulatory space?*" I have answered this question in this chapter by defining multilevel regulation in terms of specific aspects of a regulatory space. Thus a regulatory space can be called multilevel in nature:

> when both private and public actors who are located across different administrative levels are involved in the process rule-making, rule application and rule adjudication.

Thus these are the criteria for establishing multilevelness of a regulatory space. Now that I have addressed the first sub-research question, in the next chapter I theoretically explore and reconceptualize the notion of 'legal certainty'. This is necessary because I have adopted a socio-legal approach and would be studying the regulatee expectations of legal certainty. In this regard I would need to isolate some features or elements of the notion of 'legal certainty' for the purposes of reference that would guide my exploration of regulatee notions.

References

Aglietta M (1979) A theory of capitalist regulation. Verso, London/New York

Ahdieh R (2006) Dialectical regulation. Conn Law Rev 38:863

Andersson KP, Ostrom E (2008) Analyzing decentralized resource regimes from a polycentric perspective. Policy Sci 41:71–93

Atkinson MM, Coleman WD (1992) Policy networks, policy communities and the problem of governance. Governance 5:154–180

Ayres I, Braithwaite J (1992) Responsive regulation: transcending the deregulation debate. Oxford University Press, New York

Bache I, Flinders M (eds) (2004) Multi-level governance and environmental policy. Oxford University Press, Oxford, U.K

Backer LC (2011) Private actors and public governance beyond the state: the multinational corporation, the financial stability board and the global governance order. Indiana Journal of Global Legal Studies 18:751–802
Bardach E, Kagan RA (1982) Going by the book: the problem of regulatory unreasonableness. Temple University Press, Philadelphia
Bauknecht D (2011) Incentive regulation and network innovations. RSCAS Working Papers, European University Institute
Benz A (2007) Restoring accountability in multilevel governance. Paper prepared for the ECPR Joint Session Workshop (2007) Workshop 5 "Governance and Democratic Legitimacy"
Benzer M (2011) Quality of life and risk conceptions in UK healthcare regulation: towards a critical analysis. Discussion Paper No. 68, CARR
Berman H (2006) Law and revolution: the formation of the western legal tradition. Harvard University Press, Harvard, U.S.A
Bernauer T, Caduff L (2004) European food safety: multilevel governance, re nationalization, or centralization? ETH Zurich
Bickenbach F (2000) Regulation of Europe's network industries: the perspective of the new economic theory of federalism. Kiel Working Papers, Kiel Institute for the World Economy
Black J (2001) Decentering regulation: the role of regulation and self-regulation in a post-regulatory world. Curr Legal Probl 54:103–147
Blandy S, Sibley D (2010) Law, boundaries and the production of space. Soc Legal Stud 19:275–284
Boyer R (1990) The regulation school. Columbia University Press, New York
Braithwaite J (2002) Restorative justice and responsive regulation. Oxford University Press, New York
Braithwaite J, Drahos P (2000) Global business regulation. Cambridge University Press, Cambridge, U.K
Braithwaite J, Coglianese C, Levi-Faur D (2007) Can regulation and governance make a difference. Regul Governance 1:1–7
Brennan MJ, Schwartz ES (1982) Regulatory policy under uncertainty. Bell J Econ 13:506–521
Brenner R, Glick M (1991) The regulation school: theory and history. New Left Rev 188:45–119
Breyer S (1982) Regulation and its reform. Harvard University Press, Harvard, U.S.A
Brownsword R, Somsen H (2009) Law, innovation and technology: before we fast forward—a forum for debate. Law Innov Technol 1:1–73
Burke-White WW (2004) International legal pluralism. Mich J Int Law 25:963–979
Butler C (2009) Critical legal studies and the politics of space. Soc Legal Stud 18:313–332
Carter C, Scott A (1998) Legitimacy and governance beyond the European State: conceptualising governance in the European Union. Eur Law J 4:429–445
Chinkin CM (1989) The challenge of soft law: development and change in international law. Int Comp Law Q 38:850–866
Chiti E, Wessel RA (2011) The emergence of international agencies in the global administrative space: autonomous actors or state servants? In: White ND, Collins R (eds) International organizations and the idea of autonomy: institutional independence in the international legal order. Routledge, Abingdon, Oxford, U.K
Coen D, Doyle C (2000) Designing economic regulatory institutions for the European network industries. Curr Polit Econ Eur 9:83–106
de Burca G, Scott J (2006) Introduction: new governance, law and constitution. In: de Burca G, Scott J (eds) Law and new governance in the EU and US. Hart, Oxford, U.K
Dimitrakopoulis D, Richardson J (2004) Implementing EU public policy. In: Richardson J (ed) European Union: power and policy-making, 2nd edn. Routledge, London, pp 335–356
Diver CS (1983) The optimal precision of administrative rules. Yale Law J 93:65–109
Eckerberg K, Joas M (2004) Multi-level environmental governance: a concept under stress? Local Environ 9(5):405–412
Engle Merry S (1991) Law and colonialism. Law Soc Rev 25:889

Engle Merry S (1997) Global human rights and local social movements in a legally plural world. Can J Law Soc 12:247

Etienne J (2010) Self-reporting untoward events to external controllers: accounting for reporting failure by a top tier chemical plant. Discussion Paper No. 66, CARR

Falk RA (1988) To what extent are international law and international lawyers ideologically neutral? In: Cassese A, Weiler JHH (eds) Change and stability in international law-making. Walter de Gruyter, p 137

Faulkner A (2012) Commensuration and proliferation: similarity and divergence in law's shaping of medical technology. Law Innov Technol 4:165–184

Frey B, Eichenberger R (1999) The new democratic federalism for Europe. Functional, overlapping, and competing jurisdictions. Edward Elgar, Cheltenham

Grabosky P (1995) Counterproductive regulation. Int J Sociol Law 23:347–369

Gualini E (2004) Multi-level governance and institutional change: the Europeanisation of regional policy in Italy. Ashgate, Aldershot

Gunningham N, Grabosky P (1998) Smart regulation: designing environmental policy. Clarendon, Oxford

Hancher L, Moran M (1989) Organising regulatory space. In: Hancher L, Moran M (eds) Capitalism, culture and economic regulation. Oxford University Press, Oxford/New York, pp 271–299

Heritier A, Eckert S (2008) New modes of governance in the shadow of hierarchy: self-regulation by industry in Europe. J Public Policy 28:113–138

Hood C, Rothstein H, Baldwin R (2001) The government of risk: understanding risk regulation regime. Oxford University Press, Oxford, U.K

Hooghe L, Marks G (2001) Multi-level governance and European integration. Rowman and Littlefield Publishers, Oxford, U.K

Hooghe L, Marks G (2003) Unraveling the central state, but how? Types of multi-level governance. Political Science Series, 87. Institute for Advanced Studies, Vienna

Hopkins A (1994) Compliance with what? The fundamental regulatory question. Br J Criminol 34 (4):431–443

International Energy Agency (2009) Innovations in multi-level governance for energy efficiency. Information Paper (OECD/IEA, 2009)

Jachtenfuchs M (1995) Theoretical perspectives on European governance. Eur Law J 1(2):115–133

Kaye J, Gibbons SMC (2008) Mapping the regulatory space for genetic databases and biobanks in England and Wales. Med Law Int 9:111–130

Kern K (2010) Climate governance in the EU multi-level system: the role of cities. Paper prepared for presentation at the fifth pan-European conference on EU politics, University Fernando Pessoa and Faculty of Economics of Porto University, Porto, 23–26 June 2010

Kersbergen KV, Waarden FV (2004) Governance' as a bridge between disciplines: cross-disciplinary inspiration regarding shifts in governance and problems of governability, accountability and legitimacy. Eur J Polit Res 43:143

Kingsbury B, Krisch N, Stewart R (2005) The emergence of global administrative law. Law Contemp Probl 68:15–62

Kohler-Koch B, Rittberger B (2006) The 'Governance Turn' in EU studies. J Common Mark Stud Annu Rev 44:27–49

Krasner SD (1982) Structural causes and regime consequences: regimes as intervening variables. Int Organ 36:185–205

Laffont JJ (1994) The new economies of regulation ten years after. Econometrica 62:507–537

Lenschow A (2006) Europeanisation of public policy. In: Richardson J (ed) European Union: power and decision-making, 3rd edn. Routledge, London, pp 55–71

Levinson DR (2012) Scientific disagreements regarding medical devices regulatory decisions. Report of the Department of Health and Human Services, June 2012

Lipietz A (1986) Behind the crisis: the exhaustion of a regime of accumulation. A regulation school perspective on some French empirical works. Rev Radic Polit Econ 18:13–32
Loughlin M, Scott C (1997) The regulatory state. In: Dunleavy P et al (eds) Developments in British politics. Palgrave, Basingstoke
Maitland F (1898) A prologue to the history of English law. Law Q Rev 14:13
Majone G (1994) The rise of the regulatory state in Europe. West Eur Polit 17:77–101
Majone G (ed) (1996) Regulating Europe. Routledge, London
Majone G (1997) From the positive to the regulatory state. Causes and consequences of changes in the mode of governance. J Public Policy 17:139–167
Marks G (1993) Structural policy and multilevel governance in the EC. In: Cafruny A, Rosenthal G (eds) The state of the European community. Lynne Rienner, Boulder, Colorado, pp 391–410
Mayntz R (1998) New challenges to governance theory. Jean Monnet Chair Paper, 50, Robert Schuman Centre of the European University Institute, EUI, Florence
McGowan F, Seabright P (1995) Regulation in the European Community and its impact on the UK. In: Bishop M, Kay J, Mayer C (eds) The regulatory challenge. Oxford University Press
Meidinger E (1987) Regulatory culture: a theoretical outline. Law Policy 9:355–386
Moran M (2002) Review article: understanding the regulatory state. Br J Polit Sci 32:391–413
Noll R (ed) (1995) Regulatory policy and the social sciences. University of California Press, California
Ostrom E (1990) Governing the commons: the evolution of institutions for collective action. Cambridge University Press, New York
Ostrom V (1999) Polycentricity, Part I. In: McGinnis M (ed) Polycentricity and local public economies, Readings from the workshop in political theory and policy analysis. University of Michigan Press, Ann Arbor, Michigan, pp 52–74
Paraskevopoulos CJ (2006) Adapting to EU multi-level governance: regional and environmental policies in cohesion and CEE countries. Ashgate, Aldershot
Patrick E, Hertogen D, Wanyama F (2005) The emergence of multilevel governance in Kenya. Working Paper No. 7, Interdisciplinary Research Group on International Agreements and Development, Lirgiad, KU Leuven
Pauwelyn J, Wessel R, Wouters J (eds) (2012) Informal international law-making: framing the concept and research questions. Oxford University Press, Oxford, U.K
Peltzman S (1989) The economic theory of regulation after a decade of deregulation. Brookings Papers on microeconomics 1–59
Pernice I (1998) Constitutional law implications for a state participating in a process of regional integration: German constitution and "Multilevel Constitutionalism". In: Reidel E (ed) 40 German Reports on Public Law
Pernice I (1999) Multilevel constitutionalism and the treaty of Amsterdam: European constitution-making revisited. Common Mark Law Rev 36:703–750
Peters BG, Pierre J (2004) Multi-level governance and democracy: a Faustian bargain. In: Bache I, Flinders M (eds) Multi-level governance. Oxford University Press, Oxford, U.K
Princen S (2007) Agenda-setting in the European Union: a theoretical exploration and agenda for research. J Eur Public Policy 14:21–38
Rabe BG (2007) Beyond Kyoto: climate change policy in multilevel governance systems. Governance 20(3):423–444
Rabin R (1994) Federal regulation in historical perspective. In: Schuck PH (ed) Foundations of administrative law. Oxford University Press, New York/Oxford
Radaelli D (2003) The open method of coordination: a new governance architecture for the European Union. Swedish Institute for European Policy Studies
Ruiter DWP, Wessel RA (2012) The legal nature of informal international law: a legal theoretical exercise. In: Pauwelyn J, Wessel R, Wouters J (eds) Informal international law-making. Oxford University Press, Oxford, U.K

Sartori G (1994) Compare why and how: comparing, miscomparing and the comparative method. In: Dogan M, Kazancigil A (eds) Comparing nations: concepts, strategies, substance. Blackwell Publishers, Oxford, U.K
Schepel H (2005) The constitution of private governance: product standards in the regulation of integrating markets. Hart, Oxford, U.K/Portland, Oregon, p 407
Schiff Berman P (2006) Dialectical regulation, territoriality, and pluralism. Conn Law Rev 38:929
Schiff Berman P (2007) Global legal pluralism. Southern Calif Law Rev 80:1155–1237
Schmitter P (2004) Neo-functionalism. In: Wiener A, Diez T (eds) European integration theory. Oxford University Press, Oxford, U.K, pp 45–74
Scott C (2001a) Organizational variety in regulatory governance: an agenda for a comparative investigation of OECD countries. Public Organ Rev 3:301–316
Scott C (2001b) Analysing regulatory space: fragmented resources and institutional design. Public Law (Summer) 329–353
Scott C (2002) Private regulation of the public sector: a neglected facet of contemporary governance. J Law Soc 29:56–76
Scott C (2004) Regulation in the age of governance: the rise of the post-regulatory state. In: Jordana J, Levi-Faur D (eds) The politics of regulation: institutions and regulatory reforms for the age of governance. Edward Elgar, Cheltenham
Scott C (2008) The governance of the European Union: the potential for multilevel control. Eur Law J 8:59
Selznick P (1985) Focusing organizational research on regulation. In: Noll R (ed) Regulatory policy and the social sciences. University of California Press, California, p 363
Senden L (2004) Soft law in European community law. Hart, Oxford, U.K
Shore C (2011) European governance or governmentality? The European Commission and the future of democratic governance. Eur Law J 17:287–303
Snyder FG (1993) Soft law and institutional practice in the European Community. European University Institute, Florence
Snyder F (2001) Sites of criminality and sites of governance. Soc Legal Stud 10:251
Snyder F (2010) The EU, the WTO and China: legal pluralism and International Trade Regulation. Hart, Oxford, U.K
Stubbs P (2005) Stretching concepts too far? Multi-level governance, policy transfer and the politics of scale in South East Europe. Southeast Eur Polit 6:66–87
Teubner G (ed) (1987) Juridification of social spheres. De Gruyter, Berlin, pp 3–48
Teubner G (1997) Breaking frames: the global interplay of legal and social systems. Am J Comp Law 45:145–169
Ullmann W (2010) The medieval idea of law as represented by Lucas de Penna. Routledge, London
Vogel JD (2003) The hare and the tortoise revisited: the new politics of consumer and environmental regulation in Europe. Br J Polit Sci 33:557–580
Wallace H, Pollack MA, Young AR (2010) An overview. Policymaking in the European Union, 6th edn. Oxford University Press, Oxford, U.K
Walti S (2004) How multilevel structures affect environmental policy in industrialized countries. Eur J Polit Res 34:599–634
Watson M, Bulkeley H, Hudson R (2004) Vertical and horizontal integration in the governance of UK municipal waste policy. Paper presented Homeyer/Knoblauch: EPI and multi-level governance – state-of-the-art report 15 at the IDHP Berlin conference on the human dimensions of global environmental change 'greening of policies – interlinkages and policy integration', Freie Universität, Berlin, 3–4 December 2004, draft paper
Weil P (1983) Towards relative normativity in international law? Am J Int Law 77:413–442
Wessel RA, Wouters J (2008) The phenomenon of multilevel regulation. In: Wessel RA, Wouters J (eds) Multilevel regulation and the EU: the interplay between global, European and national normative processes. Martinus Nijhoff, Leiden, pp 9–47
Wilson JQ (1980) The politics of regulation. Basic Books, New York

Chapter 3
Reconceptualizing Legal Certainty: From a Principle of Positive Law to Regulatee Expectations

3.1 Introduction

This chapter addresses the second sub-research question—*What are the constitutive elements of the concept of legal certainty?* I begin with an exploration of the 'principle of legal certainty' within legal positivist literature, so as to delineate certain aspects of this principle. This is in contrast to the sociological idea of legal certainty as discussed in the scholarship of Max Weber—which I discuss in the next section. Finally given that the study is aimed at excavating regulatee expectations of legal certainty—it is imperative to isolate a set of notions that can capture or act as reference points that are commonly used while espousing legal certainty. These notions or reference points are gathered through a search of European Court of Justice cases wherein litigators (include regulatees and regulators) have used the concept of legal certainty.

In legal scholarship, the positivist presumption of a legal order characterized by a gapless system of rules that is pyramidal in structure with the Constitution at the top and all laws flowing from it, emphasizing the role played by the judiciary in plugging gaps and in ensuring abstract principles can be applied to real life situations, is well entrenched.[1] This has influenced and therefore shaped the development of the principle of legal certainty as recognized within the discourse of positive law. Positivist studies of the principle of legal certainty have focused on the concept, both from the standpoint of judicial decision-making and European legislation.[2] Securing the rights of individuals through a series of specific positive entitlements vis-à-vis the state (and therefore from public officials) are widely accepted as functional guarantees to the principle of legal certainty. Individual rights are therefore the locus of attention within the positive law concept of legal certainty.

[1] See footnote 26 in Chap. 1. See for a good overview of legal positivism Kramer (2003).

[2] Schwarze (1992) at 45–76; Raitio (2003) at 175–236; and Schermers and Waelbroeck (2001) at 65–83.

N. Chowdhury, *European Regulation of Medical Devices and Pharmaceuticals*,
DOI 10.1007/978-3-319-04594-8_3,

The focus on individual rights illuminates important aspects of the construction of legal certainty as a characteristic of the legal order. First, the discourse on individual rights emphasizes that legal certainty can be obtained by individuals if their rights vis-à-vis the state is protected within a specific legal order.[3] Second, primary focus is that on the securing of individual rights within public law.[4] Third, legal certainty is viewed as a guarantee that is a logical rational aspiration of the legal order and therefore it is the duty of the state to ensure and uphold. Fourth, legislation and administrative action are two aspects of the legal order that face scrutiny in case of delivering legal certainty. And, fifth, since legal certainty is expressed in terms of rights—there is an inherent presumption—that limited or low level of rights claims in the judicial system would be an evidence of the presence of legal certainty (and the absence of legal uncertainty) within a particular legal order.[5]

What does this mean for the concept of legal certainty? It is evident that legal positivist literature has focused attention on principle of legal certainty—by way of individual claims that are not absolute and that focus is on a series of positive obligations on the state. Consequently, it rests on two separate but interlinked presumptions. First, every legal order should ensure legal certainty for persons operating within that legal order. This is interlinked with the nature of the legal order itself—and therefore the structure of the legal order is determinative of legal certainty within that legal order. And, second (and following from the above presumption), there can be only two sources of uncertainty in a legal order—legal rules in the form of legislation and the functioning of the public administration. Consequently, sources of uncertainty cannot be located outside the legal order. All sources of uncertainty have to be endogenous to the legal order. And, therefore hypothetically it is possible to be addressed through the individual rights discourse challenging legal rules and administrative action within the specific legal order.

The idea of a nationally delimited legal order is so well entrenched in positivist legal theory, that suggestion of its limited usefulness in capturing a series of globalization related developments seems almost sacrilege. However it is difficult to ignore that states are the pre-eminent political unit and therefore the legal order as a single legal unit (if you may) is being undermined because the sovereignty and the autonomy of both respectively are in question given the pervasiveness of globalization.[6] Legal theorists have reacted to such developments by searching for global administrative law principles that provide for some notional unity of the international legal order constituting of state orders and other disparate formations.[7]

---

[3] See for allusion to individual rights as part of legal certainty; Ellermann (2012); Gribnau (2013), pp 52–74.

[4] Tridimas (1999) at 163.

[5] D'Amato (2010).

[6] See for an excellent discussion; Delbruck (1993), p. 9. See for an excellent and one of the earliest scholarship on the impact of globalization on sovereignty (and therefore nationally delimited legal orders) Sassen (1996).

[7] Krisch (2006), pp. 247–278.

Legal pluralism on the other hand views state law as constituting only one of the many instances of social ordering. There has been increasing engagement with this idea—at the global level where social ordering through transnational networks exists along with state legal orders.[8] The idea of "interlegality" has also been developed to propose for a postmodern conception of legal order that is beyond the nation state.[9] This is evidence of the inherent limitations of the concept of a nationally delimited legal order. These limitations are not only of theoretical value but may serve as an impediment in tracing the current reality of horizontal and vertical networks, partnerships and exchanges that operate between public and private actors for the purpose of law-making, law-application and law adjudication beyond states and within states and the impact on legal certainty in this context. As is evident from our discussion, legal positivist notions of legal certainty are intertwined and embedded with the idea of a nationally delimited legal order and therefore are inherently limited in usefulness. Thus given that I explore sociological notions of legal certainty it is imperative to adopt an alternative analytical category.

What is the analytical terrain within which legal scholarship needs to examine this idea of legal certainty? As discussed, the concept of legal orders being territorially delimited is limiting in significant ways. Given the increasing specialization of issues—policy fields, policy regimes, or policy domains are useful terms that can be used to discuss issue areas. However in this context I choose the notion of a 'regulatory space' to foreground the concept of legal certainty.[10]

The term is suitable due to several reasons and it is pertinent to discuss them in the context of my decision to explore sociological notions of legal certainty within a regulatory space and not a national delimited legal orders. First, it allows me to focus on not only legal rules that are issued by the state but also private rules that may influence and shape public behavior. Second, both private and public actors populate a specific regulatory space. Third, public and private actors cannot be differentiated simply in terms of their roles as regulators and regulatees respectively. It is quite possible, that private actors could also perform or participate in traditional regulatory functions viz. rulemaking, rule application and rule adjudication. And, therefore in certain instances, can play the role of a regulator. However private actors remain primarily as law-takers or regulatees—given that even if one can differentiate between private actors in terms of their roles—a considerable number of private actors will always be regulatees. Since, the basic purpose of regulation is to direct private behavior to fulfil a public purpose. Fourth, unlike policy domains or sector or area, regulatory space allows us to focus our lens on a specific aspect of the legal terrain. An aspect that may draw its unity from the basic legislations that order the space—for instance the regulatory space for the marketing authorization of medical devices is very different from the reimbursement of medical devices. The immediate and most obvious benefit of picking regulatory

[8] Mattei (1993), pp. 5–43. Moore (2008), p. 149 and Michaels (2005), pp. 1209–1259.

[9] See de Sousa Santos (1987), pp. 279–302.

[10] See Hancher and Moran (1989), pp. 271–299 and see also footnotes 39 and 70 in Chap. 1.

space over the notion of a legal order is that it allows us to focus on expectations of private actors that are not territorially situated, allowing me to capture actors that function within the regulatory space without reference to their physical location.

The focus on regulatee expectations as a function of legal certainty is well embedded in sociological theories. Thus for theorists like Niklas Luhmann, law performed a critical function of stabilizing expectations in the contemporary world that was increasingly complex and wrought by fragmentation.[11] If the primary aim of law is to guarantee predictability of outcomes (legal consequences) for persons, then the perspective of these regulatees (persons) becomes important. The perspective of economic actors is an important and hitherto an aspect that has been missing in legal scholarship. The regulatee perception of legal certainty is a critical aspect of gauging whether legal certainty is being achieved or challenged within a regulatory space. The legal positivist presumption of a nationally delimited legal order is too limiting for most legal scholars and prevents any examination of long held legal presumptions that may be disaffirmed within the contours of law as practiced and experienced today.

This chapter has been divided into five parts. First, it briefly sketches the legal positivist aspect of the development of the principle of legal certainty and highlights its organic interconnectedness with the idea of a legal order. I contrast this with other scholarship that focus on the structure of norms rather than the legal order and therefore emphasize norm design as critical in ensuring legal certainty. Second, it builds a case for focusing attention on the perspectives of regulatees by discussing Max Weber's notion of law and his idea of legal certainty—that was developed with the view of ensuring calculability for economic actors. Third, it highlights other scholarship that has embraced the regulatee perspective in exploring legal certainty. Fourth it studies ECJ case law in order to identify a set of notions that capture litigant[12] expectations of what they mean as legal certainty in European litigation. The objective of this chapter is to investigate and highlight the different aspects of legal certainty as has been developed through legal scholarship and highlight how this scholarship could be deepened by embracing the socio-legal lens.

3.2 Legal Certainty: Legal Positivist Scholarship

The legal positivist studies of the principle of legal certainty have focused on the concept, both from the standpoint of judicial decision-making and European legislation. Most such studies agree that the principle of legal certainty is a general

[11] Luhmann (1988); and Luhmann (1992), p. 1419.

[12] Litigant notions of course allude to both the regulator and regulatees. From this it is possible to identify a set of notions used commonly to construct constituent elements of the notion of legal certainty.

principle of law[13] that underlies the entire EU legal system[14] and that it protects the essential claim that the application of law to a specific situation should be predictable. Schermers and Waelbroeck have classified the specific aspects of this principle as follows[15]:

- principle of legitimate expectations
- non-retroactivity of EC legislation
- principle of acquired (vested) rights
- requirement of procedural time limits
- demand for understandable language

The principle of legitimate expectations primarily protects individuals that act in a reasonable fashion and in good faith on the basis of the law as it is. Similarly, the principle of non-retroactivity precludes the application of EU law retroactively unless in exceptional circumstances and when it is not in breach of the legitimate expectations of individuals. Further, the principle of acquired rights protects those rights which could be overturned by the retroactive application of EU law. Procedural time limits provides closure to bringing of law suits that question the legality and validity of administrative measures indefinitely and thereby jeopardizing the predictability in the functioning of the administration. Clarity and understanding of the law is especially felt in the context of EU law, wherein translation may be a difficult problem faced especially by immigrants and could prevent them from understanding the import of a decision if given in another language. However, it is important to note that although the Courts have accepted this principle as a fundamental principle of EU law, it is not absolute and does not override other administrative principles—like the principle of legality for instance.[16] In the *Duff* case[17] the ECJ summed up the main aspects of the principles of legal certainty quite well, by underlining, that

> it requires legal rules to be clear and precise, and aims to ensure that situations and legal relationships governed by Community law are foreseeable.

Although the fourth section discusses case law of the ECJ in distilling regulatee expectations of legal certainty, herein the point to be made is that the ECJ has itself accepted the legal positivist contention that legal certainty is a general principle of EC law and therefore emblematic of the legal order. The content of the principle of legal certainty has been defined in terms of specific individual rights which can be relied upon when litigating against the state. Importantly, this principle has not been

---

[13] Schwarze (1992), pp. 45–76; and Raitio (2003), pp. 175–236.

[14] This principle is derived from the national legal systems—viz. Germany, France, BENELUX countries, Italy, Spain, Poland, etc. See Maxeiner (2007), p. 541.

[15] See Schermers and Waelbroeck (2001), pp. 65–83.

[16] Case 49/59 SNUPAT [1961] ECR 53.

[17] Case C63/93 Duff, Para 20.

accepted as an absolute right and the Court has recognized that administrative decision-making requires a balancing of values.[18]

In the context of European policy and legislation, legal certainty has been embraced by the European Commission and served as a direct justification for pushing through the single market agenda by way of harmonization. Achieving consistency in legal obligations by legislating immediately binding regulations (and not directives),[19] developing standard operating procedures for national regulatory agencies via guidelines,[20] rationalizing regulatory burdens and preventing regulatory overlaps[21]; have all been pushed through in the name of ensuring greater predictability and therefore delivering legal certainty to regulatees. European legislations and policies have sought to achieve this by centralization of certain regulatory functions. As a policy and legislative goal, legal certainty has played a critical role in pushing forward with policy harmonization across sectors. The European Commission supported harmonization project, reflects the vision of a single EU legal order—which would operate through clear hierarchy and where national legal orders would functions as constituent units. Of course this is both an academically and politically disputed project—however the project itself does reiterate the presumption that legal certainty should be achieved through a constructed hierarchy of rules that mimics the hierarchy presumed within a national legal order.[22]

Two aspects within the legal order have been the focus of legal scholarship—the text of law and administrative or judicial decision making (application and adjudication of law)—on the issue of legal certainty. How should legislatures design law? Patricia Popelier conceptualizes legal certainty as a principle of proper law–making and has explored dimensions of this aspect that could raise expectations and frustrate goals especially given the absence of consensus as to the content of the principle.[23] Judicial adjudication has also been discussed in terms of ensuring consistency of interpretation and thereby contributing to legal certainty.[24]

---

[18] Groussot and Minssen (2007), pp. 385–417.

[19] For instance the European Commission has recently announced its intention to bring about a regulation for improving the current procedures for the designation of notified bodies and the harmonised conduct of audits. This is already laid down under the Directive 93/42/EEC, however given the continuing inconsistencies between member states, the Commission has supported a stronger instrument like a Regulation to address legal uncertainty. See EUCOMED (2012).

[20] European Medicines Agency (2008) *Guideline on Safety and Efficacy Follow-up Risk management of ATMPS*, Doc. Ref. EMEA/149995/2008.

European Commission (2006). Also see

[21] European Commission (2005), Financial services: Commission sets up expert group on legal certainty issues in clearing and settlement. Press Release IP/05/123.

[22] It is important to note globalization as well as specific administrative problems like expertise deficits have forced the European Commission to adopt new governance modes that emphasize regulatory partnerships both internationally and also regionally that are more heterarchical in nature. Nevertheless, the European harmonization project is wedded to the idea of hierarchically structured legal order as intrinsic to ensuring legal certainty.

[23] Popelier (2008), pp. 47–66.

[24] Betlem (2002), pp. 397–418.

Others like John Braithwaite,[25] Ofer Raban[26] and Colin Diver[27] have highlighted the issue of norm design. Braithwaite argues that in the context of complex social phenomenon or policy fields, principles as against precise rules—function better. Consistent application of rules is facilitated by a shared consensus of meanings between the law enforcement and law adjudication bodies. Thus "bindingness of the rules" themselves may have a limited or even a negative impact on legal certainty. Within the legal order, the context (policy fields) has to be considered in the design of rules. The design of rules should therefore reflect the architecture and presumptions of the policy field.

At the macro level however, the legal order provides the primary conceptual hook on which legal theorists have discussed and developed ideas on legal certainty. As mentioned in the first section, the unity of the legal order has been and continues to be an abiding positivist presumption that has shaped the practice and academics of law. Commenting on the theoretical preoccupation of academics that led them to ignore micro level problems (problems encountered in the practice of law) within private international law, Paul Heinrich Neuhaus suggests:

> The internal consistency and consequent clarity of the various theories appeared to be more important to the proponents that mere practical considerations.[28]

Similar arguments can also be forwarded in this context. Legal scholarship has made a sustained effort to establish the sancitity of the nationally delimited gapless and hierarchical legal order. This is the only explanation, for the largely singular focus on the legal order. Legal certainty has therefore remained as a function of an internally coherent and consistent legal order. An order that is hierarchical in nature and where all rules are ultimately a derivative of the Constitution—thus providing the vision of gaplessness.

The law and society movement[29] has challenged this presumption. Law or the legal order is not autonomous field. Every society has several and simultaneous ways of social ordering—religion, culture, language, etc. And each of these social orders may operate concomitantly within societies. Law is therefore just one of the ways of ordering society. Law however plays an important role—because it is also the terrain within which contest between substantive values take place. Marc Galanter has contended that this penetration—of social demands and ruptures—will create an implosion within the legal order and consequently reduce it certainty and uniformity.[30] The distinct contribution of this movement has been to view the challenge to legal certainty as a consequence of the rupture of the legal order that is driven by social pressures—highlighting that the legal order does not function in a

[25] Braithwaite (2002), pp. 47–82.

[26] Raban (2010), pp. 175–191.

[27] Diver (1983), pp. 65–109.

[28] Neuhaus (1963), pp. 795–807.

[29] See Ehrlich (1936); Malinowski (1934); Friedman (1969), p. 29; Moore (1978).

[30] Galanter (1992), p. 55.

social vacuum—and challenges to legal certainty can therefore be traced to the external context in which the legal order operates. Law is viewed therefore in reflexive manner (induced from social context) rather than a given set of prior presumptions that underlie the presumption of a nationally delimited legal order (following a deductive logic).

3.3 Review of Weber's Ideas

The question which arises is why I choose Weber for the discussion on legal certainty.[31] Apart from the obvious depth and richness of his theoretical inputs on the subject, they also represent a stark departure from legal positivist conceptions of legal certainty. Weber viewed legal certainty from outside the prism of the legal order. Given that my aim here is to explore regulatee perspectives and expectations on legal certainty in the context of multilevel regulation—Weber's ideas provides a suitable theoretical basis for supporting such the exploration of legal certainty from a regulatee perspective. Weber's focus on the calculability aspect of the law put the spotlight on the law taker or regulatee and therefore it investigates externality of law—quite different and contrary to the internal aspect of law—and the legal order—that preoccupy legal positivists. Therefore the achievement of legal certainty is seen in the context of society and not only within a limited legal order—because the legal order and society are not coterminous.

From sociology of law perspective, it is a theoretical possibility that legal certainty may be achieved by forces and developments that are taking place in the environment external to the legal order.[32] This is however unimaginable from a legal positivist perspective wherein the legal certainty is a function of the legal order—and therefore may be achieved or thwarted by structures and developments internal to the legal order. The latter presumption has of course been challenged by the law and society movement—but this challenge has not been addressed or engaged with by the majority of legal scholars. In this context, the paper explores the various aspects of concept of legal certainty—with the specific aim of highlighting its socio-legal dimensions and in the process highlighting the possibility of widening and deepening the scholarship.

Max Weber's work on Law in Economy and Society[33] is a monumental work on the role of law within economy and its function in ordering society. Weber's idea of legal certainty can be viewed from two aspects; the nature and function of law and

---

[31] I briefly discuss Habermas's idea on substantive legal certainty as a contrast to Weber's ideas and also because both Weber and Habermas's are working from a non-positivist perspective.

[32] For an interesting perspective on non-positivist approaches to legal certainty; See Bertea (2007) at 69–82.

[33] For an excellent introduction to the subject refer to Rheinstein (1954).

the development of modern state. Before interpreting[34] Weber's ideas, a caveat is necessary. Weber's ideas were developed by way of rigorous empirical work—in legal history and therefore he was able to provide rich examples for his contentions. However his vision of law is primarily that of pre-World War II capitalist western societies. The presumptions about the function of law and the economic imperatives shaping law as well as the role of the State were all developed in the context of that period. Thus his relevance of his ideas to contemporary reality has to be explored as a next step.

Social action is one of the primary concepts of Weber's thesis. He contends that all social conduct within social groups can be categorized in four ways—purpose rational, value rational, emotionally rational and traditionalistically rational. Purpose rational—refers to the idea of an economic and rational man—who only works in his self-interest; value rational means actions are guided by moral or ethical values; the other two are self-evident. Social conduct directed towards a specific goal and with reference to another person is referred to as a social relationship. Social relationships are shaped by the person's idea of what is legitimate. Thus social relationships in terms of predictability of actions are governed by their idea of a legitimate order. This legitimacy of an order can be guaranteed by faith, religion, culture, tradition, etc. Weber states:

Law will be defined as an order which depend upon an enforcement staff (emphasized in the Rheinstein text). By this Weber means legitimacy of the legal order is derived from enforceability of the order by way of coercive force. The primary effect of law (or for that matter all other kinds of social ordering) is that increases the probability of a certain action or behavior—between persons within a social group.

The two basic activities pertaining to the legal order were—law creation and law finding. He then suggests a matrix (refer to Table 3.1) for the categorization of societies according to the manner in which they create and find law.

Weber views the development of law moving in the direction of increasing rationalization—and this process is characterized by the formal dimension—generality, logical and procedure[35]—all aspects that contribute to the consistency and gaplessness of the legal order.

Probability of a certain kind of action within a social group—and therefore calculability of social conduct is what the law primarily functions to achieve. For Weber, this function of law was of primary importance in the context of capitalist economy. An early capitalist economy, based on trading required a system wherein economic action could be foreseen since it was based on a legal system that was rational. Foreseeability made it possible to enter into contractual agreements that underpin the market economy. According to Weber:

---

[34] The choice of word is deliberate—since due to the disparate nature of his book and also English not being the original language in which it was written—only interpretation is what can be attempted.

[35] Swedberg (2006), pp. 61–81.

Table 3.1 Legal typologies

	Irrational	Rational
Formal	Formal irrationality – Lack of general rules – Reliance on oracles and supernatural forces for decision making – Charismatic or revealed law	Formal rationality – Use of general rules to decide cases – Rules derived from legal concepts independent of moral or religious criteria – Positive law
Substantive	Substantive irrationality – Case by case decision making – Decision guided by external notions—ethical, emotional or political – Traditional law	Substantive rationality – Use of general rules to decide cases – General rules derived from religion, ideology, economics—rather than law – Natural law

Source: Table reproduced with minor modification from Sterling and Moore (1987), pp. 67–89

> To those who had interests in the commodity market, the rationalization and systemization of the law,... the increasing calculability of the functioning of the legal process in particular, constituted one of the most important conditions for the existence of economic enterprise[36]

From Weber's perspective, calculability of economic action is the pivot on which the legal order functions and which thereby serves as its instrumental justification. This legal certainty (in terms of calculability of law) can be best guaranteed by a hierarchic and autonomous system of gapless rules that constitutes a legal order.[37] Weber has been criticized on this account—referred to as the England Problem—by theorists who point out that the English system of common law representing a traditional type of law that was led by judicial case law—had succeeded in ensuring calculability of economic action—and therefore capitalism flourished.[38] Others have however argued that Weber's focus was not on the formal and rational legal thought but on formal justice and guaranteed rights.[39]

The following quotations of Weber, sheds some light on this:

> The tempo of modern business communication requires a promptly and predictably functioning legal system, i.e. one which is guaranteed by the strongest coercive power......modern economic life by its very nature has destroyed those other associations which used to be the bearers of law and thus of legal guaranties. This dominance of the market consociation requires on the one hand a legal system the functioning of which is calculable in accordance with rational rules.[40]

---

36 Rheinstein (1954) at 304–305.

37 Trubek (1972), p. 746.

38 Trubek (1986), p. 573. See also, Stinchcombe (1999), pp. 209–224.

39 Ewing (1987), pp. 487–512.

40 Rheinstein (1954) at 40.

> From a juridical point of view, modern law consists of legal propositions i.e. abstract norms the content of which asserts that a certain factual condition is to have certain legal consequences.[41]

The application of stable and fixed rules arranged within the framework of a hierarchic legal order that define formal rationality would seem to be a pre-requisite to the achievement of calculability that is so critical to the conduct of economic relations of the modern economy. However Weber also made the following statement:

> Systemization and codification without loss of practical adaptability could thus be achieved only for those special fields, which bourgeoisie interest had autonomously adapted to their needs and which had been empirically rationalized in the practice of special courts i.e. commercial law and law of negotiable instruments[42]

This suggests that Weber was aware that systematization and codification in the absence of what he refers to as "empirical rationalization"—process of stabilization of expectations through practice—is of limited use. Thus codification or systematization could only deliver calculability if they formalized already well-established practices that were adapted to the autonomous needs of the bourgeoisie. Ultimately Weber's primary concern was the calculability of the law. Richard Swedberg has contended that by calculable law—Weber meant three things—(1) legal texts are predictable (2) administration of law is not arbitrary and (3) contracts are legally enforced.[43] These aspects could be achieved by a formal rational legal order but could also be achieved by other systems and mechanisms. This is also evident from the above statement wherein Weber reiterates that systemization and codification—which one would imagine be required within a formal rational system—could only be achieved without any loss of practical adaptability—therefore calculability—only if there existed an empirically observed rationalization—that was spearheaded by regulatees (in this case the bourgeoisie).

Rationalization refers to the existence of regulatee consensus on the dimensions and aspects of the social relationships that governed economic conduct in a specific area—it was critical and necessary before systemization of law and codification could occur. And on the contrary, if the systemization were to occur without stabilizing of social relations—it would lead to the legal order loosing practical relevance—and therefore would fail to ensure calculability. One could not draw a direct causal relationship between formal rational legal system and calculability.

The role of lawyers as a professional class in the development of modern law is another interesting aspect of Weberian theory. Weber specifically investigated the role played by this professional class—comprising of litigating lawyers and legal theorists in developing legal science—through the different historical periods. Speaking on the general development of law through the ages—from charismatic legal revelations through "law prophets"; to empirical creation and finding of law

---

[41] Rheinstein (1954), p. 99.

[42] Rheinstein (1954), p. 282.

[43] Rheinstein (1954) at 69.

by legal honoratiores; to imposition of law by theocratic or secular powers; and finally the systematic elaboration of law and professionalized administration of justice by persons who have their legal training in the formal logic system (roman law). According to Weber this professional class plays a decisive role in developing and perpetuating—logical consistent formal legal thinking—systematization, codification of a hierarchic legal orders.

However such a legal system is incompatible with and not oriented towards the economically determined expectations of the regulatees. Further in the modern era, the legal system is no more a *de minimus* arrangement for ensuring economic exchange but is also faced with increasing demands for substantive justice—that is an outcome of the class disparities. Increasing specialization within the legal system is also a characteristic of this modern era. All these developments that challenge the rigidity inherent within the formal rational system would inevitably lead to the development of 'particularistic laws that was more expeditious and contribute to the weakening of legal formalism'.

Weber was aware that calculability of the legal system was of primary importance to a certain kinds of regulatees—i.e. those with economic power—because it was they who were the primary beneficiaries of the economic exchange in terms of profit-making. However in the context of the expanded role of the welfare state—the legal system faces the challenge of delivering substantive justice that may well come at the cost of calculability. This is also an aspect which Jurgen Habermas builds on in his book *Between Facts and Norm.*[44]

Before I elucidate on Habarmas's ideas on legal certainty it is important to note a few caveats. First, I am aware that Habermas as a discursive theorist does not automatically fit into a discussion that is focused on empirical explorations of legal certainty. Second, the focal point of Habermas's ideas is in the investigation of legitimacy of legal norms and not on legal certainty. However I choose to elaborate briefly on his ideas because he like Weber departs from a positivist paradigm. Habermas highlights the inherent indeterminacy of legal norms and argues that substantive legal certainty may be achieved if all stakeholders are guaranteed a procedural right to access the legal system. Thus although the objective of his explorations are different, he does ideate on the idea of legal certainty and suggests a procedural method which is a clear departure from positivist theories.

Habermas poses this as a rationality problem—the idea that the legal order—in terms of legal adjudication—should not only be rational (internally consistent and coherent) but should also be acceptable (by ensuring substantive justice) to all the participants of the process.[45] He develops the concept of "procedure dependent certainty of law"[46]—as a resolution to this contradictory pull of different aims. This ensures that all participants have procedural rights that guarantee them access to the

[44] Habermas (1996).

[45] Habermas (1985).

[46] Habermas (1996) at 220.

legal order. There is therefore no security of a certain substantive outcome—but predictability is ensured through a right to access the adjudication process.

Yet, Habermas is aware that a procedural guarantee is not enough to fulfil the requirements of legal certainty. And it is in this context, he develops his discourse theory of law. It is theory about how law can be legitimated. Put simply, the theory purports, that legitimacy is achieved through the discourse principle—that provides for voluntary intersubjective agreement in the law making process amongst all those affected. The resulting law can then be applied impartially based on the principle of appropriateness. For Habermas, therefore indeterminacy of legal decision making (and therefore legal uncertainty) can be limited to a considerable degree if there is a shared paradigm of the understanding of the purpose and function of law in society amongst all the citizens that make up the legal community. Therefore the substantive acceptability and embracing of the legal order by the citizens is critical to the process of ensuring legal certainty.

Other legal theorists working within the theory of argumentation and the notion of an audience—Aarnio and Peczenik for instance have suggested that legal interpretation should be undertaken with the aim of securing majoritarian support of the rational legal community.[47] Aarnio's notion of an "an ideal audience" seems to also allude to such a critical mass that may be seen as an epistemic community with a shared code of substantive values and agreement on rules of rational discourse and which operates within the legal community. In this context, legal certainty would be ensured if the law is able to conform to certain substantive values and follows a certain procedure—that is agreed and accepted by this epistemic community (that represents the majority of the legal community).

It is therefore the shared sense of values and agreement on legal procedure within the legal community—that is a pre-requisite to the achievement of legal certainty—in terms of calculability of the law. This also reflects Weber's idea of systematization and codification being conditioned upon empirical rationalization. This highlights the search for legal certainty outside the legal order—in terms of the understanding of law and the expectations from law that members of the legal community hold.

It would seem therefore that law has to perform the dual functions—that of structural consistency[48]—which allows it to provide certainty of legal transactions and—rationality—which allows it to make an intuitive appeal to validity in our eyes (and is therefore considered legitimate). This *rationality* may be derived from different sources—sovereign command in the case of Austin, Kant's universal rationalism, Rousseau's civic republicanism or certain moral principles of philosophers like John Rawls.

In the context of this book, this duality may have important empirical implications. It can be argued that greater legal certainty can be ensured if the underlying

[47] Aarnio (1987); Wroblewski (1984); and Paunio (2009), pp. 1469–1493.

[48] As discussed for legal positivists structural consistency can only be ensured through the establishment of a hierarchy of norms.

basis of legal norms are understood and accepted as legitimate. Thus the dual functions of law are not opposed but in fact may contribute to the achievement of the other. Thus legal certainty may also be a function of public acceptance of the rationality underlying the legal norms. In other words, regulatee expectations of legal certainty may also be influenced by the validity (in practice acceptance) of the norms themselves. And questions of the validity of the norms (and thus rationality); may not only allude to instrumental notions of the legal validity of the norms but could also be derived from aspects external to the law—such as the technical expertise of regulators involved in rulemaking. Following from this example, it can be argued, norms only gain validity in the eyes of the regulatees if the regulator making the norms possesses the technical expertise to formulate those norms. Consequently regulatees' perception of legal certainty within a regulatory space may be contingent on their understanding of whether the regulator has the technical expertise to formulate the norm that they are under a legal obligation to follow.

3.4 Empirical Understanding of Legal Certainty

In this section, I survey the empirical research conducted by scholars on different aspects of legal certainty. The study of legal certainty has been particularly interesting within private international law—given that the absence of a legal order. This has meant that theorists have researched on the wealth of mechanisms—both institutional and cognitive—some of which have developed by regulators and others by regulatees to ensure calculability of law. Within public law, social complexity has led to the increasing specialization of different subfields of law—this has fuelled a wealth of analysis on how legal certainty within a specific sub-field or regulatory space—can be best achieved—if legal interventions (both in terms of rule design and decision-making) are designed considering the physical architecture and the particularities of the regulatory space. In other words, legal interventions that are designed keeping in mind the physical dimensions of the space—will successfully reduce legal uncertainty.

One of the early attempts at addressing the lack of a legal order and therefore the search for unity in private international law was the Hague Conference on Private International Law that convened four times at the turn of the twentieth century.[49] The basic aim was to establish a *de minimis* rule of recognition that could be adopted by all national legal systems. This rule would ensure that in case of conflict of laws—the same legal decision would be expected for same cases.[50] Judicial

[49] The Hague Conference on Private International Law convened in quick succession 1893, 1894, 1900 and 1904. See http://www.hcch.net/index_en.php?act=text.display&tid=4 (accessed on 12 February 2013).

[50] The principle of 'duly acquired rights' under English law and "droit acquis" within French civil law in Europe.

decision-making (rather than international treaties) has in fact been the chosen vehicle for developing a commonality of purpose and effect. Courts have been pragmatic in adopting flexible and elastic terms viz. "choice of rules", "center of gravity", etc. in resolving these cases. However it is an extensive and largely disaggregated field—that is an impediment to codification.

This is also the specific area of inquiry that was spearheaded by Volkmar Gessner and his team of researchers at the University of Bremen.[51] They investigated a number of subject fields—cross border debt collection, London reinsurance market, international migrations, cross border maintenance; etc. to understand how regulatees are pursuing legal certainty within a globalized but a legally differentiated world (in terms of national legal orders). Gessner discusses Niklaus Luhmann's ideas on cognitive processes that could create stability of expectations and therefore legal certainty and other works on intercultural communications research that explore such processes. Gessner identifies "social institutions" as the key to understanding private behavior. He defines social institutions as "stable patterns of behavioral expectations on the levels of roles and programmes". Social institutions allow the actors to make choices without any operative formal and informal sanctions. *Lex mercatoria* is given as an example of commercial practice that functions in such a fashion. One of the interesting theoretical contributions of this project—is the notion of third cultures. Examples of third cultures include—the scientific communities, mafias, religious communities—that share common ethics and patterns of behavior. The diamond industry has developed an integrated and autonomous business ethics—that regulate transactions and ensure legal certainty to its members. However since the membership is tightly controlled, legal certainty becomes contingent on membership of such third cultures.

Within public law, theorists have questioned the effectiveness of adopting legal formalism—in terms of determinate legal rules (hard law) or bright line rules[52]—while regulating all kinds of social conduct.[53] This contention primarily hinges on the argument that the legal order is highly differentiated into specialized legal subfields and that legal rules and administrative decision—making has to be designed keeping in the subjective nature of the field.

Jonas Ebbesson has addressed the issue of legal certainty in the context of complex socio-ecological changes. He makes the following propositions[54]:

(i) General claims of legal certainty emphasizes the popular view of law as static and fixed (legal formalism)
(ii) Interpretation of law—is more than just statute interpretation and relevant material considerations—of the application of the law—has to be weighed

---

[51] Gessner and Budak (1998).

[52] Bright line rules is the term used to denote clearly specified and detailed legal rules that leave little to subjective interpretation.

[53] Morgan (2012), pp. 408–429.

[54] Ebbesson (2010), pp. 414–422.

into the legal decision. Legal reasoning in environmental law is broader in scope than in specific and highly defined areas such as criminal law

(iii) Law cannot predict all factual situations and therefore rules cannot be provided for all such situations in advance. Administrative decision-making may therefore have to abandon the certainty of rules—and embrace more reflexive approach through official case-by-case intervention.

He suggests that the idea that legal certainty as a function of the legal order (as forwarded within legal formalism) is a prisoner of the theoretical framework of a liberal state. Within increasingly complex societies wherein the state plays a much more welfarist (and therefore interventionist) role—legal certainty in terms of ensuring legitimacy of administrative decision-making—may be ensured through procedural approaches—e.g. the Aarhus Convention on the right to public participation in environmental decision-making. He also underlines that the uncertainty associated with environmental problems impacts across fields, and means that legal rules cannot be precisely framed—principles and standards should be the form to be adopted in the design of legal rules since they allow for flexibility. This reflects the similar arguments made by John Braithwaite discussed earlier in the paper. Such contentions have also been echoed by economists that have worked in the area of technological innovation.[55]

Other theorists commenting on specific legal orders—like China—have highlighted cultural, political and economic elements—underlining the importance of the social context in delivering "real legal certainty".[56] Socio-legal literature has therefore highlighted the importance and role of other kinds of social ordering—third cultures in providing mechanisms for accessing legal certainty especially in the case of private international law. Within public law, the fragmentation of singular legal orders into specialized domains—reflecting the factual conditions—such as transnational environmental pollution—requires a departure from basic positivist presumptions such as a gapless legal order—and adopting a more reflexive approach based on administrative discretion.

3.5 Excavating Litigant Notions of Legal Certainty: From the ECJ Case Law

Calculability of the law being the focus of this discussion—it is important to explore ways and means of gauging regulatory expectations. As is evident from the earlier discussion—lawyers and legal scholar's perspectives on legal certainty have concentrated on the internal coherence and logical consistency of the legal order which would then presumably be able to deliver legal certainty to those

[55] Braeutigam (1979), pp. 98–111.

[56] Otto (2002).

operating within the legal order. However globalization has increasingly challenged the idea of autonomous legal order and functional specializations have also undermined the unity and uniformity of the legal order. In such a scenario how do regulatees respond? Gessner and other socio-legal scholars have suggested that some are able to access specific third cultures that promote shared meaning and interpretations of social conduct. It is pertinent to point out that such socio-legal studies are operationalized via usually an empirical exploration of the notions that regulatees use to understand this concept. Unlike legal theorists and lawyers who receive legal training (includes orientation to this concept)—regulatees may not be aware or use the concept of 'legal certainty' in their functioning. In that sense legal certainty is very much a concept of legal theory—and although is being used in policymaking—still does not have ordinary purchase—in terms of familiarity with regulatees.

In this context, it is imperative to identify a set of notions that are used by regulatees—to refer to legal certainty. I explore ECJ case law to ascertain these notions—what are the notional references used to mean legal certainty. What is the content of the principle of legal certainty for regulatees—or what do the litigants (regulatees) hope to achieve by referring to this principle? The process of judicial adjudication allows regulatees (as litigants) to access the Court for disputing and establishing the correct legal interpretation. Legal positivist arguments of assessing whether legal uncertainty exists vis-à-vis the legal order in general or in specific areas of the law—draws a positive causal relationship between the scale of litigation and legal uncertainty.[57] Litigation reflects the uncertainty as to the meaning of the law amongst the regulatees and therefore the need to access the Court to clarify the interpretation. Litigation results in the creation of precedents that reduces uncertainty within the legal order.

From a sociological point of view—judicial adjudication perhaps represents the most empirical arena—wherein regulatees forward their legal arguments revealing in the process—their notions of the law in operation. Although usage of the legal semantics in the drafting of the plea may constrain the outright identification of regulatee notions—it does allow us a peek into regulatee notions—on the content of legal certainty. Once notions are identified through case law; the meaning of these notions and the value of these notions underlining the concept of legal certainty may be established via other qualitative materials such as interview, document analysis, etc.

The following paragraphs explore select case law of the ECJ on the principle of legal certainty. It has been widely used by litigants—individuals, legal persons and member states against the European Commission. Legal certainty has been interpreted to mean that the law should be public (transparent) and reasonably ascertainable; and also includes a presumption against retrospective legal provisions.

[57] Dari-Mattiacci and Deffains (2007), pp. 627–656. Also see Stinchcombe (1999), pp 211.

In Kingdom of Spain, the decision of the European Commission finding an infringement of Article 82 EC (price fixing) was contested on the grounds that it was ultra vires because it had intervened late and in a market that was already well regulated under national law.[58] Spain had brought this action of annulment, arguing that the European Commission has violated the principle of legal certainty by altering ex post the regulatory framework. The Court recognized that *legal certainty laid down the requirement that legal rules be clear and precise and aims to ensure that situations and legal relationships governed by European Union law remain foreseeable*.[59] Rule precision in textual terms so as to enable individuals to clearly ascertain their legal position (meaning, rights and obligations) was also recognized in Afton Chemical case.[60]

Reference to textual precision is not only limited to substantive legislative documents—but also to procedural documents that are placed before the Court.[61] The Court has held that

> all applications must state the subject matter of the dispute, the form of order sought and a brief statement of the pleas in law on which the application is based. Those elements must be sufficiently precise and clear......... in order to guarantee legal certainty and the sound administration of justice it is necessary, in order for an action to be admissible, that the essential matters of law and fact relied on should be stated, at least in summary form, coherently and intelligibly in the application itself.[62]

In the context of a legal dispute, it is therefore incumbent on both the parties to the dispute to produce petitions that are clear and precise and the right of legal certainty is vested in both; and realized by one against the other. The crux of the principle of legal certainty is based on the idea of individual rights and protection from excesses of the state. Therefore the primary focus is on law promulgated by the state and administrative decision-making of public institutions.

The Court in French Republic case, wherein it held that administrative acts that produce legal effects should also be clear and precise so that the person concerned is

---

[58] Case T-398/07, Kingdom of Spain v. European Commission, Judgement of the General Court (Eighth Chamber), 29 March 2012, para 94.

[59] Case C-158/07, Forster [2008] ECR I-8507, para 67; Case T-308/05, Italy v Commission [2007] ECR II-5089, para 158; and Judgement of 13 November 2008 in Case T-128/05 SPM v Council and Commission, not published in ECR, para 147.

[60] Case C-343/09, Afton Chemical Limited. v. Secretary of State for Transport. Reference for a preliminary ruling from the High Court of Justice of England and Wales, Queen's Bench Division (Administrative Court), Judgment of the Court (Fourth Chamber) of 8 July 2010. Also see, Case C-110/03 Belgium v Commission [2005] ECR I-2801, para 30; Case C-344/04 IATA and ELFAA [2006] ECR I-403, para 68; and Intertanko and Others, para 69.

[61] Case C-343/08 Commission v Czech Republic [2010] ECR I-275, para 26.

[62] Case T-19/07, Systran SA and Systran Luxembourg SA v. European Commission, Judgment of the General Court (Third Chamber) of 16 December 2010, para 107 and 108. Also see Case C-505/09 P, European Commission v Republic of Estonia, Judgment of the Court (Second Chamber) of 29 March 2012 in. para 34.

able to known without ambiguity what his rights and obligations are and to take steps accordingly.[63]

Foreseeability of law[64] (both in terms of European legislation and regulatory decisions of the European Commission), was upheld in *Belgium and Forum 187 case*[65] and *Nuova Agricast and Cofra case*.[66] In the Alcoa case, the court expounded the principle of the protection of legitimate expectations—that is logical corollary to the principle of legal certainty. It stated:

> The right to rely on the principle of the protection of legitimate expectations extends to any person in a situation in which a European Union institution has caused him to entertain expectations which are justified by precise assurances provided to him. However, if a prudent and alert economic operator could have foreseen the adoption of a European Union measure likely to affect his interests, he cannot plead that principle if the measure is adopted.[67]

European institutions therefore have an obligation to act in a consistent manner in their legal drafting and in their regulatory decisions. However given that laws do change over time,[68] this obligation is not without exemptions. The exemption ensures that in case of changes—administrative institutions should provide a reasonable notice to operators—thereby ensuring foreseeability of the changes.[69] Also the limitation period in case of administrative decisions must be fixed in advance.[70]

Upholding this right individual right to legal certainty, the Court has however qualified that right, by stating that, the claimants should have acted in good faith[71] and that they should be at risk of serious difficulties[72] if the relief is not granted. Individuals and national authorities may also adopt practices which violate European Union law, *by reason of significant and objective uncertainty regarding the implications of European Union provisions, to which the conduct of other member states or the Commission may have contributed*.[73]

---

[63] Judgement of 30 November 2009 in Joined Cases T-427/04 and T-17/05, French Republic and France Telecom SA v Commission of the European Communities, not published in ECR, para 300.

[64] Case C-305/00 Schulin [2003] ECR I-3525, para 58. Also see, Case C-199/03 Ireland v Commission [2005] ECR I-8027, para 69.

[65] Joined Cases C-182/03 and C-217/03, Belgium and Forum 187 v Commission, para 69.

[66] Case C-67/09 P, Nuova Agricast and Cofra v Commission [2010] ECR I-0000, para 77.

[67] Judgement of the court on 21 July, 2011 in Case C-194/09 P, Alcoa Transformazioni Srl v European Commission, not published in ECR, para 71.

[68] Administrative measures should only be altered by the European Union institutions, in accordance with the rules on competence and procedure. This was stated by the Court in Case T-229/94 Deutche Bahn v Commission [1997] ECR II-1689, para 113.

[69] Case C-445/06 Danske Slagterier [2009] ECR I-2119, para 34.

[70] Case 41/69 ACF Chemiefarma v Commission [1970] ECR 661.

[71] Case C-402/03 Skov and Bilka [2006] ECR I-199, para 51.

[72] Case C-2/09 Kalinchev [2010] ECR I-4939, para 50.

[73] Judgement of Court on 10 May 2012 in the Joined Cases C-338/11 to C-347/11 Satander Asset Management, not published in ECR, para 60. Also See, Case C-423/04 Richards [2006] ECR I-3585, para 42.

This clearly alludes to the conduct of administrative institutions—which also have to act in a predictable manner[74] that is reasonable ascertainable by an individual. In a separate case involving recognition and enforcement of judgments in matrimonial matters and in the matters of parental responsibility; the Court held that member states are obligated to establish clear rules and procedures for the purposes of the consent referred to in Art. 56 of the Regulation.[75]

In a recent case, *Ireland et al v European Commission*,[76] on the issue of state aid via exemptions from excise duties; the Court provided a succinct overview of the balance of rights and obligations that flow from the principle of legal certainty. It held as follows:

> Breach of the principle of legal certainty cannot effectively be pleaded if the person whose legal and substantive position was affected by the decision in question, did not observe the conditions laid down in that decision. Respect for the principle of legal certainty also requires that the institutions of European Union must, as matters of principle avoid inconsistencies that might arise in the implementation of the various provisions of European Union Law. This is all the more necessary when these provisions pursue the same objective,[77] such as undistorted competition in the common market.

Protection of individual rights being the primary basis for the principle of legal certainty, the Courts have also sought to create a coterie of supportive rights—these include the principle of equal treatment and the obligation of transparency.[78] Along with the principle of protection of legitimate expectations, these form a coterie of complementary rights that guarantee the protection of legal persons against state excesses. However the principle of legal certainty is not an absolute right. Therefore administrative institutions can amend legal provisions and alter legal decisions; but they have to do so in a manner that is transparent and consistent. This in turn will ensure that their actions are foreseeable by the individuals.

From the above discussion on case law, one is able to identify specific notions of what constitutes legal certainty. It includes the notion of *clarity, intelligibility, consistency, predictability and coherence*. It is also established by the Court, that there are chiefly two sources of violations of legal certainty. First, is the text of the law—legislations and regulatory orders. It therefore emphasizes that the administrative institutions should ensure textual precision, clarity and consistency. Second, is the issue of functioning of administrative institutions, such institutions have to take regulatory decisions in a manner that is transparent, consistent and predictable.

---

[74] Judgement of Court on 8 December 2011 in Case C-81/10 P. Also see, Case C-76/06 P Britannia Alloys & Chemicals v Commission [2007] ECR I-4405, para 79.

[75] Judgement of Court on 26 April 2012 in Case C-92/12 PPU, Health Service Executive, not published in ECR, para 82.

[76] Judgment of Court on 21 March 2012 in Joined Cases T-50/06 RENV, T 56/06 RENV, T 60/06 RENV, T 62/06 RENV, T 69/06 RENV, not published in ECR, paras 62 and 95.

[77] Case C-225/91 Matra v Commission [1993] ECR I-3203, paras 41 and 42. Also see, Case T-156/98 RJB Mining v Commission [2001] ECR II-337, para 112.

[78] Judgement of the Court on 16 February 2012 in Joined Cases C-72/10 and C 77/10, Marcello Costa and Ugo Cifone, not published in ECR, para 92.

Maintaining the unity or the coherence of the legal discipline is also the primary responsibility of these administrative institutions.

3.6 Conclusion

Legal positivists assert that legal certainty is an intrinsic characteristic of the legal order and therefore there is always a movement towards establishing stability and therefore greater legal certainty within the legal order. The hierarchical structured legal order is therefore supposed to be ideally situated in delivering legal certainty to those operating within the legal order. Sociologists of law like Weber have on the other hand focused on calculability of law and therefore on the regulatee perception and expectations of legal certainty. Other scholars, outside the legal positivist tradition; like Habermas have highlighted the importance of shared sense of values and consensus on accessing rulemaking forums as important conditions for ensuring substantive legal certainty. Thus scholars like Weber and Habermas underline that the search for legal certainty may also lead to those aspects that are external to the legal order.

Further the Law and Society movement has highlighted instances of legislative ambiguity and administrative politics that often provide broad statutory mandates—within little regulatory guidance. Regulatory agencies therefore enjoy a great deal of discretion. They are also open to politicization and regulatory capture. The point here is that the law is neither neutral nor exogenous.[79] It is especially interesting in regulatory spaces—where private actors play an important role in regulatory functions. This is in a sense could also shape their notions of regulatory uncertainty and legal certainty. The Critical Legal Studies movement has also highlighted the constitutive function of law[80]—the fact that certain regulatory spaces are uniquely constructed by the law—for instance in the case of medical devices—private standards are recognized and given the status of legal norms—thus opening up new and "non-formal" processes of 'law' making—and for ensuring calculability via participation in these processes.

The primary aim of this chapter was to discuss and explore the different dimensions of the concept of legal certainty and to specifically address the second sub-research question—*What are the constitutive elements of the concept of legal certainty?* Starting from legal positivist scholarship in terms of the principle of legal certainty—the chapter expands the debate to evaluate the utility of adopting socio-legal approaches to the study of legal certainty by focusing on calculability of the law through tracing regulatory expectations. Finally it explores ECJ case law on legal certainty and identifies the notions of *clarity, intelligibility, consistency, predictability and coherence* as constitutive of the notion of legal certainty as used of regulatees.

---

[79] Suchman and Edelman (1996), pp. 903–941.

[80] Faulkner (2009), pp. 637–646. The 'Amherst' School provided postmodern critiques of the legal system. See for instance; Sarat and Kearns (1993). For a good overview of critical legal studies scholarship, see Gordon (1984), pp. 57–125.

References

Aarnio A (1987) The rational as reasonable. A treatise on legal justification. D. Reidel Publishing Company, Dordrecht

Bertea S (2007) How non-positivism can accommodate legal certainty. In: Pavlakos G (ed) Law, rights and discourse: themes from the legal philosophy of Robert Alexy. Hart, Oxford and Portland, Oregon, pp 69–82

Betlem G (2002) The doctrine of consistent interpretation – managing legal uncertainty. Oxford J Legal Stud 22:397–418

Braeutigam RR (1979) The effect of uncertainty in regulatory delay on the rate of innovation. Law Contemp Probl 43:98–111

Braithwaite J (2002) Rules and principles: a theory of legal certainty. Aust J Legal Philos 27:47–82

D'Amato A (2010) Legal uncertainty. Faculty Working Papers, Northwestern University School of Law Scholarly Commons

Dari-Mattiacci G, Deffains B (2007) Uncertainty of law and the legal process. J Inst Theor Econ 163:627–656

de Sousa Santos B (1987) Law: a map of misreading. Towards a postmodern conception of law. J Law Soc 14:279–302

Delbruck J (1993) Globalization of law, politics, and markets – implications for domestic law – a European perspective. Indiana J Global Legal Stud 1:9

Diver CS (1983) The optimal precision of administrative rules. Yale Law J 93:65–109

Ebbesson J (2010) The rule of law in governance of complex socio-ecological changes. Global Environ Change 20:414–422

Ehrlich E (1936) Fundamental principles of the sociology of law. Harvard University Press, Harvard

Ellermann A (2012) The rule of law and the right to stay: the moral claims of undocumented migrants. American Political Science Association Annual Meeting Paper

EUCOMED (2012) Newsletter, Issue 22, June. http://www.eucomed.org/newsletternews/411/124/news/2012/06/21/Commission-unveils-plans-for-improved-oversight-of-notified-bodies-pending-revision-of-the-Medical-Devices-Directives/. Accessed 23 June 2012

European Commission (2006) Patient mobility: ways to reach more legal certainty. Health and Consumer Voice. http://ec.europa.eu/dgs/health_consumer/dyna/consumervoice/create_cv.cfm?cv_id=249. Accessed 23 June 2012

Ewing S (1987) Formal justice and the spirit of capitalism: Max Weber's sociology of law. Law Soc Rev 21(2):487–512

Faulkner A (2009) Regulatory policy as innovation: constructing rules of engagement for a technological zone of tissue engineering in the European Union. Res Policy 38:637–646

Friedman LM (1969) Legal culture and social development. Law Soc Rev 4:29

Galanter M (1992) Law abounding: legalisation around the North Atlantic. Mod Law Rev 1:55

Gessner V, Budak AC (1998) Emerging legal certainty: empirical studies on the globalization of law. Ashgate Dartmouth

Gordon RW (1984) Critical legal histories. Stanford Law Rev 36:57–125

Gribnau H (2013) Equality, legal certainty and tax legislation in the Netherlands fundamental legal principles as checks on legislative power: a case study. Utrecht Law Rev 9:52–74

Groussot X, Minssen T (2007) Res Judicata in the court of justice case law: balancing legal certainty with legality? Eur Constitutional Law Rev 3:385–417

Habermas J (1985) The theory of communicative action, volume 1: reason and the rationalization of society (English translation by Thomas McCarthy). Beacon Press, Boston

Habermas J (1996) Between facts and norms: contributions to a discourse theory of law and democracy (English translation by William Rehg). MIT Press, Cambridge, MA

Hancher L, Moran M (1989) Organising regulatory space. In: Hancher L, Moran M (eds) Capitalism, culture and economic regulation. Oxford University Press, Oxford, U.K. pp 271–299

Kramer MH (2003) In defense of legal positivism. Oxford University Press, Oxford, U.K

Krisch N (2006) The pluralism of global administrative law. Eur J Int Law 17:247–278
Luhmann N (1988) The unity of the legal system. In: Teubner G (ed) Autopoietic law: a new approach to law and society. Walter de Gruyter, Berlin
Luhmann N (1992) Operational closure and structural coupling: the differentiation of the legal system. Cardozo Law Rev 13:1419
Malinowski B (1934) Introduction. In: Hogbin HI (ed) Law and order in Polynesia. Harcourt, Brace & Co, New York
Mattei U (1993) Three patterns of law: taxonomy and change in the world's legal systems'. Am J Comp Law 45:5–43
Maxeiner JR (2007) Legal certainty: a European alternative to American legal indeterminacy? Tulane J Int Comp Law 15:541
Michaels R (2005) The re-statement of non-state law: the state, choice of law and the challenge of global legal pluralism. Wayne Law Rev 51:1209–1259
Moore SF (1978) Law as process: an anthropological approach. Routledge & Kegan Paul, London
Moore SE (2008) International law and sociolegal scholarship: toward a spatial global legal pluralism. Stud Law Polit Soc 41:149
Morgan R (2012) Ensuring greater legal certainty in OHIM decision-taking by abandoning legal formalism. J Intellect Property Law Pract 7:408–429
Neuhaus PH (1963) Legal certainty versus equity in the conflict of laws. Law Contemp Probl 28:795–807
Otto JM (2002) Towards an analytical framework. Real legal certainty and its explanatory factors. In: Chen J, Li Y, Otto JM (eds) Implementation of law in the People's Republic of China. Kluwer Law International, The Hague
Paunio E (2009) Beyond predictability – reflections on legal certainty and the discourse theory of law in the EU legal order. German Law J 10:1469–1493
Popelier P (2008) Five paradoxes on legal certainty and the law-maker. Legisprudence 2:47–66
Raban O (2010) The fallacy of legal certainty: why vague legal standards may be better for capitalism, liberalism, and democracy. Public Interest Law J 19:175–191
Raitio J (2003) The principle of legal certainty in EC law. Kluwer Academic Publishers, Dordrecht, pp 175–236
Rheinstein M (1954) Max Weber on law in economy and society. Harvard University Press
Sarat A, Kearns TR (eds) (1993) The fate of law. University of Michigan Press, Ann Arbor, Michigan
Sassen S (1996) Losing control? Sovereignty in an age of globalization. Columbia University Press, New York.
Schermers HG, Waelbroeck D (2001) Judicial protection in the European Union. Kluwer Law International, The Hague, pp 65–83
Schwarze J (1992) European administrative law. Sweet and Maxwell, London, pp 45–76
Sterling JS, Moore WE (1987) Weber's analysis of legal rationalization: a critique and constructive modification. Sociol Forum 2:67–89
Stinchcombe AL (1999) Certainty of the law: reasons, situation-types, analogy and equilibrium. J Polit Philos 7:209–224
Suchman MC, Edelman LB (1996) Legal rational myths: the new institutionalism and the law and society tradition. Law Soc Inq 21:903–941
Swedberg R (2006) Max Weber's contribution to the economic sociology of law. Annu Rev Law Soc Sci 2:61–81
Tridimas T (1999) The general principles of EC law. Oxford University Press, Oxford, U.K. p 163
Trubek D (1972) Max Weber on law and rise of capitalism. Wisconsin Law Rev 3:746
Trubek D (1986) Max Weber's tragic modernism and the study of law in society. Law Soc Rev 20:573
Wroblewski J (1984) Between legalism and finalism. Duncker und Humblot, Berlin

Chapter 4
Explanation of Methodological Choices

4.1 Introduction

In the introduction (Chap. 1) to this book I put forward the argument of how the current vertical and horizontal developments challenge the clear distinction between international law and national legal orders. Legal scholarship has sought to analyze and theorize these developments through the ideas of Global Administrative Law, International Constitutionalism, Legal Pluralism and Systems Theory. However the focus of these approaches has been to specifically explore implications of these developments in terms of legitimacy and accountability deficits that have arisen and the evolution of conflict rules between concomitant normative orders. This book focuses attention to the other (under-researched) implication—that of legal certainty. Specifically it explores these developments through the conceptualization of "multilevel regulation" and the dimensions of legal certainty (as experienced by regulatees). Following from this the primary question is:

How do regulatees pursue legal certainty in the context of multilevel European medical product regulation?

Chapters 2 and 3 provided a theoretical exploration that contributed to the conceptualization of two critical concepts—*multilevel regulation* and *legal certainty*. For the purposes of this book multilevel regulation has been defined as the "term used to characterize a regulatory space in which the process of rule making, rule application and rule adjudication is dispersed across more than one administrative or territorial level amongst several different actors, both public and private."[1] The constituent elements of legal certainty include *clarity*, *intelligibility*, *consistency*, *predictability and coherence*. I do not define 'legal certainty' because the aim is to excavate regulatee expectations of legal certainty and therefore I needed a set of notions which capture the idea of legal certainty. This set of notions is referred to as the "constituent elements of legal certainty" and they become the

[1] See Chaps. 1 and 3.

DOI 10.1007/978-3-319-04594-8_4,

basis for alluding to legal certainty in the questionnaire which is used for gathering responses from regulatees who are interviewed.

Subsequent to this conceptualization, in the previous chapters, in this chapter, I discuss in detail the selection of the two cases in the following paragraphs. In the next section (4.2) I briefly touch upon the definition of multilevel regulation in terms of the attributes and nature of the concept and also comment on legal certainty. Sections 4.3 and 4.4 examine the research methods and operationalization of the concepts respectively. Section 4.5 discusses the recruitment, sampling and the research process. Section 4.6 concludes with a review of the analytical strategy.

Why do I choose these two case studies? I have alluded to some of the reasons earlier in Chap. 1. Here I explain the reasons in greater detail. First, is the question of regulatory architecture?[2] The pharmaceutical regulatory space is hierarchical structured and the medical device regulatory space is structured in a more heterarchical style.[3] Marketing authorization of pharmaceutical products is clearly divided into national and central processes that are regulated by the EMA and the national competent authorities respectively. Their functions are governed by European regulations, directives and guidelines that provide for detailed directions as to implementation of regulatory obligations by regulatees. Most of these guidelines are generated nationally and at the European level by regulatory authorities. Marketing authorization of medical devices is a study in contrast. Although there are European directives that lay down general principles, standards that address these general principles (thereby creating a presumption of conformity) are laid down by private standardization bodies—who are in turn members of the ISO—which has a separate mandate. Further private enforcement agencies—known as ‘notified bodies’ constitute the first level of enforcement reviewers for regulatees. Thus *prima facie* these two regulatory spaces are structured differently, creating the expectation that one may be more multilevel than the other and this may have some implication for the regulatee expectations of legal certainty.

Second, together the medical devices and the pharmaceutical product categories constitute the majority of products that would encapsulate products that would be regulated under European medical product regulation. Thus the results of these two case studies would together be able to provide an authoritative guide to what can be said about the European medical product sector in general. Third, I choose to focus on the marketing authorization aspect of regulation as it is the regulatory gateway through which several other aspects of product regulation—clinical trial, manufacturing, post-marketing and vigilance—are regulated.

---

[2] In this context, I refer to regulatory architecture to mean the shape and structure of the regulatory regime governing the regulatory space including the nature of regulatory instruments to shape private action. See for other definitions of regulatory architecture, Lessig (1999).

[3] Chowdhury (2013), pp. 635–652.

Fourth and finally, both these regulatory spaces are at the cusp of regulatory upheavals that are expected to fundamentally reconstruct the regulatory architecture (this is especially true for medical devices). Various stakeholders including regulatees have been particularly involved in policy debates and regulatory meetings on this issue and opinions have differed on utility of regulatory proposals forwarded by the European Commission and that are expected to deliver greater *legal certainty*.[4] Thus the meaning and dimensions of the concept of legal certainty in terms of regulatee expectations is an important part of the ongoing policy debates that are shaping these two regulatory spaces. This allows me greater and easier access regulatee perceptions and expectations and adds currency to this book.

4.2 Conceptualization

I use the term multilevel regulation to capture both horizontal and vertical developments that are challenging our idea of a territorially delimited national legal order which is separate from an international legal order. It refers to the processes through which public regulation is being increasingly stewarded, shaped and in many cases even determined by non-state actors. Multilevel regulation can therefore be termed as my background concept.[5] I define multilevel regulation as a term used to characterize a regulatory space where the process of rule making, rule application and rule adjudication is dispersed across more than one administrative or territorial level amongst several different actors, both public and private. The relationship between the actors is non-hierarchical and may be independent of each other. Lack of central ordering of the regulatory lifecycle within this regulatory space is the most important feature of a multilevel regulation. This definition of multilevel regulation captures certain specific attributes of multilevel regulation—and therefore is the systemized concept.[6]

The attributes captured by this definition can be presented in the following manner:

- process of rule making OR rule application OR rule adjudication dispersed across more than on territorial OR administrative levels AND
- amongst several public and private actors AND
- relationship between actors is non-hierarchical

Since all the attributes are connected with each other—through 'AND' and therefore the definition is a combination of the 'family resemblance' and 'necessary and sufficient conditions' structures.[7]

---

[4] See for a discussion on the review of existing European legislation on medical devices—Chowdhury (2013), pp. 635–652; Chowdhury (2012), pp. 157–175.

[5] Robert and Collier (2001), pp. 529–546.

[6] Goertz and Starr (2003) at pp. 1–24.

[7] Tilly (1984).

If we assume the above definition of multilevel regulation the positive concept—what is the negative concept? We can refer to the negative concept as single-scale hierarchic integrated regulation (henceforth SSHIR) wherein the regulatory process (rulemaking, rule application and rule adjudication) is integrated and harmonized within a strictly specified hierarchic structure and a single government agency (operating at one administrative or territorial level) is responsible for all the three aspects of the regulatory process. SSHIR is akin to the rational myth conceptualization of the 'legal order'. Multilevel regulation should be considered as a continuous concept—this implies that it is possible for regulatory spaces to be located along the continuum between multilevel regulation (which is one extreme) and SSHIR which is the other.

Positive	⟷	Negative
(Multilevel Regulation)		(SSHIR)

Legal certainty attributes that were distilled from pleas submitted by litigants in the ECJ—includes, *clarity*, *intelligibility*, *consistency*, *predictability and coherence*. These notions were used to capture and document notions (albeit as used within the legal process) by regulatees. The questionnaire was designed therefore to refer to these attributes and regulatees were asked to explain the content and value of these attributes from their perspective. Form a regulatee point of view—litigation is always a last option—and may also not be useful especially in such cases wherein norm interpretation is plagued by scientific differences of opinion. Regulatory categorization of borderline products is an area of regulatory uncertainty—yet regulatees have by and large refrained from accessing Courts.

Legal certainty is therefore defined in this context, as the perception of regulatees within a regulatory space—that the current set of normative rules—both procedural and substantive—that operate within this space ensure clarity, intelligibility, consistency, predictability and coherence, thus ensuring calculability of the law. Following from this legal uncertainty can be defined as a situation which is unclear, unintelligible, inconsistent, unpredictable and incoherent rules which could impede the functioning of regulatees.

Here it is important to reiterate that this is an exploratory study and therefore it does not aim to establish causality between multilevel regulation and legal certainty. This is a sociological study of regulatee perception in regulatory spaces (shaped by multilevel regulation) and their expectations of legal certainty—within medical devices case study I focus on regulatees from Germany and UK. First, methodologically both represent different administrative set-ups—UK is unitary and Germany is federal. The federal nature of the German polity would mean that there would be an additional administrative level of regulatory institutions (and therefore relatively more multilevel) than in UK. Second, both Germany and the

UK have markets and medical device industries of considerable size.[8] Third, both have the largest number of notified bodies—with distinct competencies that are historically embedded—the English notified bodies are focussed on quality management system and German ones are more oriented towards product testing. Together these reasons allowed for a contrast which is an important reason for the selection of these two countries.

In the case of pharmaceuticals (the regulatory term used is 'medicinal products'), regulatees from both the centralized process (CP) (overseen by the European Medicines Agency) and the decentralized process or the mutual recognition process (MRP) were included in the sample. This was also done to gauge whether regulatees differentiated between processes on the basis of their expectations of legal certainty, given that the CP is more hierarchical in structure than the MRP.

There have been mainly three kinds of academic literature that can be argued to foreground both these case studies. First, is a regulatory studies perspective wherein regulation theorists have long argued for improving effectiveness of regulation by designing regulation that is sensitive to the structural dimensions of the regulated industry and more importantly takes into consideration the capacity and perspectives of regulatees.[9] Second are sectoral studies from the legal[10] and health and drug policy perspectives.[11] The medical devices are comparatively understudied than pharmaceuticals. However there have been some exceptions such as Prof. Christa Altenstetter who has studied the institutional politics of regulation of the medical device industry through comparative studies of European countries.[12] Third, includes studies that apply perspectives from the science and technology studies to medical technology regulation.[13]

4.3 Research Methods

The choice of research methods were driven by the research questions. The book seeks to understand social processes and subjective meanings of these processes. The book aims to explore the social process of legal certainty—how do regulatees understand this notion? And, following from this to ascertain how regulatees pursue legal certainty in the context of multilevel regulation.

[8] Germany, France and the UK constitute the three largest markets for medical devices in Europe—in that order respectively; See http://www.lboro.ac.uk/microsites/mechman/research/ipm-ktn/pdf/Sector_profile/medical-devices-the-uk-industry-and-its-technology-development.pdf (last accessed 15 June 2012) and Schmitt (2000), pp. 53–58.

[9] See Ayres and Braithwaite (1992).

[10] Hodges (2011).

[11] Abraham and Lewis (2003), Mossialos et al. (2010) and Feick (2006).

[12] See for instance, Altenstetter (2003), pp. 228–248; Altenstetter and Permanand (2007), pp. 385–405; Altenstetter (2008).

[13] Faulkner et al. (2008), pp. 195–222; Faulkner (2009); and Faulkner (2012), pp. 389–408.

Given that legal certainty is understood in terms of regulatee expectations—field interviews with regulatees and document analysis of press briefs, position papers, legislative documents, articles in trade journals and other sources; were the primary collection methods used. However an additional method adopted was an internship with a law firm (specializing in regulatory and legal advice relating to medical products)—this was taken up to explore the legal dimensions of the problem of borderline products and also to access and understand regulatee problems—through clients that approach the law firm for advice. Regulation of borderline products has been plagued by regulatory uncertainty since such products frequently escape regulatory categorization. It was expected that via this internship an understanding of both the legal dimension as well as regulatee perspectives on this problem could be accessed. And that would help assess the nature and scale of the problem.[14]

A mapping exercise was undertaken in order to ascertain whether each of the regulatory spaces is characterized by multilevel regulation. The mapping exercise is primarily done through document analysis of European legislations, pre-legislative documents, news reports, research reports written by regulatory agencies, etc.

The research process can be divided into three stages:

- Stage I: Mapping of Regulatory Spaces (Medical Devices and Medicinal Products) in terms of identification of rules, regulatory actors and the relationship between these actors.
- Stage II: Pilot Study through field research—experts interviews of regulators, regulatees and consultants working in the medical product industry (includes both medical devices and medicinal products) in Netherlands (to validate findings of the mapping exercise of Stage I) and also test interview questionnaire for Stage III: Internship with a law firm specifically to investigate the issue of borderline products
- Stage IV: Field research through interviews of regulatees in medical devices and medicinal products

The questionnaire used for capturing regulatory perceptions of multilevelness and their expectations of legal certainty was designed on the basis of the findings of Stage I and Stage II. The format and categories of the questionnaire for both medical devices and pharmaceutical case studies are the same—however in the case of some substantive issues the sub-questions differ.[15]

[14] The results of what I term as a legal excursion is discussed in detail in Chap. 8.

[15] Please refer to Annexures I and II for the medical device and the pharmaceutical case study questionnaires.

4.4 Operationalization of the Concepts

Multilevel regulation has been defined in terms of its attributes. The first step was to describe the rule making, rule application and rule adjudication processes within these two regulatory spaces. Thereafter the second step was to identify the rules governing these processes and the actors controlling these processes. The third step was to locate the territorial or administrative level of these actors. And, fourth to evaluate the relationship between the actors involved in these processes. All these aspects would contribute to qualitatively assess whether the specific regulatory space is multilevel in nature.

In the case of legal certainty, the first step was to identify a set of notions that have been used by regulatees to refer to legal certainty. This was excavated from the pleas that were considered by the ECJ in cases wherein the principle of legal certainty was discussed and adjudicated. This decision may attract criticism on the ground that these notions were not of regulatees but were in fact used by their lawyers to access the Courts—in that sense these notions represent the lawyer's interpretation of their client expectations and therefore is a credible source. These criticisms may be assuaged—by the fact that these notions were only used as reference points in constructing the questionnaire. The interview responses are the authoritative representation of the regulatee expectations—and this forms the primary data. This was an informed decision made, since using the term "legal certainty"—may not be automatically understandable to regulatees. These notions of predictability, consistence, coherence and clarity were notions that were presumed to be more accessible to regulatees.

4.5 Recruitment, Sampling and the Research Process

The units of research included a combination of people, events, institutions and documents. People included interviewees—majority of them were manufacturers (may be defined as regulatees). Additionally other important actors, viz. regulators, notified bodies, consultants and academicians were also interviewed. This was done so as assess whether regulatee expectations were different—and their assessment of legal certainty within the regulatory space—was different from the other actors sharing regulatory space with them.

First a master list of manufacturers was prepared from the following sources:

- Members of the industry associations within these regulatory spaces
- Companies that had received marketing authorization (esp. medicinal products)
- Companies that had filed responses to ongoing public consultations on regulatory reviews spearheaded by the DG SANCO (1995–2012)

Second, another list was made by identifying the names of employees of these manufacturing companies who are dealing with regulatory affairs—since it the regulatory affairs department that oversees and is most intimately involved with the marketing authorization process. This list was made on the basis of participants in DIA meetings, European Commission sponsored conferences and articles in trade journals. Also during the interview process itself, interviewees were asked to suggest names within their peer group who could be contacted for this study. Care was taken to ensure that amongst the regulatees—there was adequate representation of manufacturers who were involved with all product types and also which represented both large and medium scale manufacturers. Unfortunately no small manufacturers participated in the medical device sector—in lieu of which the industry associations representing SMEs were included. However it should be noted that in terms of market size, the regulatees interviewed represent 72 % of the general medical devices market. Also care was taken to unearth the SME perceptions of the regulatory space and also of legal certainty in particular, through the responses submitted to the surveys conducted by the DG SANCO as part of the ongoing exercise to map stakeholder perspective of the regulatory options being considered as part of the revision of the regulatory regime. All these factors have helped in limiting the impact of under-representation of individual SMEs in the interviews.

Similar problem was faced in the case of medicinal products—but could not be mitigated—because there were no industry association that represented the needs of small manufacturers—but this is the reality of the industry structure—where there has been a trend towards decreasing number of small manufacturers—except in specific therapeutic areas such as ATMPs.

Third, other actors such as the regulators from the European Commission, national competent authorities, CHMP, CAT; industry associations and, consultants were also included. Thus although the focus was on regulatee perceptions and expectations—I also wanted to know whether these were different from the views of other stakeholders—regulators and consultants in the case of pharmaceuticals; and regulators, consultants, notified bodies and industry associations in the case of medical devices.

In the case of both the case studies, first contacts with the interviewees were established through email. The email communicated the research objectives—how the regulatory spaces had evolved and inquired about their experience of the marketing authorization process. If they agreed to the request for an interview—the questionnaire was sent to them one day prior to the interview. A total of 84 email invitations requesting participation in the case of medical devices and 86 in the case of medicinal products were sent. Ultimately a total 40 interviews in medical devices and 17 interviews in medicinal products were done. Written consents in the form of email verification were sought from interviewees to record the interview.

Interviews were done on telephone and on an average lasted around 50 min. They were recorded and transcribed by me. These transcribed interviews were then shared with the interviewees. This was done to so as to assure interviewee concerns and also to ensure that there was a second level of validation of the data by the interviewees themselves. Also during the time lag between the recording and the

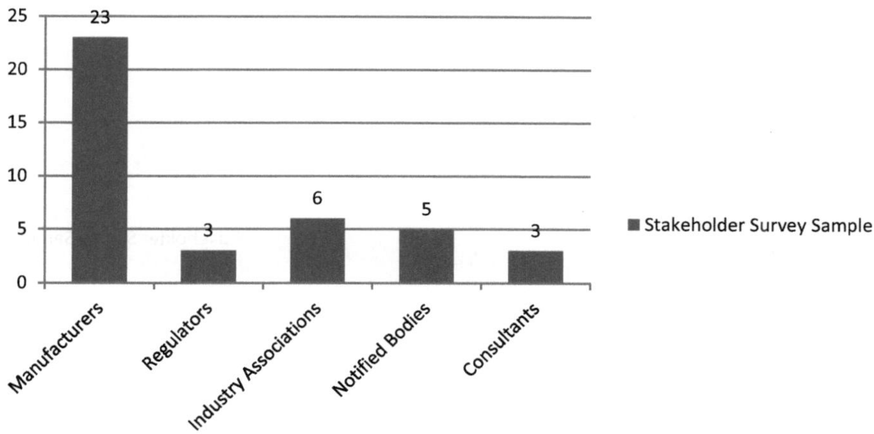

Fig. 4.1 Medical device stakeholder survey sample. *Source*: Based on survey sample of the Medical Device Case Study

transcription of the interviews—this provided a useful breather to reflect and if required ask for any clarifications. In the case of the medical device case study—36 of the 40 interviewees responded back. And, in the case of the medicinal products case study, 14 of the 17, responded back. It was presumed that those who did not respond back—did not have any reservations as to content of their interviews.

4.5.1 Medical Device Case Study

The study was designed and conducted between May to October 2011. The sample size was 40 (see Fig. 4.1 for details) and it included regulatory affairs managers of medical device manufacturing companies, national regulators like Bfarm and MHRA, European Commission, European industry associations, notified bodies and regulatory consultants. This was not a random sample. Those individuals in these organizations whose job entailed knowledge and operation of European marketing authorization processes at the company level as well as of the European policy processes, were interviewed. A representative sample of the principal stakeholders[16] in this process and also across each of the product sectors was selected.

[16] It must be noted that the focus was on regulatees (largest percentage in the sample) and regulators (Commission, National Competent Authorities) and notified bodies (that are involved in regulatory enforcement). I deliberately did not interview patient associations and other stakeholders for two reasons. First I identify 'regulatees' narrowly as those whose actions the rules aim to regulate. Thus manufacturers are identified as the primary regulatees. Second, although patient associations are important stakeholders given that they are indirectly affected by the rules—

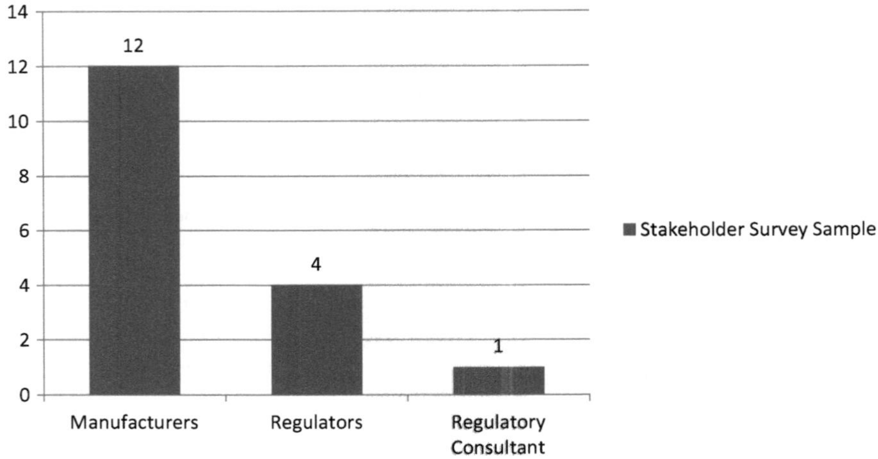

Fig. 4.2 Pharmaceutical stakeholder survey sample. *Source*: Based on survey sample of the Pharmaceutical Case study

Semi-standardized interviews were employed, rather than questionnaires. Experts were asked about their experience of the functioning of the regulatory framework. The interviews were transcribed and coded anonymously, depending on the preferences of the interviewees. The NVivo programme was used to tabulate and analyze the data.

4.5.2 Pharmaceutical Case Study

The study was designed and conducted from August, 2011 to January, 2012. The sample size was 17 (see Fig. 4.2). It included regulatory affairs managers of pharmaceutical manufacturing companies, national regulators and members of CHMP (Committee for Medicinal Products for Human Use), European industry associations, and regulatory consultants (technical consultants that advice industry). This was not a random sample. Those individuals in these organizations whose job entailed knowledge and operation of all authorization processes—viz. DCP (decentralized process), MRP (Mutual Recognition Process) and CP (Centralized Process) were approached to participate in the case study. An attempt was made also to choose a sample that represents the principal stakeholders in this process and also across each of the product sectors—biologicals, biosimilars (generics), cardiovascular, women's reproductive health, etc. The study was focused on medicinal

however patient associations have been more active on reimbursement policies rather than on marketing authorization issues.

products for human use—and therefore by definition excluded herbal and veterinary medicines.

The focus was to draw comparison between the centralized processes on the one hand, and other processes like decentralized and mutual recognition procedures. The difference between these two, is that while CP is overtly more hierarchical in nature—one agency one authorization, both the DCP and MRP processes is characterized by horizontal regulatory procedures that are structured in a heterarchical manner. This difference in architecture provides an interesting foreground to our exploration. All the interviewees had extensive knowledge and experience of both the procedures—the manufacturing companies interviewed ranged from medium scale to large companies and all of them had products/indications that were approved through the CP/DCP/MRP procedures. Additionally some of them also had insights into the US regulatory process regulated by the FDA—and therefore were able to provide a comparative perspective not only at the European level but internationally between the EU and US. The regulators were from national competent authorities who are active in the CHMP and CAT. Moreover some of the interviewees were actively involved in the ICH processes internationally.

Semi-standardized interviews were employed, rather than strict questionnaires. Experts were questioned on their experience of the functioning of the regulatory framework. The interviews were transcribed and coded anonymously, as per the wishes of the interviewees. I used the NVivo program to tabulate and analyze the data. The interview data was further supplemented by annual reports and working documents of the national competent authorities, CHMP, CAT, PDCO (Pediatric Committee) and the EMA. European Commission Annual assessment reports of the European Commission (DG SANCO), questions asked by European parliamentarians, and annual reports of the manufacturers interviewed were analyzed. Apart from this, regulatory intelligence (trade) publications like SCRIP and Clinica were also assessed to keep abreast of regulatory developments and opinions of stakeholders (specifically regulatees).

4.6 Analytical Strategy

Both the questionnaires (see Annexures I and II) were formulated on the basis of the research questions and also on the responses to the pilot study. It was divided into three parts. The first part was titled organizational details—this was to elicit information about the nature and scale of operations of the company, regulator, industry association, notified body, consultant, etc. The second part was titled regulation, stakeholders and important developments. The aim here was to document what interviewees considered to be the primary norms operating within the regulatory space, whom did they identify as stakeholders and to benchmark what they considered to be the most important regulatory changes. The changes could relate to both normative as well other physical changes in the industry. Information on all these aspects, helped validate the findings of Stage I—whether each of the regulatory spaces was multilevel in nature? And if so, what is its nature and scale. It also helped confirm the representativeness of the data set—in terms of whether any important stakeholder was missing. In the third part, the interviewees were asked about their perception of the regulatory system. Specific sub questions like whether they found it to be predictable, clear, coherent, and consistent were included. Regulatees were also specifically asked about the big challenges and problems that they faced that the compliance strategies adopted by them. It is important to note that the questionnaire was semi-standardized (this was conveyed to them at the beginning of the interview) and that interviewees had ample flexibility to add other information that they may consider valuable.

The NVivo program was used to tabulate the transcribed data. At the first stage certain themes were generated—aspects that were reiterated by the interviewees. Thereafter, the ultimate analytical categories were selected through a process of iteration—categories when seen as a set—could help envelop the entire gamut of responses in a logically related manner that would address the research questions. The linkage between the analytical categories and the research questions have been further explained in the following chapters detailing the case study results.

In order to guard against selectivity in the use of data, multiple sources of data have been used. So for instance a finding based on interviews was sought to be substantiated by research findings from journals, statements made by actors in trade journals, policy documents, etc. This is also the manner in which triangulation of the data was achieved.

So far I have laid the foundation in terms of the theoretical development of two concepts—multilevel regulation and legal certainty. In this chapter I discussed the methodological choices made at every stage of the case study. In the following chapter I discuss the results of the pilot study that formed the basis for designing of the two case studies—the results of the medical devices and the pharmaceutical case studies are discussed in Chaps. 6 and 7. These chapters address the following sub-research questions: *Is the European medical product regulation multilevel in nature*? *What are the regulatee perceptions of multilevelness of regulatory spaces*? *What are the regulatee perceptions and expectations with regard to legal certainty*? Both Chaps. 6 and 7 follow the same structure so as to aid the comparability of the two case studies.

References

Abraham J, Lewis G (2003) Regulating medicines in Europe: competition, expertise and public health. Routledge, London

Altenstetter C (2003) EU member state and medical device regulation. Int J Technol Assess Healthc 18:228–248

Altenstetter C (2008) Medical devices: European Union policymaking and the implementation of health and patient safety in France. Transaction Publishers, New York

Altenstetter C, Permanand G (2007) The EU regulation of medical devices and pharmaceuticals in comparative perspective. Rev Policy Res 24:385–405

Ayres I, Braithwaite J (1992) Responsive regulation: transcending the deregulation debate. Oxford University Press, New York
Chowdhury N (2012) Limits to the legal deliberation of science questions: a case study of borderline medical products in Europe. Pharm Policy Law 14:157–175
Chowdhury N (2013) Common market but divergent regulatory practices: exploring European regulation and the effect on regulatory uncertainty in the marketing authorization of medical products. J Eur Integration 35:635–652
Faulkner A (2009) Medical technology into healthcare and society: a sociology of devices, innovation and governance. Palgrave Macmillan, Hampshire
Faulkner A (2012) Tissue engineered technologies: regulatory pharmaceuticalisation in the European Union. Innov Eur J Soc Sci Res 25:389–408
Faulkner A, Geesink I, Kent J, FitzPatrick D (2008) Tissue-engineered technologies: scientific biomedicine, frames of risk and regulatory regime-building in Europe. Sci Cult 17:195–222
Feick J (2006) Regulatory Europeanization, national autonomy and regulatory effectiveness: marketing authorization for pharmaceuticals. MPIfG Discussion Paper 02/6, Cologne
Goertz G, Starr H (2003) Introduction: necessary condition logics, research design, and theory. In: Goertz G, Starr H (eds) Necessary conditions. Theory, methodology, and applications. Rowman & Littlefield, Lanham, pp 1–24
Hodges C (2011) The regulation of medicinal products and medical devices. In: Grubb A, Laing J, McHale J, Kennedy I (eds) Principles of medical law. Oxford University Press, Oxford, U.K
Lessig L (1999) Code: and other laws of cyberspace. Basic Books, New York
Mossialos E, Permanand G, Baeten R, Hervey TK (2010) Health systems governance in Europe: the role of European Union law and policy. Cambridge University Press, Cambridge, U.K
Robert A, Collier D (2001) Measurement validity: a shared standard for qualitative and quantitative research. Am Polit Sci Rev 95:529–546
Schmitt JM (2000) Reimbursement and pricing of medical devices in Germany. J Med Mark Device Diagn Pharm Mark 1(1):53–58
Tilly C (1984) Big structures, large processes, huge comparisons. Russell Sage Foundation, New York

Chapter 5
Pilot Study of Regulatory Uncertainty in Marketing Authorization of Medical Products in Europe

5.1 Introduction

This chapter discusses the pilot study that was conducted between September and November 2010, as a lead up to the individual case studies of the medical devices and the pharmaceutical sectors which were conducted in 2011. The primary aims of the pilot study was first, to provide a background review of regulations governing individual product sectors so as to identify specific case studies; second, to identify the critical actors operating within this regulatory space and third, to explore the concept of regulatory uncertainty in the context of these product sectors. This pilot study focuses on the regulation of marketing authorization of medical products—I use this as a generic term to refer to three product categories—medical devices, medicinal products (pharmaceuticals) and ATMPs (Advanced Therapy Medicinal Products). Legally speaking marketing authorization as a concept only applies to medicinal products (or pharmaceuticals) however in this case I use it as a catch all term to refer to the regulatory process which has to be followed by producers before products can be marketed in the European market.

Regulatory studies on marketing access in pharmaceutical regulation in the EU is concentrated in two areas—i.e., the comparative surveys of drug regulation in the EU and USA markets focusing on methodologies of drug approvals and drug safety withdrawals[1] and the impact of European procedures of marketing authorization on the operationalization of drug safety standards.[2] The Abraham and Lewis study, one of the foremost studies of European procedures of marketing authorization and their implications for drug safety in the EU. This chapter is in the same tradition. Now that the process has been unfolding for almost a decade we have luxury of hindsight, and therefore, of deepening the analysis to cover intersectoral dynamics.

[1] Kaitin et al. (1989), pp. 121–138; Parker (1989), pp. 299–309; Schweitzer et al. (1996), pp. 162–178; Bakke et al. (1995), pp. 108–117; Jefferys et al. (1998), pp. 151–156; and Abraham and Davis (2005), pp. 881–892.

[2] Abraham and Lewis (2000); Hancher (1996); and Abraham (1995).

N. Chowdhury, *European Regulation of Medical Devices and Pharmaceuticals*,
DOI 10.1007/978-3-319-04594-8_5, © Springer International Publishing Switzerland 2014

The aim of this chapter is more modest. I explore the effect of European regulation on regulatory uncertainty within these three sectors. European regulations themselves and the regulatory processes that they put into place have expanded across these three sectors. The presumption is that with the coming of common rules, regulatory uncertainty across stakeholder groups should lessen. However increasing calls for greater legal certainty and curbing regulatory uncertainty from stakeholders' questions this presumption[3] and the reiteration of the importance of legal certainty within European legal amendments[4] seem to support this contention. The three research questions are: How have European regulations shaped individual product sectors? Has that impacted regulatory uncertainty in that sector and what has been its nature and scale? What has been the impact of regulatory compliance?

The focus here is on the marketing authorization aspect. In effect this will cover a number of other areas—since marketing authorization regulation is in a sense, the gateway through which a number of other areas are regulated—meaning, it is at the stage of marketing authorization application—that the applicant has to prove conformity with obligations relating manufacturing, clinical trials and pharmacovigilance as specified under the legislations. The number of European legal instruments (directives and regulations) addressing the marketing authorization of medical products currently, stand at 11. This is excluding the number of amendments made to these instruments (well over 30) and the numerous guidelines issued by the European expert bodies, national governments and notified bodies groups. These are operationally buttressed by sets of national legislations and administrative rules. The sheer volume and the range of legal and other policy instruments regulating this sector might pose a challenge to the coherence of the regulatory system as a whole. However the volume per se may not be a problem (even though it does generate fragmentation anxieties) even though it does open up the prospect of overlaps between legal instruments and amongst regulatory authorities providing different interpretations the challenge becomes clearer. The volume is also a direct function of the multiple levels of rule creation that is characteristic of European regulation.

Rule creation, rule application and rule adjudication is scattered across multiple administrative levels depending on the particular kind of medical products. Further the specific features of the regulatory process viz. the participation of private bodies—notified bodies—functioning within the regulatory system have also had a significant impact.

Regulatory uncertainty refers to the sense of ambiguity that prevails within a regulatory space—that renders decision-making by regulatee within that space an unpredictable activity thereby hampering their functioning. Sources of ambiguity may include the structure and substance of the norms themselves, or the

---

[3] COFACE (2009); CISCO IBSG (2008); Europa Bio (2007); and DG SANCO (2009).

[4] EC (2004a) Recital 28 of Regulation (EC) No. 726/2004 and EC (2004b) Recital 7 of Directive 2004/27/EC.

institutional mechanisms that enforce those norms, the lack of a clear adjudicatory mechanism in case of dispute over interpretation of those norms, etc. Herein it is important to underline that, since regulations change over time—it is a dynamic activity—uncertainty is therefore endemic to every regulatory system. However, only when regulatory uncertainty reaches an unmanageable level does it challenge and undermine the effectiveness of the regulatory system as whole.

I interviewed (semi standardized interviews were employed) six regulatory affairs managers, regulators and drug safety scientists that deal with the European market.[5] This was not a random sample. I targeted individuals in these organizations whose job entailed knowledge and operation of European marketing authorization processes and specifically their functioning within a member state context. Their responses therefore reflect informed, rather than random opinions.[6] The interview results were supplemented by the analysis of documented statements of the principle stakeholders like the European Commission and industry bodies; as well as legislative documents.

A representative sample of the principal stakeholders across each of the product sectors was chosen. Most of the interviewees are based in the Netherlands. The Netherlands has a well-developed research based medical product industry that is globally integrated and the Dutch regulator is also actively engaged in European regulatory processes. Moreover all the interviewees are functioning at the European level and are not limited only to the national market.

---

[5] This included the following persons that have been codenamed given the these initials: EP: regulatory affairs manager of a leading MNC manufacturing and marketing medicinal products in Europe (20/9/10); ED1: quality systems and regulatory affairs manager of a leading MNC manufacturing and marketing medical devices in Europe (7/10/10); ED2: regulatory consultant to a SME which is a world leader in a niche medical device (8/10/10); ND: key person in the office of the medical devices regulator in Netherlands (14/10/10); EATMP: consultant to private companies manufacturing and marketing tissue engineering products, ATMPs and more complex medical devices in Europe (26/10/10) and PSC: key scientist with the national public research institute advising the national regulator on safety issues related to biological products and medical devices (3/11/10). As is evident, the focus of the sample is on private companies, regulators and scientists. Within companies, I have included both MNCs and a SME to bring forth the expectedly different compliance strategies and, therefore, experiences. Admittedly it may seem that medical devices sector is overly represented compared to ATMPs and even medicinal products. Although in volumes medical devices only make small part of the medical products sector; it has experienced the most far-reaching regulatory changes through the European process and more importantly currently on the anvil are the Commission's plans to introduce large-scale substantive changes to the current regulatory framework. Further, due to the large volume of medicinal products, most trained personnel in the sector are familiar with the drugs sector given that most would have started their careers within the drug industry and have then moved to the medical devices or the biological products sector. This is also an occupational necessity given the growing trend towards combination products being marketed in the EU. Thus most of the interviewees in the pilot study were aware of the developments within the medicinal products sector and therefore their comments were from a comparative perspective.

[6] Tansey (2007), pp. 765–772.

This chapter is divided into four sections. The second section provides an overview of the current regulatory system within the three product sectors—medicinal products, medical devices and ATMPs. This will provide the context for the exploration of the main questions discussed in the interviews. The third section discusses the results and, finally, the fourth section provides some conclusive comments.

5.2 Aspects of the Regulatory System

The primary aim is to identify specific aspects of the regulatory system in highlighting the institutional structures and processes that may become sources of regulatory uncertainty. This part provides a descriptive backgrounder to the results that are discussed in the following section. Please note that since a detailed overview of the regulations have been provided in Chaps. 6 and 7 for medical devices and pharmaceuticals respectively—therefore in this part I will only provide a brief background of the regulatory architecture in the two sectors alongwith a more detailed discussion of the ATMPs.

Regulations in the pharmaceutical sector has been largely kept within the purview of the member states—for instance drug pricing and reimbursement—however there has been creeping Europeanization in the area of marketing authorization, primarily driven by the public health disasters like the thalidomide tragedy. Under the current system there are two pathways of obtaining a marketing authorization. For certain kinds of high technology products, the European Medicines Agency (EMA) has mandatory control over their authorization, for others they have a choice of either going through the EMA—this is especially so if the product is to be launched in the entire European market—or producers could choose to launch the product within a member state through the national authorization process which could then be extended through the mutual recognition process to other member states. The EMA process is constitutionally dependent on the competent authorities of the national member states—since all authorization decisions are taken through CHMP (Committee for Medicinal Products for Human Use) which comprises of representatives from national competent authorities. Apart from Directive 2001/83/EC that regulates the mutual recognition process and Regulation EC/726/2004 that regulates the central authorization process, there are a host of national and European guidelines that also govern this sector.

Medical devices can be divided into three kinds: general medical devices, active implantable medical devices and in vitro medical devices. These divisions are roughly based on the invasiveness of the product category and therefore the risk posed by them. The unique characteristic of European medical device regulation is that it is one of the product categories that is regulated under the *New Approach*[7] to product regulation—it operates through a process of general principles and product

[7] See footnote 20 in Chap. 1.

standards. Regulation of risk is the basic philosophy governing product categorization.[8] Another important aspect is the involvement of notified bodies for the undertaking conformity assessment. Guidance documents like that in the pharmaceutical sector also play critical role in supporting legal regulations.

An ATMP is a medicinal product that incorporates gene therapy and somatic cell therapy or is a tissue-engineered product. ATMP regulation mandates specific provisions for these products in additional to those mandated under the Directive 2001/83/EC. The ATMP regulation (EC/1394/2007) is *lex specialis* legislation with reference to Directive 2001/83/EC that applies to medicinal products in general ATMPs fall under the list of products that follow the mandatory central authorization route of the EMA. Scholars have referred to the regulation as a form of 'regulatory pharmaceuticalisation', referring to the process by which physically disparate fields of tissue engineering, gene therapy and cell therapy was brought within a single fold,[9] thereby underlining the constitutive function of law shaping technological innovation.[10] It is important to underline that the ATMP regulation is directly applicable and binding on all member states since the beginning of 2009. However, member states continue to enjoy considerable leverage in legislating on issues such as the use of embryonic stem cells or animal cells. Recital 7 of the ATMP regulation states that it shall also not affect the right of the member states to adopt national legislation that may restrict or prohibit the sale, supply or use of medicinal products containing such cells.

A specialized committee within the EMA—Committee for Advanced Therapies (CAT)—evaluates applications for marketing authorization and prepares draft opinions on the quality, safety and efficacy of the product—to be submitted to the CMPH (Committee for Medicinal Products for Human Use) for their final approval. The CAT also advises the latter in the case of combination products or other expertise in relates areas of ATMPs. The CAT has, however, faced increasing criticism from the industry due to the slow pace of approvals.[11]

5.3 Study Results

5.3.1 How Has European Regulation Shaped Product Sectors?

Experts were asked to identify the primary legal instruments that they referred to while addressing issues of product safety and quality within the marketing authorization process (strictly speaking the term can only be used for medicinal

[8] Hodges (2005).

[9] Faulkner (2009), pp. 637–646.

[10] Faulkner et al. (2012), pp. 1–19.

[11] Clinica (2012).

products—however, I use it here to refer to licensing and followed by market launch of medical products in general). The second aspect was to discover whether there were national legislations/guidelines operating in addition to European legislations/guidelines. The third aspect was for them to identify critical actors that operated within this regulatory space. The fourth aspect was for them to identify what they thought constituted the most important changes in the regulatory regime; discuss the imperatives behind it, and their implications. Taken together, these four aspects were expected to shed light on the scale and effect of European regulations.

The key findings were first, that the European regulations were the strongest—in terms of market integration—in the pharmaceutical sector. The medical devices and the ATMP sectors witnessed medium to low level harmonization.[12] Amongst the three, only in the case of medical devices was the single market the primary rationale driving European regulations. In the case of pharmaceuticals and ATMPs it was public health and safety concerns that drove the process of European regulation, where scientific input was given primary importance in regulatory decision-making. In the case of pharmaceuticals, national regulatory divergences were sought to be resolved through a consensual decision-making within the CHMP, whereas within ATMPs, the lack of a European institutional process allows for divergent national regulatory practice. However, even in the case of pharmaceuticals pockets of divergences remain—clinical trials being an example.

Second, within pharmaceuticals, European directives 2001/83/EC and 2004/27/EC (known as the variations directive) were identified as the most important legal instruments. Further clinical trials were also singled out as an area in which through the introduction of the Good Clinical Practice Directive (2005/28/EC) led to the introduction of a new system of medical and ethical committees set up at the level of individual hospitals to validate clinical trials—this was singled out as creating a multiplicity of authorities. Interestingly the experts did not differentiate between legal instruments like directives and regulation and guidelines, thereby underlining that European regulation has also been driven by softer legal instruments like guidelines, especially in such cases where a consensus or competence was not available to the Commission to introduce a directive or legislation.

ED1 and ED2 agreed that in most cases in Europe the national legislation was a one-on-one transposition of these European directives with some additional procedural provisions (for instance in the case of NL, allowing IVDs to be sold through pharmacies). This highlights the reach and expansion of European regulation as the primary mode of legislation in this sector.

Interestingly according to ND:

[12] The criteria of classification is based on the perception of interviewees. Although there have been European regulations in all the three sectors, in the case of pharmaceuticals it has enabled harmonization, whereas in the case of medical devices and ATMPs it has met with limited success in facilitating harmonization.

> We have decided that the latest revision of the national legislation will directly refer to the European directive —— we will not write the same text into our national law'. Member states are therefore increasingly amenable to the idea of European harmonization, so much so that they even avoid textual transposition by directly referring to the Medical Device Directives.

In the context of ATMPs, the picture was radically different. Although European legal instruments like the ATMP regulation (EC/1394/2007), the three tissue and cells directives (2004/23/EC, 2006/17EC and 2006/86/EC) have been legislated, the story was different in every country. In fact, the expert provided a rough division of countries based on their regulatory frameworks.

Member states can be divided into three kinds, based on their legislative frameworks:

> NL and Irelands —— the easy ones (direct transposition of the EU directive).
> Italy —— EU plus provisions.
> Germany and Sweden —— totally different tracks —— it is treated as pharmaceutical. (EATMP)

In the case of medical devices, both ED1 and ED2 identified notified bodies and competent authorities of member states, as well as EUCOMED and EDMA as important actors. ED1 also mentioned DG SANCO in Brussels and standardization bodies (e.g., CEN and ISO) as important actors. The fact that bigger manufacturers lobby directly with the European Commission, especially given its legislative powers, is unsurprising. The influences of standardization bodies have also been pivotal in enabling manufacturers to get involved in rule-making activities. Where they (industry) have the most influence is in the standards, because there is no limit to the number of participants—they can submit a proposal for a standard to be written for a type of product, method, test material, and if it's approved by the voting system they can write the standards in consultation with other stakeholders from different countries. These standards can also be recognized as 'harmonized standards' in law. This was the thinking behind the *New Approach* to European legislation that was behind the legislating of AIMD, MDD and the IVD directives. (PSC) The role of competent authorities was also underlined in this regard as being instrumental in developing future regulatory policy: 'We follow closely national guidelines. Any submission guideline that has been developed nationally by the MEB may become a EU standard in the future' (EP). The question of RECAST[13] was also discussed and commented on at length by the experts. Most agreed that although there was some need for improvement of the regulatory system, the RECAST itself was premature.

[13] It should be noted that at the time of the study, the term RECAST was officially used by the European Commission to refer to the process of legislative changes that was under discussion with references to the medical device directives. However, since then, the European Commission (at the end of 2011) stated that the term RECAST creates an incorrect allusion to the nature of amendment of the directives, They preferred using the term 'revision', since the changes being considered could lead to fundamental changes in the regulatory structure of medical devices in Europe.

ND: There is some merit in it (RECAST), but I did have some objections against the process —— the ink was not dry on the 2007/47/EC review —— that the Commission came with a new proposal, which they had not discussed with anyone —— not with competent authorities and not with industry.
Interviewer: What do you mean by the ink was not dry?
ND: For instance in the clinical evaluation part —— we did not get enough time to work out —— see what would be the effect on companies. I know there are certain aspects which would be good to look at —— for instance the notified bodies systems and how to control the system... I think it is a good idea to get a more central approach in the sense of how competent authorities are overseeing the functioning of notified bodies.

(refers to the setting up of the Central Management Committee (CMC) by the Groups of Competent Authorities in fall 2010 as an effort to put into place a system to meet more often and make the enforcement system more efficient). Given that the announcement of the RECAST was preceded by significant amendments to the medical device directives, the timing of it has led to regulatory uncertainty as to the shape and direction of the impending changes.

5.3.2 How Has the European Regulations Impacted Regulatory Uncertainty in These Product Sectors?

The pharmaceutical sector as mentioned earlier can be characterized with as one with a high level of European regulation. One of the interviewees (ND) described it as a 'cook-book', referring to the extensive and detailed nature of the European regulations. The regulations not only include legislations in the form of directives and regulations but also guidelines issued by the EMA and the national health authorities. It is this quantum of rules coupled with their high turnover that was the primary cause of regulatory uncertainty in this sector. EP mentioned that the time-span of individual guidelines often do not match the experimentation by manufacturers. In other words, the guidelines are changed or updated at a very fast rate. And manufacturers following a specific guideline during the production process may find at the end of the process that the one they relied upon has become redundant and replaced by a new or an updated guideline.[14] However, this problem is limited to guidelines in certain areas. Therefore, although this is a cause of regulatory uncertainty, the general level of regulatory uncertainty is still low within the system.

In the case of medical devices, the interviewees were of the opinion that although the European regulations have expanded in this sector—and have led to an improvement from an earlier system of national markets—the current system remains highly fragmented. The main sources of regulatory uncertainty identified were as follows: the quality of certification of notified bodies was not uniform; national variation in administrative structures for vigilance and incident reporting

[14] European Commission (2010) *Evaluation of the European Medicines Agency*, Brussels.

nationally; the consultation process between national authorities on regulatory issues was non-transparent. The European Commission also admit that these are the challenges facing the sector[15] and are currently working on addressing them through a proposed revision of the European medical device directives, the proposals for which will be unveiled by the end of 2012. Due to these factors, regulatory uncertainty in this sector is at a medium level. It may cross the threshold on specific instances. To give an example, the disparity in the quality of notified bodies have been a subject of regulatory discussion amongst national regulators, the European Commission and the manufacturers.

The notified bodies themselves recognize this problem and have developed a Code of Conduct,[16] however only a few of the notified bodies (11 out of the 32) have signed this Code of Conduct. Lack of sustained regulatory consultations and dialogue between national regulatory authorities was also acknowledged and has been sought to be addressed through the recently set up CMC. CMC decisions in 2011 include those on classification and borderline queries, harmonized implementation on notified bodies best practice guides, and information to be provided in relation to the address of the manufacturer and of the authorized representative. These incremental steps at the institutional level have been in response to growing regulatory uncertainty. However, whether these are successful in addressing regulatory uncertainty will have to been seen in the future.

The ATMP sector has witnessed an improvement in terms of greater harmonization within the European market. A view shared by the interviewees was that European regulations should be seen in the context of a trade-off. The trade-off was between setting up a minimal test regime based on general principles and allowing member states to provide for additional national requirements. The European regulations are taken to be setting up the floor with member states free to provide for other requirements on top of those at the European level. This variation in national regulations has resulted in high levels of regulatory uncertainty that have crossed the threshold quite often. Additionally, the functioning of the CAT has also drawn criticism from the industry, in terms of the slow rate of regulatory approval.

5.3.3 How Has This Shaped Compliance Strategies?

Regulatory compliance is expected by law and that is something that companies are, therefore, legally bound to perform. The processes and methods that companies design and adopt individually and also as an industry in response to their legal obligations are important areas that can shed light on the nature of the regulatory

[15] European Commission (2011) Proposal for a regulation of the European Parliament and of the Council concerning medical devices. Commission Work Program, Roadmap for 2012 (version 3), 7 November, Brussels.

[16] NB Plus Group (2011) Code of conduct for notified bodies under directives 90/385/EEC and 93/42/EEC, version 2.7, 25 February, Brussels.

system itself at two levels. First, what are the standard responses of companies in the event that it is unclear of what is expected of it under the law? Second, it is important to note, that regulation is an interface activity that is underpinned by relationship between regulators and regulates—and in that sense it is very much a two way process where one tries to influence the other. Therefore, companies view compliance as a process that needs to be engaged with a view to the future. The regulatory system is therefore dynamic, and the industry is in a constant process of negotiation with the regulators.

Given this, two questions were asked. First, faced with an unclear regulatory situation what was their standard response—do they ask for clarification from the regulator? (And, if so, how often does that happen?) Second, what are the coping strategies they have adopted in this uncertain regulatory environment? The view from the pharmaceutical sector underlined the importance of engaging with the competent authorities of the member states; the MEB (Medicines Evaluation Board, NL) contact group with the industry was mentioned as one of the forums through which industry discusses regulatory matters that need clarification with the regulators. In comparison, the Commission was viewed as a slightly distant stakeholder, which took the lead in developing primary ideas and welcomed engagement only at the stage for public review. A point made was that comments received during the stage of public review could not drive any fundamental changes. However, the relative importance of engagement with national authorities was tempered. Sometimes companies are inhibited from asking for clarification, because it may then become the basis for issuing other guideline which may in turn lead to increase in compliance costs. (EP)

Similar views were also expressed by ED1.

> I try to avoid going to the competent authority because you can only get a formal response from them... it is not always in the interest of the company to raise things in an official way with the competent authority, because you won't want to alert your competitors to the issues as well. (ED1)

Notified bodies and peer networks (this seems to be especially the case for SMEs) as well as industry organizations like the EUCOMED were identified as other important stakeholders, who served as useful points of contact in terms of helping companies secure guidance on regulatory compliance. However, it is also important to note that bigger companies like MNCs do invest resources in cultivating a relationship with regulatory agencies, especially at the national level. They, however, view this relationship as a scarce regulatory resource, which is not to be squandered in the pursuit of minor clarifications (as EATMP stated, 'you don't want to wake up sleeping dogs'); it is more for cases of major stakes and also to secure a market advantage over rivals.

Compliance strategies are also contingent on the national context; some national competent authorities are more approachable than others.

> NL, UK, Ireland are very approachable —— Norway is less —— I asked them a question a year ago and I still don't have an answer. UK is also good at giving extensive guidelines and directions —— that's why the tissues establishment licenses cost 11,000 pounds a year. (EATMP)

The TSE Directive (2003/32/EC) was cited as a good example of facilitating interaction between the main stakeholders and thereby reducing regulatory uncertainty. Notified bodies submit a summary of their assessment (summary evaluation report) to their competent authority; this is circulated to other competent authorities and then communicated back to the notified body—often with questions. Issues are then discussed and solved between the parties.

> Experience has shown a gradual increase in the quality of reports filed. Evidence that all sides seemed to have learnt from this experience. (PSC)

This also highlights that clear and transparent spaces for regulatory conversations[17] between primary stakeholders reduces regulatory uncertainty, thereby facilitating the quality and degree of compliance.

5.4 Discussion and Conclusion

The pace and pathways of European regulation have been different in all the product sectors. One of the reasons for such diversity is the different imperatives that have driven this process in each of the sectors. Whereas drug safety has been the main motive behind the introduction of centralized authorization, the aim of the single market has been the single most important factor in shaping regulatory structures in medical devices. In the case of ATMPs technical advances had overtaken regulation and the European response has been to set up the floor and leaving the space open for national legislations. Interestingly both in medical devices and in the case of ATMPs, there is a wide variation in regulation nationally despite European harmonization. One of the factors that have impacted this variation is through the issuance of national guidelines. The industry does not make any differentiation between a legal instrument and guidelines—especially if it is issued by competent authorities. Consequently, the legal impact of both guidelines and legal instruments are equivalent.

The medical devices sector is currently in the middle of heated debate as to its functioning. In comparison to the other two sectors, this sector represented perhaps the most ambitious Europeanization program. Efficiency was sought to be promoted by putting in place a system of private notified bodies that would oversee conformity assessment that would compete with each other. However, this system has not been working optimally. More significantly, the system was designed to favor existing players in the market at the cost of new entrants. The pharmaceutical sector has seen a similar trend in terms of rapidly rising administrative burdens and compliance costs, leading to a consolidation by bigger firms that are able to better cope with it. Clearly, the Europeanization process has negatively impacted SMEs and newer entrants into the market more than big industry, although the regulatory

[17] Black (2002), pp. 163–196.

burden for both has expanded. The discussion on the question of regulatory uncertainty highlights the different sources of regulatory uncertainty within each sector. Although experts were unanimous in their opinion that the Europeanization process has enabled significant strides in harmonization of the single market, the agenda is still unfinished. An overview of the sectors illustrate a cascading effect, with the ATMPs exhibiting a high level of regulatory uncertainty, followed by medical devices and medicinal products. Such an interpretation would give credence to the conclusion that Europeanization—or legislating at the European level—would address this problem. Interestingly, that is not necessarily the case, as is apparent from the widespread industry opposition to the RECAST process in the medical devices sector. The answer lies in appreciating that the sources of uncertainty are varied across sectors. The medicinal products sector faces a problem of plenty, primarily due to the quantum and rapid amendments making it harder for companies to keep abreast. In the case of medicinal devices it is lack of institutional linkages and benchmarking that has characterized the sector. Therefore, steps like the setting up of the CMC and the EUDAMED database—where product registration would be centrally recorded and accessible to all national competent authorities—are welcome measures.

The ATMP sector, on the other hand, represents a limited free-for-all range, where the European legislations serves as a floor and the ceiling is set nationally at different levels, thus limiting the efforts for harmonization through the Europeanization process. It is interesting to note that although regulatory uncertainty is present in all sectors, in both medical devices and ATMPs it has crossed the threshold and challenged the effectiveness of the regulatory system. The wide range of legislative amendments proposed by the European Commission as part of the RECAST process is evidence of these institutional problems, and the amendments being discussed are expected to limit regulatory uncertainty to manageable levels. In the case of ATMPs, stem cells being a sensitive political issue create its own dynamic and could become an impediment to greater harmonization led by European Regulations.

Regulatory compliance seems to be driven by national engagement between industry and competent authorities. However, companies seem reticent in approaching competent authorities freely. Here also one can see a clear (perhaps not surprising) difference in the strategies of SMEs and MNCs. While the former clearly prefers the use of peer networks in discussing compliance issues, the latter prefers to make significant investments in building individual relationships with notified bodies as well as competent authorities. Given the importance of national engagement, compliance is influenced by the regulatory culture prevalent within national competent authorities. Some are more open than others, and some use this as a trade advantage. What is however surprising in the overall picture is the view that the European Commission is a distant stakeholder, with whom spaces for engagement are limited. Ultimately it is necessary to underline that the European regulations have redefined regulatory compliance in significant ways, viz. by creating new stakeholders like notified bodies and providing new mechanisms for engagement in specific sectors; it has also allowed for a (still) healthy amount of national regulatory competition.

References

Abraham J (1995) Science, politics and the pharmaceutical industry: controversy and bias in drug regulation. St Martin's Press, New York

Abraham J, Davis C (2005) A comparative analysis of drug safety withdrawals in the UK and the US (1971–1992): implications for current regulatory thinking and policy. Soc Sci Med 61 (5):881–892

Bakke OM, Manocchia M, de Abajo F, Kaitin KI, Lasagna L (1995) Drug safety discontinuations in US, UK and Spain from 1974 through 1993: a regulatory perspective. Clin Pharmacol Ther 58(1):108–117

Black J (2002) Regulatory conversations. J Law Soc 29(1):163–196

CISCO IBSG (2008) Creating legal certainty for e-health across the European Union, Engagement Snapshot. http://www.cisco.com/web/about/ac79/docs/wp/engagement/EU_Legally_eHealth_Snapshot.pdf. Accessed 4 Apr 2012

Clinica (2012) Advanced therapies: is the EU regulatory approach putting a brake on market development? 19 January, London

COFACE (2009) COFACE's Position on the proposal for a European Parliament and Council Directive on the application of patient's rights in cross-border healthcare, COFACE Position Paper

DG SANCO (2009) CPME statement on the proposal for a directive on the application of patient's rights in cross-border healthcare. Standing Committee of European Doctors, CPME/2009/003EN, Brussels

Europa Bio (2007) Companies researching and developing treatments for rare diseases welcome draft Commission guideline for providing legal certainty on market exclusivity for Orphan Medicines, press release, Brussels

Faulkner A (2009) Regulatory policy as innovation: constructing rules of engagement for a technological zone of tissue engineering in the European Union. Res Policy 38:637–646

Faulkner A, Lange B, Lawless C (2012) Material worlds: intersections of law, science, technology and society. J Law Soc 39(1):1–19

Hancher L (1996) Pharmaceutical policy and regulation: setting the pace in the European Community. In: Davis P (ed) Contested ground: public purpose and private interest in the regulation of prescription drugs. Oxford University Press, Oxford, pp 179–193

Hodges C (2005) European regulation of consumer product safety. Oxford University Press, Oxford

Kaitin KI, Mattinson N, Northington FK, Lasagna L (1989) The drug lag: an update of new drug introductions in the US and in the UK, 1977 through 1987. Clin Pharmacol Ther 46(2):121–138

Parker J (1989) Who has a drug lag? Managerial Decis Econ 10(4):299–309

Schweitzer SO, Schweitzer ME, Sourty-Le Guellec MJ (1996) Is there a US drug lag? The timing if new pharmaceutical approvals in the G-7 countries and Switzerland. Med Care Res Rev 53 (2):162–178

Tansey O (2007) Process tracing and elite interviewing: a case for non-probability sampling. Political Sci Polit 40(4):765–772

Chapter 6
Case Study on Medical Devices Regulation in Europe

6.1 Introduction

The last couple of years have been particularly eventful in the regulatory history of medical devices in Europe. In May 2008, the European Commission launched a public consultation for a 'recast' of the medical devices legislations.[1] This was met with surprise and skepticism by the industry and some of the national competent authorities (NCA) given that it came close on the heels to the significant amendments[2] that were made to the European legislations.[3] This was followed by the NCA's coming together to establish the Central Management Committee in September 2010, partially in response to the implied criticisms of the enforcement deficits within the current regulatory regime.[4] Similarly the association of notified bodies—NB-MED—developed a Code of Conduct to address the disparity in the quality of functioning between notified bodies in response to the public criticism to their functioning.[5] Then in early 2011 the industry was hit by the scandal of the poisonous PIP (Poly Implant Prothese) breast implants. Although the main industry association—EUCOMED—has sought to underline that this was a case of wilful violation of the legal obligations of the manufacturer and not as such a failure of existing regulation, questions has been raised about the fundamental effectiveness of the legislations. Reacting to this, the Environment and Health Committee of the

[1] There is a legal difference between recast and review. The former is referred to when the legislator does not propose to substantially amend the law but consolidate in one legal text different legislative instruments—e.g. directives—in the same area. To the contrary, review alludes to substantial legislative revision that would change the nature and quantum of legal obligations for regulatees. See Chalmers and Monti (2008) at 145.

[2] For instance the new Directive 2007/47/EC Directive 2007/47/EC that amends Directive 90/385/EEC on active implantable medical devices and Directive 93/42/EEC on medical devices entered into force on 11 October 2007.

[3] Chowdhury (2013), pp. 635–652.

[4] Horton (2012), p. 1060.

[5] Eisenhart (2012).

DOI 10.1007/978-3-319-04594-8_6,

European Parliament passed a resolution asking the European Commission to consider a shift to pre-market authorization system for certain types of medical devices which are in the high risk category.[6] The European Commission proposal (now for review and not recast)[7] has addressed some of the points raised in the resolution by proposing various measure. Some of these measures like the mechanism for scrutiny of certain conformity assessments and the reclassification of certain devices into Class III have been criticized by the EUCOMED.[8]

Perhaps a bit of a background is necessary to understand Eucomed's response and opposition to some of the Commission proposals. The shape, structure and regulatee capacities within the medical device sector are distinct from that of the pharmaceutical sector.

> The medical device and the in vitro diagnostic medical device sectors are estimate to comprise more than 500,000 products, covering a wide range of devices from simple bandages to the most sophisticated life supporting devices.... The ... sectors are characterized by a high degree of innovation, both incremental – once a device reaches the market, improvements may follow with 18 to 24 months – and breakthrough innovation... Not only the European Union has the largest market and some of the biggest companies of the world, but it also has an expanding ecosystem of innovative small to medium size enterprises and even micro enterprises...80 % of medical device companies and 95 % of in vitro diagnostic medical device companies being small to medium sized or micro-enterprises.[9]

The preceding quote from a Commission document gives a good idea of the nature of the medical device sector. First, unlike pharmaceuticals wherein product differentiation is based on different combinations of chemical compounds, medical device industry is highly diverse in its range of products. Second, the average innovation cycle is around 13 months—therefore a high product turnover driven by technological innovation is another feature of this industry. Third, it has one of the highest concentrations of small enterprises amongst industry sectors. All these factors are the reasons why this sector is regulated by the *New Approach* directives.[10]

---

[6] European Parliament (2012a).

[7] The proposal states that 'a fundamental review of those Directives is needed to establish a robust, transparent, predictable and sustainable regulatory framework for medical devices which ensure a high level of safety and health whilst supporting innovation' European Commission, 2012/0266 (COD).

[8] Eucomed, 'Towards a regulation that guarantees patient safety, ensures patient access and keeps innovation in Europe: Eucomed's response to the Commission's proposal for the revision of the EU Medical Devices Directives', Position Paper 30 January 2013, Brussels.

[9] European Commission, Communication from the Commission to the European Parliament, the Council, the European Economic and Social Committee and the Committee of the Regions, COM (2012)540 final, Brussels.

[10] The *New Approach* to technical harmonization and standardization is a legislative strategy through which European Directives would provide for 'essential requirements' and corresponding technical standards were to be drawn up by European Standardization bodies and were referred to as 'harmonized standards' and they would carry a presumption of conformity. See Council

The medical devices regulatory system is therefore unique in terms of the non-prescriptive nature of the directives and the use of third party assessors for undertaking conformity assessments. This is distinct from prescriptive nature of pharmaceutical regulations. Adoption of the *New Approach* for medical devices regulation reflects these unique characteristics of the medical device sector. And the current proposals for the review of the legislations do not take into account these unique characteristics; this is evident from the industry opposition to some of the proposals. Thus for instance, Andy Vaughan, a standards consultant for the ABHI (Association of British Healthcare Industries) referred to the current regulations as a, "clever system of product regulation" and "very flexible and efficient method for ensuring safe products reach the patients."[11]

There is a clear difference of opinion between industry associations like EUCOMED which see the existing regulatory framework fundamentally robust but which could do with some improvements and the regulators like European Commission that favor a more structural shift—as is evident from the adoption of the word *review* instead of *recast*. Underlying this difference in opinion may be elementary differences between regulators and regulatees as to their idea of what kind of regulatory architecture would deliver legal certainty.

This chapter has been divided into six parts. In the following Sect. 6.2, I provide an overview of the historical development of regulations in the medical device sector. This provides a useful background to Sects. 6.3–6.5, in which I address the following sub-research questions—*Is the European medical device regulation multilevel in nature*? *What are the regulatee perceptions of multilevelness of regulatory spaces*? *What are the regulatee expectations with regard to legal certainty*? Section 6.6 includes an analysis of the regulatee responses in the two preceding sections and concluding remarks.

6.2 History of Regulation in the Medical Device Sector

There was great diversity amongst European countries in how medical devices were regulated prior to the harmonization through European directives in the early 1990s. However there was one common feature that was shared by most countries—medical devices regulation evolved within the pharmaceutical regulatory framework before ultimately splitting into a legally autonomous framework.[12] Although there were Council directives that referred to certain kinds of medical

Resolution of 7 May 1985 on a new approach to technical harmonization and standards, Official Journal C 136, 04/06/1985 P. 0001–0009. Also see footnote 20 in Chap. 1.

[11] EUCOMED, 'A new regulatory framework for medical devices', November 2011, Brussels.

[12] This is also reflected in the present day since in a number of member states there is a common regulator for both medical devices and pharmaceuticals. For instance the in the UK it is the MHRA (Medical and Healthcare Products Regulatory Agency).

devices[13]—the most significant development was in 1985, when the Commission adopted the *New Approach* to legislative harmonization.[14] The *New Approach* was designed to catalyze harmonization efforts in legislative areas that are characterized by product diversity driven by technology innovation. This legislative approach is distinct from the earlier more prescriptive approach wherein detailed rules were provided in legislations and there was a greater risk of it being rendered redundant when the product turnover was high and driven by incremental innovation.[15]

There are four fundamental aspects to the *New Approach*—first, private organizations competent in the standardization[16] area have the duty of drawing up technical specifications (term used is 'harmonized standards') required for the production and placement on the market of products that are in conformity with the 'essential requirements' specified in the Directives; second, these technical specifications maintain their status as voluntary standards; third, although non-mandatory, national authorities will presume conformity with the 'essential requirements' if products are manufactured in conformity with these harmonized standards (thus the producer has a choice of not manufacturing in conformity with the harmonized standards, in that case however he is under an obligation to prove that his products conformed to the 'essential requirements' of the Directive).

The Active Implantable Medical Devices Directive (AIMDD) represents the first case of application of the *New Approach* to the field of medical devices.[17] This was followed by the Medical Devices Directive (MDD) in June 1993 and came into force from June 1998.[18] And finally the In Vitro Diagnostic Devices Directive (IVDDD) that was passed in October 1998 and became mandatory in December 2003.[19] The largest percentage of medical device products falls within the remit of the MDD. The MDD operates on the basis of risk classification of medical device. Products are categorized into four risk classes—Classes I, IIa, IIb and III—starting from lowest to the highest risk category on account of the vulnerability of the human body. The manufacturer is the one who chooses the risk classification for their devices. As a general rule, Class I devices is under the sole discretion of the

[13] See for instance Directive 76/764/EEC of 27 July 1976 on the approximation of the laws of the Member States on clinical mercury-in-glass, maximum reading thermometers.

[14] See footnote 20 in Chap. 1 and footnote 10 in this chapter.

[15] European Commission (2000).

[16] Agreements were signed between the EC and CEN and Cenelec in November 1984, in which the latter were recognized as the competent bodies for the adoption of harmonized standards in accordance with the general guidelines on cooperation between the Commission and these two bodies.

[17] Council Directive of 20 June 1990 on the approximation of the laws of the Member States relating to active implantable medical devices (90/385/EEC). OJ L 189, 20.7.1990, p. 17.

[18] Council Directive 93/42/EEC of 14 June 1993 concerning medical devices. OJ L 169, 12.7.1993, p. 1.

[19] Council Directive 98/79/EC of the European Parliament and of the Council of 27 October 1998 on *in vitro* diagnostic medical devices. OJ L 331, 7.12.1998, p. 1.

manufacturer, for Class II devices; notified bodies need to be consulted at the production stage; for Classes IIb and III which constitute the high risk category, notified bodies need to review the design and the production of the devices.[20] Currently the Commission is considering two proposals for Regulations—one on medical devices (that would replace the AIMD and the MDD) and the other on *in vitro* medical devices that would replace the IVDDD.

6.3 Is the Medical Device Regulatory Space Multilevel in Nature?

As mentioned in Chap. 1 and then discussed in detail in Chap. 2, I define multilevel regulation as a term to denote a regulatory space—where all the critical aspects of the regulatory lifecycle—i.e. rulemaking, rule application and rule adjudication is dispersed across multiple administrative and territorial levels and amongst both public and private actors. In the following sections I identify actors involved in these activities, their location in terms of the administrative level and the quality of their interaction.

6.3.1 Rule Making

The primary rules that regulate the medical devices sector are the three Directives. Since they are directives and not regulations—the implementing national legislation also play an important role. Standards play a critical role in *New Approach* directives given that it is the technical specifications that create a presumption of conformity and therefore provide a substantive incentive for regulatees to adopt them in meeting their regulatory obligations. Another important part of the rules are guidance documents such as the MEDDEVs (Medical Device Guidance Documents) that are published by the European Commission and that promote common approach to the implementation of the procedures as laid down in the Directives. I start with the mapping rules regulating this sector because this provides us with the basis for which to identify the actors that involved in rulemaking.

The European Commission (DG SANCO)[21] plays a very important role as it is not only the principal architect of the Directives but it also play an active role by periodically publishing interpretative documents that clarify provisions of these Directives. They also are the prime movers in undertaking legislative amendments and revisions of the regulatory structure as is evident from the discussion in Sect. 5.1.

[20] The IVDD follows a different structure under which the annexure contains detailed guidance in terms of a list of products which require intervention of a notified body.

[21] Director General for Health and Consumers, European Commission.

They host a number of stakeholders groups (of mixed membership)[22] that author the guidance documents. The other public regulator is the NCAs. They draft the national implementing legislations; they also publish national guidelines on the implementation of the directives and also participate actively in rule-making activities (e.g. guidance documents) at the European level.

Amongst the private actors, the foremost bodies are the European Standardization Organizations (ESOs). The ESOs share a relationship with the EC, wherein the latter grants them the status of ESOs, thereby recognizing their function and mandate for producing voluntary standards across industries. It must be noted that only a few of the standards produced are given the status of 'harmonized standards'—meaning they carry a presumption of conformity. The ESOs may draft such standards either in response to a specific request by the EC or they themselves could suggest standards to the EC for recognition as harmonized standards. The grant of the status of a 'harmonized standard' is based on the assessment by the EC that the standard will enable the implementation of either partial or full, some of the 'essential requirements' as provided under the Directives. Every harmonized standard includes an Annex Z—which explains the manner in which the standards fulfil the 'essential requirements'.

It is important to appreciate the institutional structure within which the ESO's function. The ESOs in fact function within well-structured parts of global entities. Thus for instance the CEN is part of the ISO network, and works in close cooperation with the ISO. This cooperation is governed by the Vienna Agreement and since this agreement there has been tremendous growth in the joint development of standards by ISO and the CEN.[23] This institutional affiliation creates a proclivity towards international harmonization of standards. And, at times this may be at odds with their obligations to produce harmonized standards that are by nature regional standards specifically designed to fulfil certain 'essential requirements' of Directives (for a concrete example the formal challenge to ISO 13485 discussed in Sect. 5.4).

Another facet that merits close attention are guidance documents. Although strictly speaking, guidance documents do not have the same status as a law—e.g. like a directive or a regulation for instance—they do represent a broad consensus on how the directives should be interpreted and therefore are intended to shape the actions of both regulators such as the NCAs as well as regulatees. These consensus documents are issued primarily by actors that are involved in rule making and rule application functions within the regulatory structure. Although *prima facie* there is no clear hierarchy between the different actors issuing guidance documents—viz. EC, NCAs, Notified Bodies and also industry associations. Given that the drafting team of MEDDEVs includes all the primary stakeholders there is a functional consensus on the ground—that MEDDEVs will be accorded pre-eminence in the

---

[22] This would include groups such as the Medical Devices Expert Group (MDEG) which includes national experts, representatives from NCAs and industry associations.

[23] CEN Annual Report 2011.

field of guidance documents. The MEDDEVs are issued by the Medical Device Expert Group (MDEG). It is an expert body of the Commission and includes representatives of competent authorities of Member States, standardization bodies such as the CEN and CENLEC, industry bodies like EUCOMED and EDMA and the Notified Bodies Expert Group. The MEDDEV Guidance documents are considered and accepted as definitive consensus positions on a wide range of issues such as classification of devices, translation procedures, definition of accessory, etc. The MDEG functions through several sub-groups—Market Surveillance Operation Group; Vigilance Expert Group; and New & Emerging Medical Device Technologies Working Group. The Notified Bodies Operations Group (NBOG) is another important body set by the Commission, that issues guidance documents (the moniker used is NB-MED). These documents could also be elevated to the rank of MEDDEVS if the MDEG grants then approval. The last rung of this hierarchy is taken by the national competent authorities of member states.

As an aside it is important to flag off the role of the GHTF. The GHTF was set up by regulators from USA, Canada, European Union, Japan and Australia in cooperation with industry bodies to take forward the agenda of international regulatory harmonization. It was disbanded in late 2012 and was restructured as the IMDRF (International Medical Device Regulators Forum) which is designed to prioritize the role of public regulations (indeed the name is a strong indication) in harmonization efforts (however not to the exclusion of industry—but not in the role of partners).

6.3.2 Rule Application

As is the case in *New Approach* directives, independent assessors—known as notified bodies are the first in line enforcers of rules. Their primary role is to review the measures taken by regulatees to ensure that they fulfil their regulatory obligations—this procedure is formally referred to as the conformity assessment. With the exception of high risk Class III medical devices—NCAs are not involved in this stage. NCAs are however the primary actors involved in the authorization and appointment of notified bodies within their territory. They are therefore oversee the functioning of the notified bodies—and if found wanting are in a position to withdraw the authorization from the notified body.

Two important aspects of conformity assessment within this regulatory space should be noted. First, the manufacturers are free to choose any notified body operating within the European Union. Thus there is no territorial linkage between manufacturing site and the location of the notified body. Although it must be noted that most of the bigger notified bodies maintain national offices in all of the bigger markets (viz. Germany, France, UK and Netherlands). One implication of this is that national regulators face curious situation wherein design and production is sought to be influenced through control of notified bodies. Thus in the UK, the MHRA is in a position to influence the compliance of manufacturers even outside the UK through the BSI (British Standards Institution) which is one of the biggest notified bodies in Europe. Whereas NCAs of smaller member states like Malta do not have any notified bodies and therefore have limited influence over their manufacturers. Second, the manufacturer shares a contractual relationship with the notified bodies—where the former chooses the latter to undertake assessment of design and manufacturing through product testing and inspection audits. Critics have argued that although handing over conformity assessment to private actors has brought down cost of approval of medical devices, the commercial relationship may compromise public interest.[24]

Nevertheless given that it is the NCAs which have to oversee the designation and the performance of the notified bodies, they have the primary responsibility to ensure that notified bodies function in the public interest. The oversight of NCA's have however been persistently criticized. The lack of uniformity in the designation and monitoring of notified bodies amongst NCAs has been identified as one of the prime reasons for the widely differing quality in the performance of notified bodies.[25]

6.3.3 Rule Adjudication

Rule adjudication is referred to the process through disputes over the interpretation of rules is mediated and settled.[26] There is a need to differentiate between rule adjudication and legal adjudication. Legal adjudication refers to an institutional process that involves the use of professional groups such as lawyers or arbitration experts in settling a dispute over the correct interpretation of rules. Rule adjudication on the other hand refers to not only legal adjudication but also regulatory processes and institutions that have been established within the primary purpose of delivering uniform interpretation of rules. Legal adjudication is therefore a species of rule adjudication in the context of regulatory spaces.

Allowing for a mechanism for resolving disputes that involve interpretation of rules is critical specifically in context of legislative instruments like a Directive, because it allows member states flexibility in adopting national implementing acts that may diverge as to the mechanisms for achieving the intent of the Directive. This mechanism is represented in the MDEG which is hosted by the European Commission and which is a conglomeration of several working groups, comprising

[24] It has been contended that the notified bodies "individual Notified Bodies will be under commercial pressures to not be perceived as more 'difficult' than others" and this may lead to a race to dilution of oversight. See Feldschreiber and Robinson (2012).

[25] European Commission, Medical devices: European Commission calls for immediate actions—tighten controls, increase surveillance, and restore confidence, (IP/12/119) Press Release, Brussels.

[26] See for a brief explanation of rule making; rule application and rule adjudication in footnote 71 in Chap. 1.

of representatives from NCAs, industry bodies, independent experts and the European Commission. MEDDEVs are the foremost guidance documents that are produced by the MDEG. The MDEG works on the principal of consensus and only issues guidance documents or status reports once consensus is reached. Therefore their outputs reflect industry best practice and consensus amongst the principal regulators and regulatees. Significantly, the MDEG status reports or MEDDEVS do not have a legal status and is therefore non-binding in nature. In fact all MEDDEVs carry similar disclaimers:

> This guideline is not legally binding, since only the European Court of Justice can give an authoritative interpretation of Community law. It has been elaborated by an expert group including experts from Member States' Competent Authorities, the Commission' services, as well as industry trade associations. It is therefore intended that the document will provide useful guidance which should assist common positions to be taken throughout the European Union. Due to the participation of the aforementioned interested parties and of experts from Competent Authorities, it is anticipated that these guidelines will be followed within the Member States and, therefore, ensure the uniform application of relevant Directive provisions.[27]

However as is evident from the above quote, that although strictly speaking the outputs of MDEG is not legally binding, there is a clear expectation that these will be followed by both regulators and regulatees and thereby assist in harmonization. Both NCAs and notified bodies are involved in activities that require rule interpretation. The former has considerable flexibility in interpreting the provisions of the Directives and the latter has tremendous authority for rule interpretation on a case-by-case basis for conducting conformity assessment. Therefore the regulatory structure of the *New Approach* itself provides ample legitimate opportunity to these actors to be involved in rule interpretation. In this context, the lack of a firm legal basis for the MDEG which is mandated with the function of achieving consensus in areas of differing rule interpretation (in effect performing rule adjudication) creates significant potential for uncertainty. Nevertheless there are the Courts which are tasked with the primary responsibility of rule adjudication—however surprisingly given the potential for uncertainty with the other mechanisms—there have been limited number of cases that have reached the Courts.[28]

It is clear from the formal review of the rulemaking, rule application and rule adjudication activities that both private and public actors operating at national, European and international level are involved in these three activities. And the relationship between these actors is primarily heterarchical in nature. Thus medical

---

[27] Guidelines on Medical Devices: IVD Medical Device Borderline and Classification issues, MEDDEV 2.14/1 revision 2 January 2012.

[28] There have been three cases on medical devices in the ECJ so far. These include Brain Products GmbH vs. Bio Semi VOF and Others (Case C-219/11. European Court Reports 2012); Kemikalieinspektionen v Nordiska Dental AB (Case C-288/08. European Court reports 2009 Page I-11031) and Medipac-Kazantzidis AE v Venizeleio-Pananeio (PE.S.Y. KRITIS) (Case C-6/05. European Court reports 2007 Page I-04557). Similar trends are evident in the national Courts—partial study of this aspect was carried out in case study on borderline products presented in Chap. 7.

devices as a regulatory space would fall in the multilevel side of the continuum which has multilevel regulation and nationally delimited hierarchical legal order located at both ends of the spectrum.

6.4 What Is the Regulatee Perception of Multilevelness?

6.4.1 Rule Making, Rule Application and Rule Adjudication

A set of questions were posed to the regulatees. The first set relates to their perception of nature of rules (and whether the formal identification of rules conforms to the regulatee perception of 'rules' that regulate this space) and was there any possibility of overlap between different rules and therefore uncertainty given that a number of actors were involved in rule making and rule application. Second, what was their perception of the distribution of rule interpretation competences to NCAs and notified bodies and did they appreciate the functioning of the MDEG in the context of rule adjudication. And a third set of responses which were made during the interviews was in relation with the nature and quality of relationship that regulatees shared with regulators and notified bodies. This emerged as an important aspect as perceived by the regulatees because although the formal review may allude to a certain archetype of linkage (heterarchical or hierarchical)—in practice it is their perception of this aspect which is critical to gaining insights into multilevelness.

On the question whether, there was a hierarchy between guidelines issued by the different European bodies and the national authorities; notified bodies contended that there was clear hierarchy in operation between guidelines—with MEDDEVs being at the top of the order. Manufacturers seems to agree, and considered MEDDEV guidance same as directives, since they were recognized by all the principal stakeholders—notified bodies, national regulators, European commission—and therefore expected to be followed. Justification would be demanded from manufacturers in case the applicable MEDDEV was not followed. Thus a significant burden of proof was carried by manufacturer, almost akin to a legal obligation. National guidelines—especially from the MHRA—were usually made in areas where the MEDDEV was silent. One of the interviewees from a notified body pointed out that "*MHRA guidance has gone down in recent years because the European guidance has improved over the years*." Regulatee perception of what they consider 'binding' is important because that helps identify the 'rules' and thus rule makers and in determining multilevelness in rule-making.

Manufacturers tend to follow a maximalist approach in conforming to guidance documents—"take the European consensus and localize from there." Overall although there existed minor differences between national interpretations of MEDDEVs, MEDDEVs were treated as the primary reference documents and were given as much value as the Directives themselves. The regular updating of

MEDDEVs also ensured that they were adapted to current developments and therefore remained applicable and useful for manufacturers. Thus the identification of MEDDEVs as 'rules' in the formal review discussed in the earlier section is shared by regulatees. And interestingly even though MEDDEVs do not have any formal legal status but given that they are consensus documents developed by MDEG and involve both regulators and regulatees—they represent agreement amongst the actors within this regulatory space and are therefore considered important rules.

Another aspect of rulemaking is standards. Standards were identified as playing a pivotal role in the context of medical devices. The EN ISO 13485 (quality management) and EN ISO 14971 (risk assessment) horizontal standards, are amongst the harmonized standards, that are universally used across all manufacturing products, including medical devices. However harmonized standards form only a small percentage of standards and manufacturers also use a large number of non-harmonized product standards, although they do not allow for a presumption of conformity. Designation of a harmonized standard, was no guarantee for clarity—EN 14820 (Single-use containers for human venous blood specimen collection) was identified as an example of a badly written standard that was open to many interpretations. This also serves to underline easy presumptions such as harmonized standards are based on a consensus between regulators and regulatees and therefore ensure predictability. Lack of consensus may also be reflected in poorly drafted harmonized standards and therefore of limited utility. Thus standardization is a specific instance of rule making which is characterized by multilevelness wherein harmonization by itself is not a guarantee for delivering clarity and predictability.

Manufacturers and notified bodies were concerned about the legal challenge for the deharmonisation of the 11 harmonized standards (including EN ISO 14971) and EN 13485 mounted by the European Commission and the Swedish national competent authority (MPA) respectively. The challenge was mounted because the regulators remained unconvinced by the Annex Z of the standards—explaining how each standard the essential requirements under the EU medical device directives. The regulatees underlined that these were global standards that do not only respond to EU law.[29] The EU challenge was considered still legitimate, but the more substantive Swedish challenge to EN ISO 13485 reflected a myopic view of a national competent authority. Standards are not mechanically applied by companies and notified bodies tend to take a maximalist approach of ensuring that companies fulfil the basic objective of the standards within the given circumstances. The action of the MPA thus reflected a lack of practical understanding and distrusting of manufacturers. Recently however, following the revision of the EN ISO 13485 and EN ISO 14971 (still on-going), the threat of deharmonisation has receded.[30] However this development reflects the limited nature of control over rule-making by regulators especially in the context of globalized standards that penetrate into European law via formal recognition.

[29] This also underlined the institutional structures of the ISO that embeds the ESOs.

[30] Maxwell (2012).

Interestingly regulatees suggested, that this legal challenge for deharmonisation is the indirect fall out of the decreasing participation of regulators in the standardization process (due to resource constrains) and therefore the use of ex post mechanisms for influencing the development of standards. A vital aspect of rule-making—i.e. standardization; is now dominated by private actors—viz. manufacturers (mostly big manufacturing). Most manufacturers considered it imperative to get involved in standardization processes to better understand and influence the process. This and other factors like limited involvement of SMEs and other societal stakeholders, was the impetus behind the European Commission's proposal for adopting a Regulation for European standardization activities[31] allowing for better public control over standardization activities both at the European as well as internationally. Formally the ESOs operate within well laid out institutional arrangement between the European Commission and themselves. However given that the ESO are also embedded within the ISO institutional structure—creates an impetus towards the adoption of global standards which may not conform to the requirements of the European Union. This illustrates that the ESOs may experience contradictory pulls in its functioning—the legal challenge to deharmonization being a concrete example of this.

This highlights an important facet of standardization. Regulatees perceive multilevelness in rule making—they are of course aware that the process of adoption of harmonized standards is supposed to address the predictability and clarity deficits that private standard setting may suffer from (by giving them some legal status although not making them binding). However they are also acutely aware that the process of extending recognition to standards—by denoting them as harmonized—is a fragile process that is in many ways contingent on continued participation of regulators in the standard setting process. In case this is disrupted then it leads to *ex post* challenge which was witnessed in the case of the two formal challenges mounted by the European Commission and Swedish authorities. This reveals that the process of formal recognition until supported by substantive participation of regulators will not robust enough to contain the ruptures in rule making (standardization) which arise due to multilevelness.

On the issue of rule application, at the European level two areas in which national divergences exist were in vigilance reporting (e.g. timing of vigilance reports) and registration requirements (e.g. registration in the Italian Repertorio[32] was mentioned by several interviewees as an additional burden that was not mandated under the directives). A comparison was also made between UK and Germany in terms of national requirements and regulatory culture.[33] Germany has

[31] European Commission (2011).

[32] All medical devices sold in Italy must be registered in an Italian database ("Repertorio") administered by the Ministry of Health through its new system, NSIS. This requirement is a national regulation with no relation to the fact that the product might already be CE marked.

[33] For instance the UK regulatory culture is based on the philosophy of quality assessment of industrial processes whereas in Germany the large number of independent product testing laboratories are a testament to a regulatory culture with a focus on product testing and verification. I use the term to refer to the shared sense of social beliefs and presumptions that guide and shape

additional national requirements on the post-marketing issues that are embedded within the decentralized institutional supervision of länder authorities. It was pointed out, that the UK has followed a light touch form of regulation, eschewing additional national requirements—and this was also reflected in the case of medical devices. Manufacturers operating in the German market faced more multilevel regulation than those in the U.K. One of manufactures in fact had taken a strategic decision to locate their European Authorized Representative in Germany in order to leverage themselves under the prevailing circumstances. Another proof of the distinct regulatory cultures is that the bigger notified bodies (e.g. BSi and TUV product services) maintain two offices—one in UK and the other in Germany to handle national specific requirements. This decision to maintain a separate national office despite being a single European market reflects the perception of notified bodies that there are operational differences between these two markets that require dedicated personnel. This illustrates that national differences exists when it comes to rule application and thus reinforces multilevelness.

6.4.2 Regulatory Relationships

Formally there are three sets of relationship between regulators and regulatees. First, between the notified bodies and NCAs that appoints and oversees them. Second, between manufacturers and NCAs (specifically in the case of Class III high risk medical devices and borderline products) and third is between manufacturers and notified bodies that undertake conformity assessment for their products. The European Commission is an important actor specifically in terms of hosting the MDEG and in drafting legislative proposals—however it does not share a regulatory relationship with any of the other actors—regulators or regulatees. The first and second relationship is formally structured in a hierarchical fashion, whereas in the case of the third, it is non-hierarchical.

Notified Bodies remarked that there were regular interactions with the NCAs [specifically the Bfarm (Bundesinstitut für Arzneimittel und Medizinprodukte—German for the Federal Institute for Drugs and Medical Devices) and MHRA] and the competences of the notified bodies were regularly reviewed. This was not always the case, and NCAs especially the bigger ones (MHRA and Bfarm) have matured with time. An interviewee from a leading notified body remarked:

> I was not party to the first audit; – but I can only imagine if you are not an auditor and you have to go and audit an auditing organization – then it is very hard – they know all the

individual action within this regulatory space. Of course culture may be defined both at the macro and micro level. I use it to allude to a national practice and belief systems that guide social action in the medical device regulatory space. For a detailed theoretical analysis of this concept see Meidinger (1987), pp. 355–386.

tricks – I think by now organizations like the MHRA have matured to the level that they are partners at the same level of inspection and auditing than the organizations that they have to look at – that is a major change.

Most manufacturers agreed that they have to "*appease*" competent authorities and notified bodies. However they also mentioned that share an open and constructive relationship with the MHRA. A manufacturer shared their experience in the case of contaminated heparin from China that confronted the MHRA. In that particular case, MHRA had sought the help of the manufacturer. They had helped them decide their risk assessment of these devices marketed in the UK. Availability of other regulatory discussion forums like the Committee on the Safety of Devices (CSD) that work in an advisory capacity to the MHRA, which manufacturers can also access; was identified as important forums for facilitating a congenial relationship with the national competent authorities. In comparison, the Bfarm, was termed non-collaborative and "antagonistic". One of the companies faced a vigilance issue with a customer in Freiburg, they were struggling to get access to the device to finish the analysis—they approached the Bfarm for assistance. But, their request was turned down on the basis that they had not finished the investigation. The interviewee said that "*Manufacturers therefore faced a stalemate that did not benefit anyone*."[34]

Unlike with national competent authorities, manufacturer's relationship with notified bodies is conducted in the spirit of negotiation and discussion. To quote a manufacturer:

sometimes when we have a difference of opinion – we just have to sit down and present our case – we bring our expertise and we will sit down just facing each other – and say that – well we have three hours to get a consensus – because that is a European tradition – you present your case and let your counterpart present their case and you discuss it.

A number of manufacturers pointed out that this was unlike the regulatory style adopted by the USFDA, wherein legal interpretation is an outcome of unilateral decision, and not the result of a discussion. Manufacturers also appreciated the European system because there is a closer link between inspectors and assessors within notified bodies—which is missing in the FDA.[35] Manufacturers also felt that shared backgrounds with personnel from notified bodies allow them to discuss issues between "*engineer to engineer facilitating the creation of credible expectations in both sides*".

It is apparent that due to common educational and technical qualifications, manufacturers identify with notified bodies and view themselves as members of a larger epistemic community—*engineers*—who share technical knowledge and a set of presumptions that allows them to evolve a close working relationship which stabilizes expectations that one has from the other.

---

[34] Since incomplete analysis of the problem due to the lack of access to the device would not benefit the patient, the manufacturer or the NCA.

[35] See for a comparison of the regulatory architecture and institutional styles between Europe and USA, Kramer et al. (2012), pp. 848–855.

In case of any disagreement with the notified bodies, manufacturers would first approach the industry associations, to explore whether this was a common predicament faced by other manufacturers. If so they would ask the industry associations to liaison with the NCA—this would ensure a better hearing. This also highlights that interactions between manufacturers and NCAs were a valuable resource which was only accessed when manufacturers had a very strong case and that to through the industry associations—so as to bolster their case and to prevent being isolated on an issue by regulators.

A revealing example was provided by a manufacturer highlighting the changing relationship between manufacturers and competent authorities. The manufacturer was marketing radiation equipment in the European market. He faced some uncertainty, because there was inadequate guidance on the reporting requirements for radiation exposure. Despite repeated demands for guidance, regulatory authorities both in UK and others like the FDA had not provided any guidance. When asked what could be the reasons for this procrastination—given that radiation exposure was not a new area, he replied:

> My uninformed guess as to why this may be the case is because they do not have enough experience, clinical or working knowledge to formulate the guideline. Certainly we would be happy to work with any competent authority to have this clarified.

Further, commenting on the process of interaction with the MHRA, the manufacturer said:

> we are quite happy to have discussions.....the Competent Authority will start to explain their process – the reasons they have reached that decision – but in my experience their explanation is not as thorough as ours. We are able to produce good quality documentation and a full risk assessment process.......they will give us an opinion and explain their opinion – but not with the level of detail we are able to provide.......they are making individual decisions that are not based on what I call firm foundation.

This reveals an important aspect of the changing relationship between regulators and regulatee. The fact that the regulatee have far greater domain knowledge in their own specific products, allows them greater insight and therefore confidence in challenging the decision-making authority of the regulator. The simple fact that regulatees—manufacturers—possess greater domain knowledge is of course nothing new. However in the context of medical devices it assumes importance because—the regulatory architecture privileges such domain knowledge in rule making functions. Therefore in the case of the medical device directives (and indeed all *New Approach* directives) by adopting a standards based regulatory regime—it gives indirect recognition to the critical role of domain/technical knowledge in rule making. Manufacturers have internalized this recognition—and this has allowed them to gain confidence and challenge regulatory decisions on technical grounds. I refer to phenomenon as positional identity.[36]

---

[36] Positional Identity is a phrase used in cells and tissue research within biology. Here I use this expression to refer to the a growing self-realization of manufacturers that as possessors of technical knowledge—the regulatory space allows them greater authority vis-à-vis regulators.

This can be characterized as an inverse pyramid. Wherein there is a clear hierarchy of regulatory authority with manufacturers at the bottom, followed by notified bodies in the second rung, and finally the National Competent Authority and the European Commission, making up the top rung. On the other hand, domain knowledge is most prevalent with manufacturers, followed in decreasing levels, by notified bodies, national competent authorities and lastly the European commission. Inverse pyramids may also exist in other product regulatory system, but it is especially strong in product categories such as medical devices, which is technologically driven with high product turnover across an equally diverse product range. This aspect makes it difficult for regulatory authorities to competently track and address regulatory issues.

The *New Approach* to law making was brought about in recognition of this inherent limitation of the rule-makers, struggling to keep abreast of product development. The *New Approach* provided a number of arenas (e.g. standardization) where it privileged domain knowledge over regulatory authority. This allows manufacturers—who indeed have greater knowledge of their products, to challenge regulatory authority in a manner that is quite uncommon in other jurisdictions (for e.g. under the FDA). Moreover, it dilutes the strict roles between regulators as producers of rules and regulatees as passive consumers of those rules as seen in classic regimes of command and control.

6.5 What Are the Regulatee Perceptions and Expectations of Legal Certainty?

Questions that were posed to regulatees in this regard included, whether the regulatees perceived the system to be clear and intelligible in terms of their legal obligations and how often did they face a situation wherein they had to take external advice; did they find the regulatory system to be predictable in terms of decisions rendered by regulatory authorities; did they face any specific areas of regulatory uncertainty and what were their demands and expectations from the regulatory system.

Majority of manufacturers referred to national differences in product classification and vigilance reporting protocols; as specific aspects which were leading to problems of inconsistency and thus impeding harmonization and the proper application of the Directives. Biological indicators being classified as a medical device in France and as an accessory in UK, was quoted as an example. These differences were also deemed irresolvable due to a lack of any institutional mechanism that would establish consensus or take a final decision. Referring to the lack of legal authority of the MDEG (Medical Devices Expert Group on Borderline and Classification) to make any authoritative decision on product classification, a manufacturer noted:

we require a decision rather than allow it to be sitting in a working party without any statutory authority.

However, stakeholders agreed that the issue of borderline products affected less than 10 % of total products. So the scale of the problem in the present context is marginal. Nevertheless it has been noted that there is a trend towards more combination products[37] and survey results indicate that around 30 % of all new products under development are combination products. Thus if regulatory intervention to address product classification issues is not made at this stage—inconsistency relating to product categorization will be a problem that will continue to grow and plague this sector.

Overall most manufacturers agreed that the system is clear and coherent and the regulatory system is predictable for the most part, since it is based on clear classification of risk. This makes it relatively easy to identify products that fall within a specific risk category and therefore the regulatory obligations that are required to be implemented. Interviewees were of the opinion that the European regulatory system is based on trust; unlike that of the US system; where the FDA considers regulatees to be crooks until proven otherwise. It was also pointed out that the European system also serves as a *sui generis* system that has been adopted in parts by a number of other medical device regulatory systems—like that in Australia and the Canada.

There is however a nervous expectation on the part of all the manufacturers interviewed as to the legislative proposals which the European Commission is expected to unveil for the amendment of the three medical device directives in the coming months. Since the first announcement of the proposal for recast in 2008, the Commission has had two public consultations (in 2008 and 2010) on a slew of proposed amendments to the three directives. Subsequently the Commission announced the measures that it is considering to propose, would better be described as a 'revision' since it is expected to suggest a number of fundamental changes to address the challenges facing the current system; viz. varying level of public health protection, categorization problems for products based on new technologies, scarcity of expertise; and national variation. All problems that reflect inconsistency and lack of coherence—that would seem to increase regulatory uncertainty.

Following the PIP (Poly Implant Protheses) crisis concerning the usage of substandard materials in breast implants; there have been several institutional interventions at the European level. First, was the risk assessment of PIP breast implants that was delivered in early February 2012 by SCENIHR (Scientific Committee on Emerging and Newly Identified Health Risks). It found inconclusive evidence of PIP silicone breast implants carrying greater risks in comparison to

[37] Combination products are the trade name for "borderline"—products—the latter being a regulatory reference. Both the names refer to the same characteristics of products using more than one principal modes of action and therefore use of this criterion for product differentiation is rendered unreliable. Thus giving rise to the problem of products falling into more than one regulatory product category.

other breast implants. However the political fall-out of this has been widespread. Second, DG SANCO Commissioner John Dalli's announced[38] (European Commission 2012) a number of 'immediate actions' addressing perceived regulatory deficits. These actions were addressed to the member states and were to be taken on the basis of existing legislation; and as a prelude to the coming into place of the revised directives in the near future. These actions include; ensuring consistency amongst member states in the recognition of notified bodies, better coordination in the supervision of notified bodies; use of unannounced checks of manufacturer premises by notified bodies, improving vigilance systems and leveraging tools for traceability of medical devices. Third, the Environment and Public Health Committee of the European Parliament passed a unanimous resolution calling for the establishment of a breast implant register, more stringent checks and product traceability tools.[39] Most importantly it has advocated for a premarket authorization system for high-risk devices; similar to the system operating for pharmaceuticals.

Interestingly manufacturers and notified bodies, although they do agree partially with the Commission's prognosis, they do not support a fundamental revision of the system. In the context of the varying level of quality of notified bodies—they squarely lay the blame on the national competent authorities—since many "*member states look at it as a national right to have notified bodies*".

EUCOMED has argued that the current system is fundamentally an effective system that has ensured innovation and public health through faster access to health technologies[40] and therefore improvements should be in the nature of better application and enforcement of the existing rules. It has opposed the suggestion to have a centralized agency like the EMA or have the EMA extend its mandate to include medical devices. Centralization it believes is not the answer, but greater harmonization. Centralization itself will not guarantee access to expertise, as even within the EMA, there is continued dependence on external experts. Manufacturer's mistrust of the EMA stems from their experience with national competent authorities. Most national competent authorities that are mixed agencies (that regulate both drugs and devices) have shown a marked propensity towards adopting a drug orientation to the regulation of devices. Notified bodies have also tried to address the criticisms levelled, by drawing up a Code of Conduct.[41] However, till date only eleven out of the total number of thirty bodies have signed the code.

On the other hand, the national Member States have formed the CMC a in September, 2010 partially in response to the criticisms of the European Commission of the lack of coordination as an imperative for recast and the results of the public consultation. Currently the set-up is that of a talking shop wherein competent authorities can exchange information and ensure consistency of approach and

---

[38] European Commission (2012) Commissioner Dalli calls for immediate actions concerning the safety of medical devices. Speech/12/77. 9 February.

[39] European Parliament (2012b).

[40] EUCOMED (2011).

[41] Team NB (2011).

interpretation with reference to the medical device legislations. Statements made by the representatives of some of the larger NCAs, like that in Germany, UK and Netherlands; suggest that the CMC is an ambitious platform that will widen its sphere of actions in the near future.[42]

Following the European Parliamentary Committee resolution, EUCOMED responded, by supporting most of the proposals, with the exception for pre-market approval. It pointed to a fundamental difference between medical devices and pharmaceuticals which made it impossible to undertake clinical trials (in the case of certain medical devices like hip prosthesis). In such circumstances, clinical evaluations would be based on existing clinical data. Further, the delivery and performance of medical devices is based on a number of factors—including the skills and experience of physician, the quality of hospitals, etc. In fact, one of the surprising findings of the study was that, a substantial number of manufacturers felt that the impending revision of the medical device directives was causing regulatory uncertainty—since the expectation of certain changes—has influenced the present interpretation of regulatory requirements. Therefore, the expectation which way the revision would go was already influencing regulatory authorities—specifically national competent authorities and notified bodies—in their decision-making.

6.6 Analysis and Conclusion

This chapter explored three aspects of the medical devices case study. The first aspect was a formal review of the regulatory space in terms of establishing multilevelness. Second, was to delve into regulatee perception of multilevelness and whether they conform to my formal review. And third, was to explore regulatee expectations with regard to legal certainty. I summarize the main findings in the following paragraphs.

The formal review of the regulatory space concentrated on three aspects—rule making, rule application and rule adjudication. Guidance documents are considered to be equivalent to formal legal rules and since multiple actors (NCAs, MDEG and Notified bodies) issues their own guidance documents—this creates a case of multilevelness. Standards also play a critical role and they operate within a well laid down institutional framework wherein the European Commission recognizes the expertise of ESOs and adopts standards developed by then 'harmonized standards'. Further multiple legislative instruments adopted by member states to implement the directive also create scope for multilevelness. In the case of rule application the NCAs are the primary body for appointing notified bodies. There are a number of European guidelines governing the appointment of notified bodies, however there is diversity amongst NCAs on how notified bodies are appointed and thereafter supervised. This is due to the difference in resource capacities between

[42] 2011–2012 Annual Report of the HMA (Heads of Medicines Agency) Strategy.

the NCAs. In the case of rule adjudication, similar problem is faced because the adjudicatory mechanisms—MDEG—does not enjoy legal basis although there is a clear expectation that because the MDEG process involves both regulators and regulatees and is based on consensus, it would be followed by everybody. This however is not the case, since there have been instances of difference in which same products have been categorized differently by different NCAs. Thus overall I make the argument that this regulatory space lies on the multilevel side of the continuum.

Regulatee perceptions of multilevelness partially conform to the findings of the formal review. Although guidance documents are perceived to be as important as formal legal rules and despite there being a multiplicity of guidance documents issued by several actors both at the European and national level; regulatees were of the opinion that there was no overlap because there was consensus amongst all actors that MEDDEVS were the most important and that all other guidance documents were secondary to the latter. This was also evident in the fact that NCAs (not always but) in most cases drafted guidance documents to clarify MEDDEVs or when the MEDDEVs were silent on a certain issue. Standards were a different issue—regulatees agreed that although there was an institutional process governing the recognition of 'harmonized standards' by the European Commission—this partnership was weakened by the 'formal proceedings for deharmonization' that was launched by the European Commission. They looked at this more in terms of an *ex post* challenge by regulators vis-à-vis standard setting activities s in which the regulators themselves were outvoted or did not participate. It was also underlined that NCAs and the European Commission did not appreciate the fact that ESOs were part of the ISO structure and their primary aim is the global harmonization of standards. This was cited as another instance of multilevelness in which actors did not share a hierarchical relation—which therefore resulted in fragmentation tendencies. In the case of rule application, regulatees were happy with the functioning of notified bodies and appreciated that due to shared technical qualifications and educational backgrounds, they were able to discuss and debate issues from a common perspective with their technical evaluators. Regulatees were also vocal on their relationship with regulators. Although most regulatees reiterated that they had to *appease* regulatory authorities underlining the hierarchical nature of this relationship. However from their statements it is clear that the *sui generis* nature of the *New Approach* affords them ample opportunity to discuss, debate and question decisions of regulatory authorities based on their domain expertise. Thus the development of positional identity has made the relationship between regulatees and regulators more non-hierarchical.

Regulatee expectations of legal certainty centered on borderline products and specific aspects like vigilance reporting requirements as provided by NCA; which they found to be plagued by inconsistency. The lack of legal basis for MDEG classification decisions has also contributed to unpredictability. On other hand, regulatees recognized that the European system was based on a clear system of risk identification—which made product categorization relatively easier. Further the consensual nature of key regulatory process like the MDEG decision-making framework and the standards setting activities. This coupled with growing positional identity has meant that regulatees find the current system clear and predictable. This is also amply evident from their opposition to fundamental changes in the current system that is being proposed by the European Commission.

References

Chalmers D, Monti G (2008) European Union Law. Cambridge University Press, Cambridge, U.K. p. 145

Chowdhury N (2013) Common market but divergent regulatory practices: exploring European regulation and the effect on regulatory uncertainty in the marketing authorization of medical products. J Eur Integration 35:635–652

Eisenhart S (2012) European Commission plans greater oversight of notified bodies. Emergo Group Blog. http://www.emergogroup.com/blog/2012/11/european-commission-plans-greater-oversight-notified-bodies. Last accessed 16 Apr 2013

EUCOMED (2011) A new EU regulatory framework for medical devices, November. http://www.eucomed.org/uploads/Modules/Publications/111118_eu_mdd_position_paper_eucomed_final_version.pdf. Last accessed 21 Apr 2012

European Commission (2000) Guide to the implementation of directives based on the new approach and the global approach. http://ec.europa.eu/enterprise/policies/single-market-goods/files/blue-guide/guidepublic_en.pdf. Last accessed 14 Apr 2013

European Commission (2011) Proposal for a Regulation of the European Parliament and of the Council on European Standardization and amending Council Directives 89/686/EEC and 93/15/EEC and Directives 94/9/EC, 94/25/EC, 95/16/EC, 97/23/EC, 98/34/EC, 2004/22/EC, 2007/23/EC, 2009/105/EC and 2009/23/EC of the European Parliament and of the Council. http://ec.europa.eu/enterprise/policies/european-standards/files/standardization/com-2011-315_en.pdf. Last accessed 21 April 2012

European Parliament (2012a) European Parliament resolution of 14 June 2012 on defective silicone gel breast implants made by French company PIP, 2012/2621(RSP), Brussels. http://www.europarl.europa.eu/oeil/popups/ficheprocedure.do?lang=en&reference=2012/2621(SP). Last accessed 12 Apr 2013

European Parliament (2012b) PIP breast implants: "learn the lessons of this fraud". Press Release, 26 April. http://www.europarl.europa.eu/sides/getDoc.do?pubRef=-//EP//NONSGML+IMPRESS+20120423IPR43732+0+DOC+PDF+V0//EN&language=EN. Last accessed 21 Apr 2012

Feldschreiber P, Robinson T (2012) PIP and hips. Do we need a new regulatory system for medical devices? (July 25, 2012) Lexology. http://www.lexology.com/library/detail.aspx?g=1e97243d-fb34-4208-8ecd-86456742fcfd. Last accessed 14 Apr 2013

Horton R (2012) A serious regulatory failure, with urgent implications. Lancet 379:1060

Kramer DB, Xu S, Kesselheim AS (2012) Regulation of medical devices in the United States and European Union. N Engl J Med 366:848–855

Maxwell A (2012) EU standards deharmonisation threat recedes. SCRIP Regulatory Affairs, 13 March. http://www.rajpharma.com/regulatoryregion/europe/EU-standards-deharmonisiation-threatrecedes-327994?autnID=/contentstore/rajpharma/codex/7ac969ae-6c57-11e1-ab65-4737e25c5eed.xml. Last accessed 14 Apr 2012

Meidinger E (1987) Regulatory culture: a theoretical outline. Law Policy 9:355–386

Team NB (2011) Code of Conduct Medical Notified Bodies v2.7, 25 February. http://www.bsiamerica.com/upload/MS-Assessment+Certification/Subject-Areas+Sectors/Healthcare+MedicalDevices/Documents/Code%20of%20Conduct%20Medical%20Notified%20Bodies%20v2%207%20(25feb2011).pdf. Last accessed 5 May 2012

Chapter 7
Case Study on Pharmaceutical Regulation in Europe

7.1 Introduction

> The Pharmaceutical industry as a whole – both originators and generics manufacturers – should get a faster return on investments in research and development and operate in a legally predictable environment.[1]

Speaking on the European Commission Strategy for the Pharmaceutical Sector, Commissioner John Dalli made this statement. It underlines the value of a predictable and therefore calculable legal environment for the functioning of manufacturers. And, it also highlights the responsibility of the regulators—in this case the European Commission and the NCA's of the member states to provide such an environment.

The regulatory system for marketing authorization of pharmaceuticals in Europe is uniquely structured. It allows manufacturers to obtain marketing authorization for accessing the European market, through multiple regulatory pathways operating at the European and national levels. The institutional structure governing marketing authorization includes the European Commission, the EMA and the NCAs of the member states. Thus relationships between the EMA and NCAs are not hierarchically structured. This is in sharp contrast to the more hierarchically structured regulatory systems such as led by the USFDA—that follow the principle of—one agency in one regulatory field.

International harmonization through regulatory networks such as the ICH have also contributed to this multilevelness of regulatory system. The growing complexity of pharmaceutical products have compelled regulators to access professional health networks in search of harnessing scientific expertise for regulatory decision-making.

Currently, the pharmaceutical regulations are at the cusp of many important changes that will influence and will reshape the future direction of the system.

[1] European Commission (2012). http://ec.europa.eu/commission_2010-014/dalli/docs/speech_04062012.pdf (Accessed on 11 June 2012).

N. Chowdhury, *European Regulation of Medical Devices and Pharmaceuticals*, DOI 10.1007/978-3-319-04594-8_7,

These include the adoption and implementation of pharmacovigilance legislation (Regulation EU No 1235/2010 and Directive 2010/84/EU) that seeks to completely overhaul and rationalize responsibilities for post-authorization monitoring of pharmaceutical products. Last year, the European Commission had also developed a proposal for a revision of the clinical trials directive (2001/21/EC) to address the divergent national practices and streamlining reporting procedures.[2] Enlarging the sphere of conditional marketing authorizations, improving the consistency of scientific review processes, and facilitating relative effectiveness assessments; are some of the current issues that are under discussion.[3]

The chapter has been divided into six sections. I start with an overview of the history of regulations (Sect. 7.2) in this sector which provides a useful background to the regulatory philosophy and in helping understand the development trajectory of the regime. Section 7.3 discusses the formal review of the regulatory space in terms of rulemaking, rule application and rule adjudication in order to determine the multilevelness of the space. Section 7.4 examines whether the results of the formal review is shared by the regulatees in terms of their own assessment of multilevelness of pharmaceutical regulatory space. Section 7.5 discusses the key regulatee responses that reveal their perceptions and expectations with regard to legal certainty. Finally Sect. 7.6 analyses the regulatee responses in the two preceding sections and provides some concluding remarks.

7.2 History of Regulation in the Pharmaceutical Sector

Public health crises, like the thalidomide tragedy, had acted as a catalyst to regulate issues like the grounds for market access of new pharmaceuticals and pharmacovigilance at the European level.[4] Directive 65/65/EEC was the first European legislation addressing these issues by laying down safety, efficacy and therapeutic benefit as the three grounds for granting market access to pharmaceuticals. These general principles form the basis of the scientific analysis that the EMA conducts. Scientific knowledge is the foundation for regulating market access of pharmaceutical products (and also food products) in Europe. The argument that only few of the member states have sufficient access to scientific expertise (especially in the case of newer areas like biotechnology and nanotechnology products) have been made to support widening of the EMA's competences in this area.[5]

[2] European Commission (2010) Annexes to the Communication from the Commission to the European Parliament, the Council, the European Economic and Social Committee and the Committee of the Regions, Commission Work Program, COM(2010) 623 final, Brussels. See http://ec.europa.eu/atwork/programmes/docs/cwp2011_annex_en.pdf (Accessed on 11 June 2011).

[3] European Medicines Agency (2010) Roadmap to 2015. London.

[4] Permanand and Vos (2010); Altenstetter (1992); and Krapohl (2007), pp. 25–46.

[5] Permanand (2006); Permanand et al. (2006), pp. 87–90; Everson et al. (2000); Regulation (EC) No 1394/2007 of the European Parliament and of the Council of 13 November 2007 on

Yet, it is important to remember that public health as an area of social policy has been zealously guarded as a national competence by member states (indeed this continues to be the case of drug pricing and reimbursement policies) and that Community's competence in this area has mostly expanded as a consequence of the "spill over"[6] from the single market agenda. It was only in 2009 that the supervision of the EMA was moved from the industry to the health and consumer affairs director general.[7] The member states do not favor complete centralization of marketing authorization within these three sectors. This debate should not necessarily be framed, as if centralization necessarily leads to a loss of competence—because even in the case of centralization—viz. in specific kinds of medicinal products—it is the member state experts that formulate policy and leads regulatory decision-making through the CHMP within the EMA. Still admittedly the moving up of competences to a European body does precludes (or at least creates the pressure) of desisting from following divergent policies.

Post 1965, the Commission made several follow up attempts at harmonization of market authorization requirements and the procedural aspects, through the mutual recognition procedure (established in 1975) and the concertation procedure in 1987. From the 1990s to early 2000 saw the adoption of numerous legislations pertaining to good manufacturing practice, labelling, clinical practice and patient protection. The EMA (earlier known as the European Agency for Evaluation of Medicinal Products) was set up in 1995, it took over the functioning of the CPMP (Committee for Proprietary Medicinal Product) in order to provide a single window clearance for certain kinds of products—eventually leading to the establishment of the mandatory centralized authorization process in 2004[8] for biotechnological and other higher technology products. However, applicants (for marketing authorization of medicinal products) can also choose this route if they can prove that their product is innovative—in terms of either fulfilling some public health need or therapeutic efficacy.

Marketing authorization is the gateway through which various aspects of manufacturing and distribution of medicinal products in Europe is regulated. In effect, this is the checkpoint at which manufacturers have to prove their compliance with a number of regulatory obligations relating to clinical trials, manufacturing and pharmacovigilance. Unlike in the case of medical devices, pharmaceutical regulation is based on the principle of pre-market assessment. This assessment is commonly known as the benefit-risk balance. Every assessment for the grant of

advanced therapy medicinal products and amending Directive 2001/83/EC and Regulation (EC) No 726/2004.

[6] Armstrong (2002); Baeten (2003); Barani (2006); Duncan (2002), pp. 1027–1030; Duncan and Farrell (2005).

[7] European Commission. (2009) *President Barroso unveils his new team.* 27 November. Press Release: Brussels.

[8] Regulation (EC) No 726/2004 of the European Parliament and the Council of 31 March 2004 laying down Community procedures for the authorization and supervision of medicinal products for human and veterinary use and establishing a European Medicines Agency.

marketing authorization has to find a positive benefit risk balance—potential risks are outweighed by the therapeutic efficacy of the product. General conditions for the grant of marketing authorization are laid down under Directive 2001/83/EC and Regulation EC/726/2004. The Good Clinical Practice, Good Manufacturing Practice and Good Clinical Practice for investigation medicine products are guidelines that lay down best practices that should be adopted. Additionally, manufacturers of orphan drugs,[9] medicinal products for pediatric use[10] and ATMPs[11] have to follow special rules for such kind of products. Special provisions are also laid down for medicinal products incorporating human blood and plasma,[12] human tissues and cells[13] and GMOs.[14]

Currently, there exist a total of four regulatory pathways through which manufacturers can access market authorization for their products. As mentioned above, the CP is administered by the European Medicines Agency in London. It allows the manufacturer to submit single application and which if granted would allow access to all markets in the EU. The number of products on the mandatory CP list has gradually been expanded to include auto-immune and viral diseases since 2008. It is also open for generic medicines that are based on centralized products, once the data exclusivity period for such products are over. The simplest pathway is the national procedure (NP), wherein the manufacturer applies to one member state, to access that specific national market. The third pathway is MRP[15] in which the manufacturer applies to other member states to recognize the marketing authorization granted under the national procedure by the ‘reference member state’. There is a time limit of 90 days laid down for this procedure. The fourth pathway is the DCP[16] was introduced in 2005 and allows manufacturers to simultaneously apply in all member states where MA is sought. The applicant will choose a reference member state, which will have to make the assessment in 120 days and which

---

[9] Regulation (EC) No 141/2000 of the European Parliament and of the Council of 6 December 1999 on orphan medicinal products.

[10] Regulation (EC) No 1901/2006 of the European Parliament and of the Council of 12 December 2006 on medicinal products for paediatric use and amending Regulation (EEC) No 1768/92, Directive 2001/20/EC, Directive 2001/83/EC and Regulation (EC) No 726/2004.

[11] Regulation (EC) No 1394/2007 of the European Parliament and of the Council of 13 November 2007 on advanced therapy medicinal products and amending Directive 2001/83/EC and Regulation (EC) No 726/2004.

[12] Title X—Special Provisions on medicinal products derived from human blood and plasma (Articles 109 and 110) of Directive 2001/83/EC.

[13] Directive 2004/23/EC of the European Parliament and of the Council of 31 March 2004 on setting standards of quality and safety for the donation, procurement, testing, processing, preservation, storage and distribution of human tissues and cells.

[14] Commission Directive 2003/63/EC of 25 June 2003 amending Directive 2001/83/EC, providing for the obligation to undertake environmental risk assessment by manufacturer using GMOs in medicine products.

[15] Directive 2001/83/EC of the European Parliament and of the Council of 6 November 2001 on the Community code relating to medicinal products for human use.

[16] Directive 2004/27/EC of the European Parliament and of the Council of 31 March 2004.

will have to be recognized by other member states in 90 days unless there is a potential public health risk.

In the case of the third and fourth pathways—the relationship between the national competent authorities is not hierarchical in nature—so there is a possibility of disagreement over the benefit risk assessment in the case of specific applications for authorization. However there is a strict time limit for notifying of any disagreement to the CHMP.

The centralized procedure is managed by the European Medicines Agency. Interestingly the EMA does not have an additional or separate contingent of scientific experts to assess the applications for marketing authorization. It is the CHMP that is primarily responsible for preparing EMA's opinion on all relevant questions regarding marketing authorization of medicinal products under CP. The CHMP members are nominated by the NCAs of the member states in consultation with the management Board of the EMA. Along with the CHMP, there are five other scientific committees—Committee for Medicinal Products for Veterinary Use (CVMP), Committee for Orphan Medicinal Products (COMP), Pediatric Committee (PDCO), Committee on Advanced Therapeutics (CAT) and Committee on Herbal Medicinal Products (HMPC). The CHMP oversees the functioning of the CAT and PDCO, since it is upon the latter's recommendation that scientific opinion is sought from these specialized scientific committees and it is the coopted members of the CHMP that make the membership of these two specialized committees. Apart from these six committees, the CHMP is further assisted by three standing working parties (QWP, BWP and SAWP)[17] and five temporary working parties that focus on different aspects. The CHMP is therefore the most important body overseeing the marketing authorization process under CP. Its rules of procedure mandate that CHMP should function through consensus, but in case of a disagreement, majority voting is adopted. Further unlike in other regulatory fields, where European regulatory agencies function separately from national regulatory agencies of the member states, within pharmaceuticals, it is the CHMP which is the primary driver in the EMA. The CHMP represents an amalgamation of the national competent authorities. Therefore the EMA largely functions as a secretariat and substantive decision-making is subsumed within the CHMP. This unique regulatory structure therefore represents a mechanism for resolving disagreements between member states rather than a centralization of regulatory authority.

There are four aspects to CHMP's role: first, is the preliminary assessment of products seeking EU wide authorization. Variations of initial applications are also overseen by the CHMP. Every authorization under the CP is followed by the publishing of the European Assessment Report that elaborates on the scientific grounds for the positive approval of the CHMP. The second and relatively new aspect is the scientific advice facility that was unveiled in 2011 through the establishment of the Scientific Advice Working Party (SAWP). The SAWP

[17] The acronyms refer to Joint CHMP-CVMP Quality Working Party, Biological Working Party and Safety Working Party respectively.

functions under the CHMP[18] to provide scientific advice, protocol assistance[19] and qualification of novel methodologies to manufacturers. The scientific advice procedure is prospective and not legally binding in nature. The third is monitoring of safety of authorized medicines. Pharmacovigilance activity of marketing authorization holders is also tracked through assessing adverse drug reaction reports (ADRs) and if necessary, recommending changes in the medicine's marketing authorization (including suspension and withdrawal) to the European Commission. Fourth, in both the MRP and DCP, the CHMP arbitrates disputes[20] between member states in cases of disagreement on the marketing authorization of particular medicines. It is also the body that investigates the veracity of measures initiated by the member states for protection of public health ('community referral procedure').

Interestingly the formal process of authorization mandates, that the CHMP decision on authorization is formulated in terms of a recommendation to the European Commission, which the latter has to adopt.[21] However there have been some instances in the past, the European Commission has refused to simply accept the CHMP recommendation. The most recent incident is that concerning the application of marketing authorization for Glybera, a treatment for the inherited disorder lipoprotein lipase deficiency (LPL).[22] In January this year, the European Commission refused to adopt CHMP's recommendation rejecting Glybera. Thereafter it had resent the file back to CHMP asking it to reconsider. The CHMP has voted again to refuse the grant of marketing authorization to Glybera.[23] What is noteworthy is the process of rejecting this application; it has also gone against the advice received from CAT—which had recommendation approval under strict conditions of usage.

[18] The SAWP is a permanent working party of the CHMP and holds the distinction of being the only working party to be established under EU legislation. Specifically Article 56(3) of European Parliament and Council Regulation (EC) 726/2004, which provides that "The Executive Director, in close consultation with the Committee for Medicinal Products for Human Use and the Committee for Medicinal Products for Veterinary Use, shall set up the administrative structures and procedures allowing the development of advice for undertakings, as referred to in Article 57(1)(n), particularly regarding the development of new therapies. Each committee shall establish a standing working party with the sole remit of providing scientific advice to undertakings." BWP and QWP stands for the Biologics Working Party and Quality Working Party of the CHMP respectively.

[19] Refers to a special form of scientific advice available for companies developing medicines for 'orphan' or rare diseases.

[20] Article 30 of Directive 2001/83/EC—states that "...if Member States have adopted divergent decisions concerning the authorisation of the medicinal product or its suspension or revocation, a Member State, the Commission or the applicant or the marketing authorisation holder may refer the matter to the Committee for Medicinal Products for Human Use."

[21] Council Decision of 28 June 1999 laying down the procedures for the exercise of implementing powers conferred on the Commission, OJ L 184, 17.7.1999, pp. 23–26. See Art 5(3).

[22] Nuala (2012), p. 474.

[23] European Medicines Agency (2012) *European Medicines Agency maintains recommendation not to grant a marketing authorisation for Glybera*. Press Release EMA/CHMP/264472/2012.

This incident highlights the unclear hierarchy that operates between the specialized committees assisting the CHMP and also between the CHMP itself and the European Commission. Although the European Commission has the formal competence to decide on the recommendation of the CHMP, in practice it has been a mere rubber stamp—given that it is the CHMP recommendation is a scientific assessment that has in a sense received political approval of the NCA via the established consensus procedure. However as the Glybera case illustrates the European Commission has overruled the recommendation and has asked the CHMP to reconsider. The question that remains open is whether authorizations should be based on scientific assessments of risk-benefit balance—as is the case under the legal regime—or should other considerations relating to access to medicine be also factored into such decisions.

7.3 Is the Pharmaceutical Regulatory Space Multilevel in Nature?

The three aspects investigated were rule making, rule application and rule adjudication activities. The research question sought to explore multilevelness of this regulatory space—whether the rule making, rule application and rule adjudication activities are distributed across administrative levels vertically and also whether the regulatory authority is also shared between public and private actors.

7.3.1 Rule Making

The primary legal acts regulating this space, are Directive 2001/83/EC and Regulation EC (No) 726/2004. Both these instruments together regulate all aspects—clinical trials, manufacturing, clinical evaluation and pharmacovigilance—of marketing authorization. The DCP and MRP processes are regulated by the Directive and therefore it allows for some degree of flexibility to be adopted by national implementing act in shaping national implementing procedures. Guidelines also play a critical role in this space; primarily because the sheer scale of regulatory obligations require clarity and simplification that guidelines can help achieve. Guidelines are issues by actors operating at international, European and national levels. Internationally the ICH is a very important platform for regulatory harmonization. The ICH includes both regulators and regulatees as equal members. However, although industry has been very active in flagging issues for harmonization—they have been only partially successful, as the adoption of common guidelines ultimately depends on the agreement between regulators (EMA, FDA and Ministry of Health, Labour and Welfare, Japan).

Table 7.1 Regulatory space of marketing authorization of pharmaceuticals

Regulatory life cycle	Administrative levels	Actor responsibility	
		Primary	Oversight
Rule making	International – Guidance documents	ICH (involves regulators and regulatees)	
	European – Directives & regulation – Notice to applicants – CHMP guidelines	CHMP European Commission	
	National – National implementing acts – National guidelines on clinical trials – Administrative guidelines	National competent authorities (NCA)	
Rule application	International (None)		
	European – Assessment of applications in CP	EMA (CHMP—CAT & PDCO)	European Commission
	National – Assessment of applications in NP, DCP & MRP – Clinical trials – Pharmacovigilance	NCA	
Rule adjudication	International (None)		
	European – CAT/PDCO assessments – DCP and MRP process conflicts	CHMP ECJ	
	National – NP applications	National Courts	

Source: Based on preliminary mapping exercise conducted as part of the Pharmaceutical Case Study

At the European level, the European Commission (DG SANCO) is the primary driver of legislative developments. It has also issued guidelines—Notice to Applicants—explaining the procedural requirements such as renewal procedures, dossier requirements for Type IA/IB variation notifications, summary of product characteristics, package information and classification for the supply, etc. The CHMP also issues guidelines but those focus on scientific issues regarding demonstration of quality, safety and efficacy. Nationally, the NCAs also issue guidelines on administrative requirements regarding the DCP and MRP processes (Table 7.1).

7.3.2 Rule Application

In the context of rule application, there is clear division of regulatory authority between the EMA and the NCAs. The former working through CHMP oversees the CP and the latter oversees the DCP and MRP processes. The NCAs are also at the forefront of enforcement of pharmacovigilance procedures. The oversight of the CP is provided by the European Commission—which has the final authority in adopting the recommendations made by CHMP. Given that the benefit-risk assessment undertaken by the CHMP is a scientific assessment—under the usual scenario the European Commission accepts the recommendation of the CHMP for the grant of MA. However as was pointed out, like in the Glybera case, there have been instances in which wherein the European Commission has refused to accept CHMP recommendation and have taken the unprecedented step of asking the CHMP to reconsider its decision. Such instances seem to be driven by political factors—the access to medicine—rather than a challenge to the scientific assessment of the CHMP. It would be interesting to watch how this latest disagreement (in the case of Glybera) is resolved—given that the regulation only permits scientific assessment as the basis of determining MA applications. However in terms of regulatory hierarchy—the CHMP decision is in the form of a recommendation to the European Commission—which reserves the right to accept or reject it.

Both in the case of clinical trials and pharmacovigilance—the European Commission has been keen to harmonize national differences between the NCAs. The newly introduced Pharmacovigilance legislations and the proposed revision of the clinical trials directive 2001/20/EC is with a view to address these national differences.

7.3.3 Rule Adjudication

Rule adjudication[24] should be seen in two contexts. First, that between the CHMP and other specialized committees like CAT and PDCO. In the case of ATMPs, pediatric drugs and general pharmaceuticals, it is the CHMP that has the final authority. However there could be cases in which the CAT and PDCO disagrees with CHMP on scientific grounds. In such cases the only way out to resolve is by majority voting. However one can envisage that growing complexity of pharmaceutical products will raise the credibility and authoritativeness of scientific assessments made by CAT and PDCO and this would force CHMP to defer to the

[24] Rule adjudication is defined as adjudication of disputes on differing legal interpretations of the same provisions of law.

specialized jurisdiction and authority of the latter.[25] Second, the CHMP also plays a critical role as an arbitrator for disputes involving the DCP and MRP processes—here again the principle of majority voting is adopted to resolve such matters. The European Court of Justice has played a marginal role in resolving disputes relating to marketing authorization applications.[26]

The above discussion suggests that in this regulatory space, rule making, rule application and rule adjudication activities are legally ordered by the European legislations. In the case of rule-making—although ICH guidelines are formulated by both regulators and regulatees—the process is hostage to the agreement between regulators—and therefore it is they that form the pivot on which the process revolves. Therefore only when regulators across the three jurisdictions agree—do guidelines get formulated and percolate down to the regulatory space. Both in the case of rule application and rule adjudication—it is the public authorities/regulators that are the primary actors. In this context, if we were to revisit the definition of multilevel regulation—it refers to the distribution of regulatory authority amongst actors operating across administrative levels and also between public and private actors. It is evident that the regulatory space of marketing authorization of medicinal products in Europe is characterized by a limited scale of multilevelness. Although there are multiple levels of regulatory authority—the functions are well distributed between the actors. The only space wherein private actors (in the form of regulatees) play a role is in rule making—ICH guidelines—however, their authority is limited to agenda setting—because the drafting and adoption of guidelines is dependent on consensus amongst regulators. Another aspect that negates multilevelness is that the same group of people perform multiple functions vis-à-vis their membership of different bodies. The primary actors are the members of NCA who are represented in the CHMP and who are also co-opted for membership of CAT and PDCO. This enables the members to respect the separate mandate and work distribution between the different actors. Thus the commonality of membership reinforces the distribution of regulatory authority amongst actors as provided under the European legislations. Rule interpretation is therefore monopolized by a common set of experts that function as regulators—acting either through NCAs or in the CHMP, and thereby limiting the possibility of divergent regulatory interpretations which may have led to regulatory uncertainty.

---

[25] In 2010, EMA set up the Consistency Group, to review all draft guidelines before they are discussed in the CHMP to ensure regulatory and scientific consistency. For details see EMA (2010) *Reflection paper on working parties (WP) CHMP/EMA group analysis and proposals*, EMA/315270/2010, Adopted by CHMP in May 2010.

[26] Most of the cases has been on patenting issues—specifically the legal status of Supplementary Protection Certificates under the patent law. One exception is a recent case on marketing authorization—Judgment of the Court (Third Chamber) of 19 April 2012, *Artegodan GmbH v European Commission et Federal Republic of Germany*. Case C-221/10 P.

7.4 What Is the Regulatee Perception of Multilevelness?

The regulatees overall agreed with the formal review of the multilevelness in the pharmaceutical regulatory space. With reference to rulemaking several manufacturers agreed that there exists operational distribution of mandates—at the European level, the CHMP focuses on scientific issues, and the DG SANCO on administrative issues. Manufacturers also underlined that common and circulating membership between these different bodies—ICH, European Commission and CHMP and NCAs has meant that there is a de facto acknowledgement of the individual competences and responsibility regarding the contents of guidelines produced and this would seem to create the necessary impetus to avoid conflicts. With reference to ICH guidelines interviewees commented that some of the earlier guidelines were so general (reflecting continuing disagreements between regulators and therefore inability to agree to specific language and commitments) that they were useless—and therefore increasing focus has shifted to toxicology issues that are more horizontal in nature.

In the case of rule application manufacturers identified NCAs as the most important entities and agreed that the CHMP process was driven by the NCAs. The consensual system that guides decision-making procedures in the CHMP is based on national expertise and is therefore the policy stand taken by key NCAs in the context of rule application was considered to be a good indication of how issues would stack up in the CHMP. Thus although formally it was the EMA which regulated and oversaw the CP, manufacturers were clear that it was ultimately the NCAs coming together as the CHMP which took a lead in rule application. It was also pointed out that in terms of volume the maximum authorizations is through the DCP/MRP process and that explains why NCAs play a relatively more critical role in rule application than the EMA. In the context of rule adjudication, here again the majority of manufacturers underlined the critical role played by CHMP. Queries about the marginal role of the ECJ in adjudicating disputes over rule application elicited the following response. Manufacturers suggested that the marginal role of the ECJ was because the CHMP procedure is working relatively effectively and this explains the limited manner in which ECJ has been accessed. The fact that the CHMP is a consensus body with the adequate regulatory and scientific expertise is also an important factor that may drive preferences for CHMP adjudication rather than litigation through the ECJ.

Thus overall the regulatees seem to agree with the results of the formal review of multilevelness. They agreed with the assessment that the regulatory space of pharmaceuticals was characterized by low levels of multilevelness because the distribution of competences was ordered through the European legislations and the fact that there was a common community of experts—that acted as regulators—with common membership of NCAs, CHMP and the ICH meant that there was a clear understanding and consensus between key members which limited fragmentation and regulatory conflict between multiple authorities which were formally located at different administrative levels.

7.5 What Are the Regulatee Perceptions and Expectations of Legal Certainty?

The question posed to manufacturers was whether they had a clear preference for one amongst the three regulatory pathways CP, DCP and MRP? This question regarding the choice of regulatory pathway is expected to reveal whether there is a perceived degree of multilevelness between these pathways and if that influences the regulatee perception in terms of consistency, predictability, clarity, coherence and intelligibility. Thus do regulatees differentiate between regulatory pathways on the basis of to what extent each is expected to deliver on these aspects that contribute to legal certainty. This is key to understanding regulatee expectations of legal certainty. Two caveats need to be made—NP was not considered because the coverage is limited to a particular member nation—whereas DCP/CP/MRP can be compared in terms allowing coverage of the EU market. Second, manufacturers were asked their preference—when they had the opportunity to exercise this preference—so products in therapeutic areas where CP is mandatory (viz. AIDs, Cancel, Viral diseases, etc.) was logically excluded.

The responses of manufacturers can be split into two categories. One set of manufacturers especially large generic manufacturers admitted to a clear preference for CP. They preferred the CP over the MRP and DCP processes because the timelines for approval was strictly followed in the former and therefore the process was clearer and relatively more predictable.

> Whereas in the latter – although the process was well laid down in guidelines – NCAs frequently deviated from them, this was not the case with the central authorization procedure wherein the EMA usually stuck to the strict deadlines

The quality of scientific assessments and streamlined procedures for maintenance of licenses were also identified as reasons for this preference.

The other set of manufacturers explained this clear cut choice by generic manufacturers—as expected—because the clinical development evidence of the product is very straightforward and well known given that they have undergone a process of clinical evaluation when for the first time marketing authorization was granted. And thus therapeutic efficacy and other clinical indicators are quite well known. Thus generic manufacturers of off patent drugs are in a unique position of benefitting from applying for marketing authorization through the CP process because there is little uncertainty with regard to clinical evaluation process as that is well known. And, in such cases the CP ensures coverage of the entire European market—without any uncertainty as to the scientific assessment. Manufacturers however commented that involvement in the CP requires a certain threshold of resources—which may not be available to SMEs. The EMA seems to be also aware of this issue—since has established a dedicated SME office in 2005 to implement a slew of measures to facilitate access of CP for SMEs.[27]

---

[27] Commission Regulation (EC) No 2049/2005 of 15 December 2005 laying down, pursuant to Regulation (EC) No 726/2004 of the European Parliament and of the Council, rules regarding the

The other set of manufacturers underlined that the choice of regulatory pathways was a function of therapeutic area and product specificities and therefore not motivated by perceived differences between regulatory pathways in terms of legal certainty. In case of a new therapeutic indication—usually a two-step strategy is adopted. At first, the manufacturer would try and get a positive approval from a NCA and then extend through the DCP or MRP processes. A critical difference between the CP and MRP/DCP processes is that, in the former the manufacturer is allocated the rapporteurs by the CHMP itself, whereas in the latter—the process allows the possibility of choosing a specific NCA to perform the scientific assessment.

Contraceptives were cited as an example in which the political climate (conservative or liberal government) determined whether individual member states granted marketing authorization.[28] It is in this context that CHMP allocation of rapporteurs is perceived to be fraught with risk. In such cases, therefore the manufacturers would prefer to reserve this choice—so as to pick an NCA which it could expect to be supportive of their application. Further, due to the rapid increase of administrative burden in drug development on both sides of the Atlantic—drug development is frequently pursued through partnerships. In such cases, both the DCP and MRP allows for greater flexibility in the distribution of markets between partners. Regulators interviewed also agreed with this view that all the processes had their strength and weaknesses. The CP brought in a certain sense of predictability, because since all NCAs have a right to vote in the CHMP, one or two negative votes could not hold up the MA for the manufacturer. Similarly in the MRP, being armed with a positive opinion—increases predictability to a great extent.

Despite the clear difference of opinion between two sets of manufacturers—both agreed that the existence of multiple regulatory pathways was in itself a positive—since it allowed manufacturers flexibility in choosing a specific pathway. Another aspect that was stressed was that as long as reimbursement policies differed between member states, companies would always use the MRP/DCP processes to target bigger markets first to launch their products.

Although the manufacturers perceived the CP to be marginally better in terms of ensuring consistency, predictability and clarity, ultimately the respondents did not distinguish between the regulatory pathways based on these factors. It is the result of a strategic choice—that is largely determined by the market structure, reimbursement policies, therapeutic indication and existing business partnerships. This finding seems to be reinforced by the earlier assessment that this regulatory space is

---

payment of fees to, and the receipt of administrative assistance from, the European Medicines Agency by micro, small and medium-sized enterprises.

[28] For instance in the recent case of Europe wide review of the drug—Diane 35—initiated at the request of the French pharmaceutical regulator—ANSM, it was noted that this drug which is also used as a oral contraceptive, marketing authorization has been given for different uses by different member states. So although in many member countries they are authorized as a contraceptive for women with acne and hirsutism; in France they were only authorized for treatment of acne. See WHO Drug Information Vol. 27, No. 1, 2013.

characterised by very low levels of multilevelness. Regulatory uncertainty is limited—one cannot differentiate between regulatory pathways on the basis of perceived differences of clarity, consistency, predictability, intelligibility and coherence. Thus the choice of which regulatory pathway to adopt was entirely dependent on a combination of factors.

The interviewees were unanimous in their opinion that at a systemic level, they found the regulatory space to be predictable, consistent, coherent and clear—however they did identify some pockets of the system that were characterized by regulatory uncertainty. A majority of manufacturers criticized the functioning of the PDCO. They accepted and appreciated the rationale behind the specific regulatory obligations—like submission of a Pediatric Investigation Plan—they viewed the demands of the PDCO as

> Too academic. Their theoretical expectations do not match practicalities.

Practical realities referred to included—the demand for pediatric plan too early in the development process—at a stage where manufacturers themselves were not in a position to discuss the development strategy. And also the ethical complexities of testing on children were not appreciated by the PDCO. The fact that this criticism was shared by many manufactures was evident from the dedicated working group on pediatrics that was set up by the EFPIA to lobby for greater transparency and consistency in the functioning of PDCO. A survey of the early experience of pediatric regulation carried out amongst 34 manufacturers has suggested a number of procedural changes that are aimed at addressing structural inadequacies.[29] The other general complaint was that the quantum and turnover of guidelines issued by the EMA. Manufacturers stated that despite the extensive guidelines, given the complexity of the process itself:

> There will always be situations where we will have to ask for clarifications.

This is an important response in as much as it seems, to indicate that regulatees view legal certainty as an outcome of a process. Consequently their expectations of legal certainty are not of an absolute value—but more in terms of a process through legal certainty may be gained. Specifically in the context of a highly technological field such as pharmaceuticals wherein research is evolving—regulatees understand and empathize with the ground reality that there cannot always be a situation wherein there is absolute ex ante clarity on rules—therefore the admission that there will always be situations wherein clarifications will be sought.

The rapid pace of rule making and the cumulative impact of the rule in terms of administrative burden was another recurrent theme that manufacturers underlined as a negative fallout of regulators drive for ensuring greater legal certainty. The regulatees seem to differ on this with regulators—who seem to believe that greater legal certainty can be ensured through greater number of rules.

---

[29] EFPIA (2011).

The new Pharmacovigilance legislation was also identified as another instance of overzealous legislation, that failed to take into account the impact on companies. Manufacturers however reiterated that the text of the law was clear—it was only rule application by NCAs that discrepancies and differences crept up. The clinical trials directive was seen as another such an example.[30] One manufacturer described the directive as a

> Mixed blessing – whereas in Italy and Spain it made things simpler. In the case of Germany during pre-legislation – we had to submit documentation without any regulatory feedback. And now discussion is required – and usually the regulator always suggests amendments to the protocol

Thus although overall the legislative texts are clear—devil quite simply seems to lie in the details. Manufacturers felt that at product specific levels the regulatory obligations become unclear as to whether something requires the approval of regulator. In such situations, manufacturers take a conservative approach—maximalist in nature—*let us submit it nevertheless.*

This also helps partially explain the increasing administrative burden on companies. At the sectoral level higher regulatory costs have led to greater consolidation by bigger conglomerates—since the financial threshold for competing in this regulatory space has grown up dramatically. The European Commission is aware of this problem (both at an overall level and specifically in the context of pharmaceuticals)—and has established a High Level Group of Independent Stakeholders on Administrative Burdens to discuss issues and explore solutions.[31] The regulators interviewed also agreed to the overall impression that the administrative burden was steadily rising. He described it as follows:

> I compare the whole regulatory systems as a Christmas tree because over the years both industries and regulators have added beautiful balls to this tree and for good reasons but if you now look at this tree from a distance you see it is unstable and it is overloaded and there is tons of reasons to pull out some of these balls that were important in the past but are not important today anymore because we have other ways of looking at the same problems. And I think the challenge for all of us is how to pull out the unneeded balls in this Christmas tree but maybe also to add some new ones we really need and at the moment we are in my view in this transition phase where everybody looks at this tree and say well we have to pull out something but nobody dare because if you pull out in an erratic way then the whole tree falls apart and nobody is happy. And this analogy from the Christmas tree I use it very often in lectures and discussions on the topic. It is a very helpful way of looking at it because it also highlights that the balls in the tree had their own merit in the past. The people were not stupid when they put it on the tree because those regulators and industry people had done a good job at that point of time. But the times have changed and the situations have changed and I think also the products have changed and also the dossiers have changed. So there is a

[30] The HMA (Head of Medicines Agencies) Strategy II stated that consistency of implementation (in other words rule application) is required in that area of clinical trials. HMA (2010) *A Strategy for the Heads of Medicines Agencies, 2011–2015.*

[31] http://ec.europa.eu/enterprise/policies/smart-regulation/administrative-burdens/high-level-group/index_en.htm.

> real need for transition and we require the regulatory science to really reengineer the whole system.

The industry had also made this point earlier, while participating in the consultation process initiated by the EMEA-CHMP think-tank group on innovative drug development. Speaking on guidelines it had stated[32]:

> More and more Guidelines and Points to Consider tend to be considered as kind of rules/laws. More flexibility and creativity should not be discouraged . . .. Guidelines do not take into account real innovations . . ..innovations do not fit into the guidelines usually. Regulators tend to add but never remove requirements.

This succinctly demonstrates that although the principal stakeholders—regulators and regulatees are aware of the problem—the political costs of seeming to reduce regulatory burden or even rationalizing them seem too high in the context of the pharmaceutical regulatory space. Similar concerns are reflected on the debate on greater transparency—in terms of access to clinical trial data. Public health activists have argued that full clinical trial reports of authorized drugs should be made publicly available to allow for independent analysis of the benefits and risks.[33] Regulators have however argued that "unrestricted availability of full datasets may facilitate publication of papers containing misleading results, which in turn lead to urgent calls for regulatory action."[34]

A majority of manufacturers in fact expect a gradual hardening of regulatory burden—and adopting more precautionary approaches—symbolic of policy measures such as adopting the 'safety first' principle. Risk aversion would then drive regulatory philosophy rather than a benefit-risk balance.

However in terms of regulatory uncertainty, for a majority of pharmaceutical products the manufacturers perceived the regulatory environment to be predictable, consistent, intelligible, coherent and clear. For regulators the outstanding challenge

> Is that the regulatory system is built historically for classical chemical drugs and also for larger pharmaceutical companies – this is evident from the dossier requirements – and upfront costs can be prohibitive

Solutions currently being actively debated include an expansion of the conditional approval system—which would allow manufacturers to access a targeted population at a much faster pace—with the additional obligation of providing proof of efficacy in the targeted population. However regulators reiterated that although there is a need to address specific areas of regulatory uncertainty

> Scientific assessment has to be more consistent, evidence based and data driven – but it will always remain inherently a value driven subjective exercise

[32] EMEA (2007) *Innovative Drug Development Approaches*. Final report from the EMEA-CHMP Think Tank Group on Innovative Drug Development. EMEA/127318/2007, p. 22.

[33] Doshi et al. (2012), p. e1001201.

[34] Eichler et al. (2012), p. e1001202.

This highlights both the technical and personal nature of the assessment and thus there is always some probability of it being unpredictable and influenced by personalities of the assessors themselves.

Another critical area that was highlighted by regulatees was the question of access to regulatory advice by way of early contact and regular interaction between the regulators and regulatees. A majority of manufacturers agreed that over the last decade or so the EMA has become more transparent and accessible—so much so that it is easier to predict a shortlist of potential rapporteurs who would be assessing the application for marketing authorization. However others did differ on this—they contended that the EMA's default position is to distrust the industry and it does not look at the industry as 'stakeholders'—and this is evident from the lack of consultation with the industry specifically in the preparation of regulatory reports—consultations usually happen once the reports has already been finalized—and before publication. Perhaps it was to address the distrust that a majority of manufacturers underlined the importance of building trust between the EMA and the industry. Forums such as the DIA have been instrumental in providing a 'neutral forum' for interaction between professionals employed both in the industry and within regulatory agencies. Collaborative platforms—European Healthcare Innovation Leadership Network and Innovative Medicines Initiative (IMI)—have played an important role in allowing regulators and regulatees to come together and work in collaborative projects and help bridge the trust deficit.

The scientific advice procedure was singled out as critical in gaining predictability in the final clinical evaluation of the application. One of the interviewees remarked:

> Scientific advice procedure is widely used – It gives us a feel and flavor of what to expect from national authorities and heightens predictability

Manufacturers usually adopt a two stage procedure—first, scientific advice from national authorities and then from the CHMP. Manufacturers seem to prefer bigger and more well established (read western European) NCAs, since they have both the expertise and the experience. In deciding to submit MA applications through the DCP and MRP procedures, they show a marked preference for bigger NCAs—since given their good reputation—the chances of acceptability of their assessments is greater.

On the whole manufacturers understand and appreciate that different—NCAs—have different experience, competence and preferences and that the European harmonization is an ongoing project. Therefore they take a sympathetic view of difference in the national assessments of similar (or even same) products—and view it not as a problem of consistency and more a question of subjective assessment that will always permeate pharmaceutical regulatory decision-making. They understand and accept that the European harmonization project will move incrementally and therefore have resigned themselves to the differences in rule application and conflicts in rule adjudication that may arise in the context of member states.

7.6 Analysis and Conclusion

The three sub research questions which were addressed in this chapter were as follows: Is the pharmaceutical regulatory space multilevel in nature? What is the regulatee perception of multilevelness? What are the regulatee perceptions and expectations with regard to legal certainty?

The formal review of the regulatory space indicated that the regulatory space was well structured by the European legislations. Although the ICH was an important actor involved in rule making that operated at the international level—it did not contribute to the multilevelness because the ICH process was driven by European and other international regulators. In the case of rule application there are some differences between national regulators primarily because the DCP/MRP process is regulated nationally and therefore the national regulators have greater flexibility in designing local specific responses. Nevertheless the CHMP—which is the body that includes all national regulators and which functions on the basis of consensus (failing which majority voting is adopted)—has played a critical role in harmonizing rule application and rule adjudication. Therefore overall the formal review revealed that there is low level of multilevelness in the regulatory space of pharmaceuticals.

Regulatee's perception of multilevelness conformed to the findings in the formal review. Although there were specific pockets of uncertainty—clinical trials, pharmacovigilance—primarily due to divergences in rule application between national regulators, a majority agreed that the role of the CHMP has been critical in addressing these divergences.

On the issue of regulatee expectations with regard to legal certainty the key finding is that although the regulatees find the centralized process to be marginally more predictable than the DCP/MRP process, primarily owing to adherence of timeline. This however has not influenced the choice of regulatory pathways. Regulatees understand and appreciate that the European harmonization is an incremental project and that therefore problems of consistency in rule application between national regulators may crop up. Regulatees also underlined that the nature of the pharmaceutical regulatory space is such that there will always be science related questions—as part of the clinical evaluation process—that would need clarification. In this context therefore, regulatees underlined that there is no expectation of absolute *ex ante* clarity. And this is precisely the reason why communication pathways are critical in between regulators and regulatees. For instance the Scientific Advice Procedure was identified as critical in ensuring a direct access channel between regulators and regulatees.

References

Altenstetter C (1992) Health care in the European Community. In: Hermans G et al (eds) Health care in Europe after 1992. Dartmouth Publishing, Leiden

Armstrong KA (2002) Mutual recognition. In: Barnard C, Scott J (eds) The legal foundations of the single European market. Hart, Oxford

Baeten R (2003) Health care on the European political agenda. In: Degryse C, Pochet P (eds) Social developments in the European Union. ETUI, Brussels

Barani L (2006) Hard and soft law in the European Union: the case of social policy and the open method of coordination. The Constitutionalism Web-Papers

Doshi P, Jefferson T, Del Mar C (2012) The imperative to share clinical study reports. PLoS Med 9:e1001201

Duncan B (2002) Health policy in the European Union: how it's made and how to influence it. Br Med J 324:1027–1030

Duncan B, Farrell AM (2005) The emergence of EU governance in public health: the case of blood policy and regulation. In: Steffen M (ed) Health governance in Europe. Routledge, London

EFPIA (2011) EFPIA survey on impact of the paediatric regulation on marketing authorization holders (Jan 2007 – Jun 2010), presentation made at the EFPIA/EMA Info Day, 23 May. http://www.ema.europa.eu/docs/en_GB/document_library/Presentation/2011/05/WC500106718.pdf

Eichler H-G, Abadie E, Breckenridge A, Leufkens H, Rasi G (2012) Open clinical trial data for all? A view from regulators. PLoS Med 9(4):e1001202

Everson M, Majone G, Metcalfe L, Schout A (2000) The role of specialised agencies in decentralising EU governance. Report presented to the European Commission

Krapohl S (2007) Thalidomide, BSE and the single market: an historical-institutionalist approach to regulatory regimes in the European Union. Eur J Polit Res 46:25–46

Nuala M (2012) Agency defies advice and rejects gene therapy for third time. Nat Biotechnol 30:474

Permanand G (2006) EU pharmaceutical regulation: the politics of policymaking. Manchester University Press, Manchester

Permanand G, Vos E (2010) EU regulatory agencies and health protection. In: Mossialos E et al (eds) Health systems governance in Europe. Cambridge University Press, Cambridge, U.K

Permanand G, Mossialos E, McKee M (2006) Regulating medicines in Europe: the European Medicines Agency, marketing authorization, transparency and pharmacovigilance. Clin Med 6:87–90

Chapter 8
Case Study on Borderline Medical Products in Europe

8.1 Introduction

Medical products include pharmaceuticals, medical devices and cosmetics. All these three kind of products have enjoyed public visibility—unsurprising given their potential health impacts. In terms of the scale of regulatory burden, it is highest in the case of pharmaceuticals, followed by medical devices and then cosmetics. Current regulatory debates on medical devices in fact surround this specific issue—that whether medical devices should also be regulated in a similar manner as pharmaceuticals. The medical device industry associations have opposed this move. However one area in which all the principal stakeholders agree that further clarity is required is in the case of borderline products.

Borderline products refer to products that escape regulatory categorization, in other words products which may fall under two or more regulatory product categories. Borderline product also includes those kinds of products that may fall across sub-categories within single products. For instance in the case of medical devices, subcategories could mean active implantable medical device, in vitro medical device or a general medical device. It includes risk categories—Class I, IIa, IIb and III. Thus borderline products would also include those that fall across sub-categories—however in this chapter the focus is on the former kinds of products.

Despite guidance existing at the EU level, national Courts have had difficulties dealing with borderline cases. ECJ has been called upon to clarify borderline products in the context of pharmaceutical, cosmetics and it has ruled on this issue in recent times in the context of the preliminary reference from the German Bundesgerighthof—*BrainProducts Gmbh v. Bio Semi V.O.F. and Others*[1] and

[1] Case C-219/11, Judgement of the Court (Third Chamber) in Brain Products GmbH v Bio Semi VOF of 22 November 2012.

N. Chowdhury, *European Regulation of Medical Devices and Pharmaceuticals*,
DOI 10.1007/978-3-319-04594-8_8,

that from the Finnish Korkein hallinto-oikeus –n *Laboratoires Lyocentre*[2] case. In the former case the ruling failed to clarify as to what constitutes borderline products and lay down some general principles of assessment and regulation, especially in the context of the medical device regulation. In the latter case, the ECJ upheld the right of competent authorities of member states to provide for divergent product classification—thus the same product could be classified as a medical device in one member state and as a medicinal product in another member state. It further clarified that in cases where a competent authority chose to classify a product as a medicinal product already classified as a medical device in another member state, then it has to follow the Article18 (wrongly affixed CE marking) and where appropriate Article 8 (safeguard clause). It also held that within the same member state, a product that is similar to a medicinal product (in terms of containing an identical substance and same mode of action) cannot be marketed as a medical device unless there is some specific characteristic that allows it to be categorized as such—and in this case the verification will be done by the national court on a case-by-case basis. As is evident this opportunity was also left unused by the ECJ to bring more clarity to this issue.

Although there is a definition of "medical device"—that does capture most kinds of the medical devices in the market—borderline products that escape easy categorization have continued to be a problem. This was also an opportunity lost to revisit the jurisprudence developed by the ECJ in the *Hecht Pharma*,[3] *BiosNaturprodukte*[4] and most recently in *Chemische Fabrik Kreussler and Co. GmbH*.[5]

In this chapter I analyze the challenge that borderline products pose to the regulatory structure and propose ideas for national courts to deal more effectively with cases involving borderline products. There are four parts to the book that I forward here. First, that the notion of "borderline products" is itself unhelpful. I explore the idea of border area—that has been proposed by Erik Vollebregt.[6] A "border area" is not only a factually more accurate representation, but it is also of greater utility and allows a relatively more determinative framework for categorizing products that seemingly escape such categorization. Second, the established jurisprudence of the ECJ on this is delineated so as to highlight the paucity of expertise that is required to resolve—what is essentially a science question. Following from this I raise the question, whether the judges are equipped to dispense

[2] Case C-109/12, Judgement of the Court (Fourth Chamber) in Laboratoires Lyocentre v Lääkealan turvallisuus– ja kehittämiskeskus, Sosiaali– ja terveysalan lupa– ja valvontavirasto of 3 October 2013.

[3] Case C-140/07, Judgement of the Court (First Chamber) in Hecht-Pharma Gmbh v. Staatliches Gewerbeaufsichtsamt Luneberg of 15 January 2009.

[4] Case C-27/08, Judgement of the Court (Fifth Chamber) in Bios Naturprodukte Gmbh v. Saarland of 3 April 2009.

[5] Case C-308/11, Judgement of the Court (Fifth Chamber) in Chemische Fabrik Kreussler and Co GmbH v. Sunstar Deutschland GmbH of 6 September 2012.

[6] http://medicaldeviceslegal.com/2011/04/04/from-borderline-to-border-area/ (last accessed 25 September 2012).

with such questions. Third, the legal status of MEDDEVs[7] and the Manual on Borderline and Classification[8] are explored. Together these two kinds of publications are critical tools that are used extensively by both regulators and regulatee to oversee and perform compliance with the directives. They are produced by expert bodies and are supposed to represent the state of the art. However their legal status remain unclear—of course they are clearly non-mandatory—but do they create certain expectations? Domestic courts of the member states vary considerably on the authoritative value of these documents. Fourth, the impending revision and the surrounding discussions will also have far reaching implications for how this issue is addressed institutionally within Europe. I assess the proposals, currently on the table, with regard to this issue.

This chapter is divided into six parts. In Sect. 8.2, I explain borderline versus border area. A crucial part of the criterion for medicinal products is that they should have a pharmacological, immunological or metabolic mode of action—though legally fixed, this is a scientifically evolving category. In Sect. 8.3, I trace the ECJ jurisprudence on the definition of medicinal products, medical devices and cosmetics. And, its acceptance of the fact, that science is not binary and evolves with time. I discuss three possible interventions for better equipping the judges to take science based decisions in this area. Section 8.4 evaluates the legal status of the non-binding guidance documents that play a critical role in this area. Although not mentioned in the legal text of the Directives—they are explicitly recognized in the context of the New Approach directives, in playing a useful function by generating, independent, scientific and state of the art opinion on a range of technical issues. Section 8.5, discusses the implications of the legislative proposals in the Review undertaken by the European Commission. Finally Section 8.6, concludes the explorations in this chapter.

8.2 Borderline Versus Border Area

Article 2(a) of the Council Directive 93/42/EEC defines medical devices as:

Any instrument, apparatus, appliance, software, material or other article, whether used alone or in combination . . ...intended by the manufacturer for the purpose of:

[7] To reiterate MEDDEVs are guidance documents, representing consensus on a range of issues contained in the medical devices directives. They represent the consensual position of national competent authorities, European Commission, notified bodies, industry associations and other interested parties. Although not legally binding, they are expected to be followed because they set the industry benchmark for standard practice. They are published by the European Commission.

[8] The Manual is published in the name of the Working party on Borderline and Classification—a dedicated expert group of the European Commission—and comprised of Commission services, experts of Member States and other stakeholders—who meet on a regular basis to discuss borderline and classification cases in order to ensure a uniform approach. The focus is on a case-by-case analysis of borderline products, rather than on laying down horizontal general principles.

- Diagnosis, prevention, monitoring or alleviation of disease,
- Diagnosis, monitoring treatment or alleviation of or compensation for injury or handicap,
- Investigation, replacement or modification of the anatomy or the physiological process,
- Control of conception

and which does not achieve its principal intended action in or on the human body by pharmacological, immunological or metabolic means, but which may be assisted in its function by such means.

The definition of medical devices is a negative definition—simply speaking: a medical product that does not have a medicinal mode of action is a medical device. It then captures all such products, which do not strictly fall within the scope of the definition of medicinal products. The question of the primary mode of action is a determinative factor in separating medical devices from medicinal products. When the science on the primary mode of action is inconclusive, the hierarchy clause in the Medicinal Products directive provides that the product should be seen as a medicinal product.[9]

Article 1.2 of the Council Directive 2001/83/EC defined medicinal product as:

(a) Any substance or combination of substances which may be used in or administered to human beings either with a view to restoring, correcting or modifying physiological functions by exerting a pharmacological, immunological or metabolic action, or to make a medical diagnosis.
(b) Any substance or combination of substances which may be used in or administered to human beings either with a view to restoring, correcting or modifying physiological functions by exerting a pharmacological, immunological or metabolic action, or to making a medical diagnosis.

The first case, that the ECJ got an opportunity to directly address this issue of borderline products was in 2005 in *HLH Warenvertriebs Gmbh and Orthica BV v. Bundesrepublik Deutschland*.[10] The issue was the distinction between medicinal products and food additives. The classification of the product in one member state was binding on all other member states. First, on the question of determining product classification, the Court upheld the jurisdiction of national competent authorities to decide on a case-by-case basis taking into account all characteristics of the products, *in particular its composition, its pharmacological properties, in the*

[9] Article 2.2 of Directive 2001/83/EC states that; "in cases of doubt, where, taking into account all its characteristics, a product may fall within the definition of a 'medicinal product and within the definition of a product covered by other Community legislation the provisions of this Directive shall apply'." This puts the medicinal products regulation at the top of the hierarchy. This clause is referred to as the 'rule of doubt'.

[10] HLH Warenvertriebs GmbH (C-211/03) and Orthica BV (C-299/03 and C-316/03 to C-318/03) v Bundesrepublik Deutschland, Judgment of the Court (First Chamber) of 9 June 2005.

extent to which it can be established in the present scientific knowledge.[11] Relying on its earlier jurisprudence,[12] the Court also held that, ancillary factors like, the manner of usage, scale of distribution, familiarity to consumers and associated risks should also be considered. There are twin ways of defining medicinal product—by presentation and by function. The pharmacological properties of the product are the basis for ascertaining whether it is a medicinal product. The risk to health is an autonomous factor, which should be considered independently. Most importantly the Court accepted that the current level of harmonization is incomplete (represents an unfinished project) and thus differences in product categorization may exist between European member states.

Hecht Pharma was the next case in which the ECJ addressed the question of what is a medicinal product by function. The classification of a food additive ("red rice") was in question. The first issue was whether the Medicinal Product Directive (2001/83/EC) applied to a product—where it has not been positively established that it is a medicinal product by function—without it being possible to exclude the possibility that it could be a medicinal product. The Court held that the directive does not apply to a product in whose case, it has not been scientifically established that it is a medicinal product by function. The Court interpreted the "rule of doubt"[13] as including ancillary factors (discussed above) that are relevant in determining product classification. Further, except for substances or combination of substances intended for medical diagnosis, a product cannot be regarded as a medicinal product—if it contains active substances, which if used as intended—will be incapable of *appreciably* restoring, correcting or modifying physiological functions by exerting a pharmacological, immunological or metabolic action (emphasis added). The threshold at which a product is capable of doing so is left to be determined by competent authorities of member states. Specifically the Court rejected the distinction between the capacity to exert pharmacological action and the capacity to modify physiological functions.[14] Most importantly the advocate general in his opinion also underlined that—the creeping extension of the scope of Directive 2001/83 to include extraneous products would be detrimental to the free movement of goods.[15]

This was followed closely by the judgment of the ECJ in *BIOS Naturprodukte Gmbh v Saarland* in which the Court got a chance to revisit the concept of

---

[11] HLH Warenvertriebs GmbH (C-211/03) and Orthica BV (C-299/03 and C-316/03 to C-318/03) v Bundesrepublik Deutschland, Judgment of the Court (First Chamber) of 9 June 2005, paragraph 30.

[12] Case C-369/88 Delattre [1991-ECR I-1487], paragraphs 26 and 35; Case C-60/89 Monteil and Samanni [1991-ECR I-1547], paragraph 29; Case C-112/89 Upjohn [1991-ECR I-1703], paragraph 23; Case C-290/90 Commission v. Germany [1992-ECR I-3317], paragraph 17; Case C-150/00 Commission v. Austria [2004-ECR I-3891], paragraph 64.

[13] Article 2.2 of 2001/83/EC—"in cases of doubt, where, taking into account all its characteristics a product may fall within the definition of a 'medicinal product' and within the definition of a product covered by other legislation, the provisions of this directive shall apply."

[14] Hecht Pharma, paragraph 44.

[15] Opinion of the Advocate General Trstenjak—delivered on 19 June 2008 (1) Case C140/07 Hecht-Pharma GmbH v Staatliches Gewerbeaufsichtsamt Luneburg. Paragraph 68.

'medicinal product by function' and also the relevance of dosage in the final determination. The product concerned was incense tablets (referred to 'Weihrauch H 15 Tabletten' in the trade). The court reiterated that *the pharmacological, immunological or metabolic properties of a product constitute, in fact, the factor on the basis of which it must be ascertained, in light of the potential capacities of the product... whether it may be used in administered to human beings with a view to restoring, correcting or modifying physiological functions.*[16] The normal conditions of usage of the product were an important factor in determining its effect—and the fact that a higher dosage may have a significant physiological effect is irrelevant. That the product under normal circumstances may carry a health risk is not sufficient reason for its categorization as a medicinal product.

In *Brain Products* case the primary point of contention is whether a product intended to be used for a non-medical purpose can be categorized as a medical device. The product in question is called 'Active Two'—it is a system than can record electric signals from the brain, heart and muscles—and is primarily used by researchers in the area of cognitive sciences. The promotional material related to the device explicitly states that the product cannot be used for diagnosis or treatment in the medical sector. Brain Products is a manufacturing competitor of BioSemi (manufacturers of Active Two) and has challenged the product categorization and argue that it should be regarded as a medical device and certified as so—notwithstanding the *intended use*. (Emphasis added).

The Advocate General's opinion on this issue can be divided into three parts—the literal as against the systematic and teleological interpretation; determinative value of the manufacturer's intended use of the product; and the logic of necessary outcome. First, a literal interpretation of third indent of Article 1(2) (a) would mean that only products intended for medical use are included. In comparison if we were to adopt a literal interpretation, certain functions of the product—can fall within the definition of the first indent—"investigation of a ... physiological process".[17] However he argues that from the legislative text it is apparent that only products used in a medical setting—therefore used by doctors on patients—are included. Legislative reference in the Annexes also seems to underline the medical aspect of the product requiring certification. Second, product categorization by the manufacturer albeit a subjective element—but is important—because disregarding this would make it impossible to delimit medical devices as a product category—given the variety of functionally equivalent products that medical profession uses—which can also be used in other fields. Nevertheless he adds a caveat that, "any product which, by its very nature, is clearly intended to be used solely for a purpose of a medical nature *will have to be regarded as a medical device*."[18] (Emphasis in the original).

[16] *See* BIOS Naturprodukte, footnote 4 in this chapter, paragraph 20.

[17] Case C-219/11 ECJ. The Advocate General Mengozzi's opinion was delivered in this case on 15 May 2012. Paragraphs 23–29.

[18] Case C-219/11 ECJ. The Advocate General Mengozzi's opinion was delivered in this case on 15 May 2012. Paragraph 63.

Third, the Advocate General contends that if Active Two were to be accepted as a medical device—then it would never get certification since, it is used for research and therefore does not provide any individual benefit—and therefore it is impossible to undertake a benefit risk balance—which is a prerequisite for the certification of a medical device. All these factors, have led him to suggest to the Court that "A product which is intended by the manufacturer to be applied for human beings for the purpose of investigation of a physiological process constitutes a medical device, within the terms if the third indent of Article 1(2) (a) of Directive 93/42/EEC, only where it is intended for a medical purpose."[19]

This logic of the advocate general was accepted by the Court and based on this it ruled as follows:

> The third indent of Article 1(2)(a) of Council Directive 93/42/EEC of 14 June 1993 concerning medical devices, as amended by Directive 2007/47/EC of the European Parliament and of the Council of 5 September 2007, must be interpreted as meaning that the concept of 'medical device' covers an object conceived by its manufacturer to be used for human beings for the purpose of investigation of a physiological process only if it is intended for a medical purpose.[20]

Thus underlining that manufacturer's intention is the determinative factor in this context. This is in distinct from the reasoning used to determine medicinal product categorization—wherein both the function of the product and the manufacturer's intended use of the product is considered cumulatively.

In *Chemische Fabrik* case, the product in contention is a mouthwash solution, which is sought to be categorized as a medicinal product. In this case the Court held, first, that the guidance document on the demarcation between the Cosmetics Product Directive[21] and the Medicinal Products Directive[22] may be taken into account for the purpose of defining the term "pharmacological action." And second, the Court opted for a broader definition of "pharmacological action" as constituting interaction between the substance in question and any cellular constituent present within the user's body (and not just the cellular constituent of the user's body).

The requirement of pharmacological, immunological or metabolic mode of action is a legal concept that needs to be scientifically supported and this scientific support can evolve over time as science evolves. The above discussion shows the developing case law in this area. It is clear from the case law that the criterion of medicinal product based on the mode of action is a binary criterion. This binary choice must however be scientifically supported—and science as is recognized by the Court is under a process of development—and therefore necessarily imprecise and subject of discussion. The problem with scientific evidence is that, as with

[19] Hecht Pharma. Paragraph 65.

[20] See Brain Products. Paragraph 34.

[21] Council Directive 76/768/EEC of 27 July 1976 on the approximation of the laws of the Member States relating to cosmetic products, OJ L 262, 27.9.1976, p. 169 as amended.

[22] http://ec.europa.eu/consumers/sectors/cosmetics/files/doc/guidance (last accessed on 23 September 2012).

scientific theses, it can be subjected to falsification and discussion, about which side has the most correct scientific argument. In this context, the problem of the concept of 'borderline products', is evident. It is used largely as a descriptive category to refer to those products which may fall under two or more product categories as delimited under the directive.

To deal with this problem I argue that the concept of border-area as developed by Eirk Vollebregt is a better tool for capturing the present reality of products escaping regulatory categorization. It also has an additional function of aiding in differentiating between the kinds of products that fall on the borderline and others which may share common characteristics with multiple product categories—but lean towards a certain product category in terms of both presentation (design and features) and function.

Figure 8.1 depicts that by adopting the concept of border area—allows for more design flexibility in two ways. First, it captures a larger number of products with multifunctionality and unclear modes of action. Second, it differentiates between neat borderline products and those which may display dual characteristics but which fall within a clear product category—i.e. it helps to locate medical devices with pharmaceutical characteristics and pharmaceutical products with medical device characteristics. Thus is provides for a finer and cleaner product categorization. A borderline area therefore can do more justice to scientific debates. Since it allows for the building a more extensive categorization with flexibility to reflect scientific developments. Therefore, it is possible that a product currently on the borderline may move towards a more device type or pharmaceutical type of product. This flexibility is especially critical in a sector like this where product development is fast and continuously evolving. The concept of borderline area will also enable the competent authorities to track product development across medical devices and pharmaceuticals with reference to these kinds of products.

Another aspect is the application of the hierarchy clause in the border area. Inconclusive scientific deliberation on whether a certain product is a medical device or a pharmaceutical presents the only circumstance under which the rule of doubt or the hierarchy clause can be applied. The border area should facilitate more conclusive scientific deliberation and will dissuade the application of the clause in the first instance. Advocate General Trstenjak's opinion in *Hecht Pharma* and *Commission v Germany*[23] and Opinion of Advocate General Geelhoed[24] 25 in *HLH Warenvertrieb and Orthica*, have reiterated that the 'creeping' extension of the scope of Directive 2001/83 to include extraneous products would be detrimental to the free movement of goods.

[23] Case C319/05 Commission v Germany [2007] ECR I9811, paragraph 43.

[24] C 211/03 Opinion of Advocate General Geelhoed in HLH Warenvertrieb and Orthica, paragraph 36.

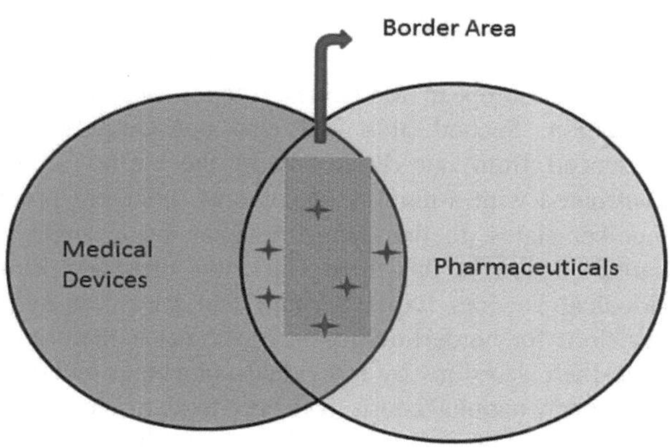

Fig. 8.1 Pictoral representation of border area between medical devices and pharmaceuticals. *Source*: Chowdhury (2012)

8.3 Judicial Decision-Making on Science Issues

The ECJ in its case law has recognized that in many areas science is insufficiently developed to provide clear cut binary answers to legal questions on whether a product is a medical device or a pharmaceutical or even a food stuff. Legislatively this problem has been recognized and partially addressed through Article 2.2—rule of doubt. However this is not a satisfactory resolution—because it essentially transforms the lack of science to provide binary answers to regulatory categorizations, into additional regulatory burden for manufacturers. Therefore in case of doubt, apply the greatest regulatory burden (pharmaceutical rather than medical devices)—this is a better to be safe than sorry approach.

I look at this problem from the aspect of judicial decision-making. The judges are primarily facing a situation where both the parties are able to marshal enough scientific evidence to support their contention. And a judge being usually a legal specialist is unable to sift through and adequately assess the validity of the claims made. Scientific expertise is normally not the forte of judges, which makes them ill-equipped to assess legal questions that are based on the resolution of competing scientific claims. This debate between a generalist and a specialist judge, is in some ways treading old territory. The establishment of separate patent courts—wherein the judges have specialist expertise in the subject—have been successful in bridging this gap and addressing this problem. Therefore the question here is, how best to equip judges to make decision-making in these kind of cases where access to scientific expertise is essential. Herein I consider solutions ranging from, that which require institutional interventions in the Court, to others that make greater use of referencing procedures.

One of the suggestions for accessing scientific expertise by the judiciary has been the establishment of a European supranational body—with both the scientific expertise and the authority to pronounce on borderline products on a case by case basis. Essentially this means the pushing up of product categorization capacities—that are currently under the purview of competent authority—to that to a European body. There are two direct benefits to this solution. First, this would allow for pooling of scientific resources at the European level—similar to what has happened under the European Medicines Agency (EMA) with regards to pharmaceutical regulation. Second, this will also considerably hasten harmonization. As is evidenced from our discussion in the earlier section—the Courts have been confronted with a number of cases of divergent product categorization between member states. In that sense, decision by a single European body will enable harmonization in this area. Currently there are European level expert bodies (Medical Devices Expert Group) that take case-by-case product categorization decisions for borderline products—however there have been frequent departures from their decisions by individual competent authorities. This could also be the reason why national courts have been loath to accept the authority of these bodies. It is therefore clear, that if such a body is established at the European level—it should include representatives of all member states and have the authority to take binding decisions on product categorization. The Courts would therefore have to refer to such authority in case of any doubt.

Another alternative, could be in terms allowing for intervention by the amicus curiae—to be represented by the competent authorities. The competent authorities have considerable scientific expertise and are also have the legal obligation to act in public interest—and therefore ideally placed to provide a balanced and impartial scientific advice to the Court. Such a procedure is possible in the Netherlands. Article 44 and article 44a of the Dutch Code of Civil Procedure respectively, allows the public prosecutor and the European Commission to intervene in cases. Further in cases being discussed in the appeals Court, the national competent authorities (in this case the IGZ)[25] could intervene in pending cases through the public prosecutor. The law therefore provides for such a procedure, which can be used by the competent authorities to provide impartial scientific advice in cases involving borderline products.

Another interesting framework, which could be explored, is that of the cooperation between national courts and the European Commission in competition law. Article 15 of the Regulation EC/1/1003[26] provides for a number of mechanisms through which national courts can formally cooperate with the European Commission in ongoing cases. First, national courts may ask the Commission to provide information in their possession or an opinion on interpretation of the law. Second, the commission itself may also take *suo moto* action to submit written observations to the national court on an ongoing case and if permitted by the court, can also make oral observations. Such a framework for interaction could also be established in the case of medical devices—especially in the context of borderline products. National

[25] The Competent Authority for all medical devices in the Netherlands is the Dutch Health Care Inspectorate (IGZ).

[26] Council Regulation (EC) No 1/2003 of 16 December 2002 on the implementation of the rules on competition laid down in Articles 81 and 82 of the Treaty.

courts in such cases can access scientific information and opinion of the Commission.

Both the Joint Research Centre and the European Medicines Agency are well established public institutions with scientific expertise and could be tapped by the Commission to provide unbiased opinion on such cases. Information requests from Commission could also include other borderline cases that are also ongoing in other member states. This would also help achieve some consideration of parallel national developments and held dissuade contradictory regulatory developments. In the review of the medical devices directives, part of the discussion there is how to effectively deal with borderline products by implanting a supranational procedure to decide on the qualification of a product.[27] As referred to earlier parallels exists between this problem and that faced by judges dealing with patent issues (prior to the setting up of patent courts). Specialized courts with judges with scientific training and/or expertise could be another alternative. This is of course a resource intensive solution. Depending on the scale of the problem—this will however, provide a long-term solution to the problem. As technological convergence becomes a growing reality—products with multi-functionality will become the norm—and the obvious outcome would be regulatory gaps. And technical knowledge will become critical in plugging these regulatory gaps—through judicial orders.

As mentioned earlier the Medical Devices Expert Group was established with the purpose of specifically fulfilling this function of plugging regulatory gaps by undertaking a case-by-case analysis of borderline products to determine which regulatory regime will be applicable. However their effectiveness has been limited by the non-adoption of their reports (in some instances) by national competent authorities, resulting in national variation in borderline and classification—i.e. determining the regulatory status of products.[28] Further, national courts have not been forthcoming in relying on their documents. This failure to consider European publications on border-line products have stemmed from the lack of understanding of the *New Approach*[29]—and the inability to appreciate the role played by guidance documents in the functioning of the medical devices regulatory regime. The following section traces the reaction of the national judges to the unique regulatory architecture of the *New Approach* by reviewing the legal status of these relevant European publications through selective national case law.

[27] See Council Conclusions on innovation in the medical device sector, OJ 2011/C 202/03.

[28] European Commission, Proposal for a Regulation of the European Parliament and of the Council concerning medical devices and repealing Directives 90/385/EEC and 93/42/EEC. Last modified 7 November 2011. Available on the internet; http://ec.europa.eu/governance/impact/plannedia/docs/2008sanco081proposalmedicaldevices en.pdf (last accessed on 29 November 2011).

[29] European Commission. Guide to the implementation of directives based on the New Approach and the Global Approach. Luxembourg: Office for Official Publications of the EC; 2000. ISBN 92-828-7500-8.

8.4 Regulatory Status of EU Guidance Documents

Before elucidating the status of MEDDEV guidance documents, it would be helpful to briefly explain what they are and understand their utility. The MEDDEVs are described on the commission website as:

> guidelines…(that) aim at promoting a common approach by manufacturers and Notified Bodies involved in the conformity assessment procedures according to the relevant annexes of the Directives, and by Competent Authorities charged with safeguarding public health.[30]

These are documents that comment on a range of issues—from conformity assessment to market surveillance and clinical investigation. These are consensus statements arrived at by the principle regulatory participants (notified bodies, competent authorities of member states, European Commission and the industry). As the moniker suggests, these are not legally binding. However there is an expectation that given that they represent a broad consensus on critical issues in the Directives that need elucidation, they would be followed by all the parties involved. This would help fostering uniform application of the legal requirements as provided under the directives. Another important aspect of the MEDDEVs is its currency. MEDDEVs are regularly updated. Therefore they perform a useful function of allowing regulatory authorities (in this case the Commission) to steer the developments in a manner that responds to product developments appropriately. Also as a soft law instrument it harnesses the regulatory capacity (in terms of technical knowledge) of the primary participants as well as creating an ownership dividend for regulatory decisions of the Commission.

The most pertinent document in this context are the MEDDEV 2.1/3 on borderline products, drug-delivery products and medical devices incorporating, as integral part, an ancillary medicinal substance or human blood derivative. This was last updated in December' 2009. And, the Manual on borderline and classification in the Community Regulatory framework for medical devices contains guidance on a number of specific borderline products. In response to a parliamentary question by a MEP—Anneli Jaatteenmaki—the Commission stated:

> In order to ensure a uniform approach within the Community, the Commission services have drafted a Manual that represents the agreed position of the Medical Device Expert Group 'Borderline and Classification' (6) on specific borderline products or categories of products. This Manual will be regularly updated in the light of the discussions of this group. Once endorsed by the Medical Device Expert Group 'Borderline and Classification' the Manual will be published on the Commission's website.
>
> In order to update the MEDDEV guidance 2.1/3, the Commission services have undertaken a broad written consultation of stakeholders through the involvement of the abovementioned expert group, which includes experts from Member States' competent authorities, the relevant Commission services, the European Medicines Agency and industry trade associations. These stakeholders were asked to send their written contributions on the draft revised guidance by the end of January 2008. Due to the participation of the

[30] Available on the internet; http://ec.europa.eu/health/medical-devices/documents/guidelines/indexen.htm (last accessed on 16 October 2011).

> aforementioned interested parties and of experts from competent authorities, it is anticipated that this guidance will be followed within the Member States and, therefore, will ensure uniform application of the directives.[31]

This reveals some important aspects to the status of such publications—in the eyes of the Commission. First is that the aim of these publications is to facilitate the uniform application of the medical devices directives. Second, the Commission expects to be confronted with these problems intermittently and therefore stresses the need to periodically update the manual. Third, the fact that the output is based on wide consultation with stakeholders that represent the principal interested parties—the Commission states creates an expectation of ownership and therefore compliance with the guidance. These aspects reveal that the Commission taking into consideration the regulatory architecture of the medical devices anticipated certain gaps and therefore created an institutional grouping that not only collated expertise but was also representative of distinctive interests—to provide periodic guidance. Thus although these publications are strictly non-binding—there is a de facto expectation of compliance. Does that impose an obligation on member states to act according to the MEDDEV? This will ultimately depend on the national laws of individual member states—that govern policy documents—and Commission lacks the necessary competence to decide on such issues. It ultimately falls under the jurisdiction of national authorities and Courts to rule on this issue.

The status of MEDDEVs is relatively clearer than the Manual. Although both address exactly the same issues, the Commission is technically the author of the MEDDEV—whereas the Manual is only published by the Commission. The MEDDEV is drafted and published by the Commission after consultation with interested parties. These documents are non-binding—but the Commission may rely on them in the course of fulfilling its obligation to give reasoned decisions.[32] However, these documents cannot overrule or pre-empt European or the national courts in the interpretation of European statutes. MEDDEVs therefore only binds the Commission and then too—in so far as it relies on them for justifying their decisions. In *Portela v Commission*, a direct action that was filed in the Court of First Instance, seeking that the Commission should direct a notified body to act in accordance with a MEDDEV was dismissed.[33] Therefore, it is still very much an open question whether the MEDDEVs create any sort of obligation to act in accordance or just to be taken into consideration.

The Manual is authored by a group of experts—Medical Devices Expert Group on Borderline and Classification—comprising of experts from industry, trade association, competent authorities and notified bodies. The Commission is only the publisher

---

[31] E-0355/08, Answer given by Mr Verheugen on behalf of the Commission to the written question by Anneli Jaatteenmaki. http://www.europarl.europa.eu/sides/getAllAnswers.do?reference=E-2008-0355&language=EN (last accessed on 28 November 2013).

[32] Case T-349/03, Corsica Ferries France SAS v Commission of the European Communities. Paragraph 66.

[33] Case C-85/09 P. Order of the Court (Fourth Chamber) of 29 October 2009 in Portela v Commission, OJ C 55 of 07.03.2009, p. 25.

of the Manual if it is found to be agreeable to all the participating parties. Therefore the Manual does reflect a consensus position of all the interested parties—who are stakeholders in the regulatory system and would then be expected to have de facto obligation to apply the findings of the Manual. In the following paragraphs I review the findings of the national Courts on the status of these two documents.

In the *Hyaltech* judgement[34] the Court deliberated on the authoritative value of MEDDEV Guidance. The petitioners had relied on MEDDEV guidance document (No. 6/2 of process) to support the manufacturer's intent as being determinative of product classification. The judge did not support this interpretation. He contended that Guidance was clear that although the manufacturer's claims should be taken into account while determining the principle intended action of the product—it cannot contradict scientific data. Therefore the manufacturer's claim and the scientific data presented by him cannot be the sole criteria for determining product categorization. It was reiterated that MEDDEV documents were authoritative in terms of collating expert opinion; however, it was not binding on a tribunal or a court of law. Despite the MEDDEVs being valuable and a persuasive document, it was a supplement to the Directive, and one could not rely on its words if it suggested an irrational means for deciding on an important issue. Specifically, in reiterating the authority of the Competent Authority (in this case the MHRA), it was noted, that the MEDDEV guidance

> cannot reasonably be interpreted as exhaustive and as fettering the discretion of the licensing authority to examine material which may be relevant to their determination of a matter concerning the vitally important object of the protection of the public health.[35]

The principle of deference results from the recognition that the generality of judicial training impedes it from assessing technical matters. Legislatively the New Approach also reflects this principle. First, by breaking up rulemaking activities into general principles (essential requirements) as legislated under the Directives and harmonized standards (developed by private standardization bodies but recognized by the European Commission). This is a form of legislative deference to technical expertise of non-public actors. The MDEG is also another such grouping that functions at the European level in providing expert advice on a wide range of issues to do with the implementation of the directive. The obvious question is "who do you defer to"? The national courts recognize the competent authorities as repository of technical expertise and therefore are willing to defer to their judgment in specific technical questions—they however seem unwilling to extend this recognition to expert technical bodies like the MDEG.

National courts therefore are aware of their technical limitation and therefore the necessity to defer to the technical expertise of expert bodies—but they only recognize public bodies at the national level—i.e. the Competent Authorities. Thereby ignoring two primary principles on which this regulatory system is based. First, that private

---

[34] Hyaltech Ltd, Re Judicial Review, 2009 SLT 92. Paragraph 71.

[35] Opinion of Lord Macphail, In the petition of Hyaltech Limited, Petitioners for Judicial Review of a decision of the Medicine and Health Products Regulatory Agency. 2007 CSOH 84.

parties play an important role in enforcing public functions and their expertise is sought to be tapped in developing regulatory disciplines within this system, at the European level. Second, the European directives represented efforts at legislative harmonization and fostering the single market. The institutional architecture of the competent authorities overseeing enforcement activities of notified bodies and developing regulatory disciplines through working parties comprising of principle participants, are there to secure these two principles. The national courts perceives themselves (and rightfully so) as arbiter of legal disputes—but are unwilling to take cognizance of the multilevel regulatory framework that is operational in this field. The repeated reference to the public health function of the national Competent Authorities seem to focus attention on an unwarranted assumption that consideration of technical expertise of bodies operating at the European level, may limit (or even undermine) the regulatory authority of national the former from performing their regulatory duties. The refusal to engage with the principle underlying the regulatory architecture of medical devices in Europe and thereby viewing through a prism of a false trade-off, belie the still ill-defined and uncomfortable role that national courts inhabit in the European integration project.[36]

Another option is to follow the Article 18 procedure. Article 18 of the MDD relates to the wrongly affixing CE marking. This can happen in borderline product cases, where the manufacturer incorrectly categorizes the product as a medical device and therefore affixes a CE mark. In such a case, it allows the member state to take institute infringement action against the manufacturer and restrict or prohibit the placing on the market following the Article 8 procedure. The Article 8 procedure is the safeguard clause, under which the members have to intimate the Commission in cases of withdrawal of CE marked products from their domestic market following such an infringement. The European Commission has to make a final determination of the correct application of the safeguard clause, this includes discussion with other member states. This is a cumbersome procedure that can only triggered by action by national competent authorities and essentially an ex post remedy, rather than an ex ante regulatory determination of product classification that is accessible by individual manufacturers.

8.5 From Recast to Review

In May 2008, the European Commission announced its plans for the RECAST[37] later renamed Review, of the three medical device directives along with the six amending directives. The aim of the Commission is to modernize and simplify legislation.

[36] Golub (1995); Pollicino (2010), pp. 65–111.

[37] RECAST refers to the codification of law into a single legislative act. There can be horizontal or vertical codification. Horizontal codification is bringing together all related acts on same or similar subject, and, the latter refers to collating of principle act along with its amendments into a single act. However this also envisages not only textual collation but also substantial changes in the act itself.

Non-uniform levels of protection of public health, expertise deficit alongwith textual fragmentation were identified as the main reasons for embarking on this process.[38]

The Council of the European Union recently discussed the impending Review, in a High Level Meeting in the June 2011.[39] With regard to product categorization and classification issues in the current regulatory system it was stated[40]:

> a simple and rapid mechanism must be set up for accelerated adoption of binding and consistent decisions and the implementation thereof on the determination of products as medical devices and the classification of medical devices in order to address the growing number of "borderline" cases between medical devices and other products subject to different regulatory frameworks (the framework for pharmaceuticals in particular, but also those for cosmetics, aesthetic products, food or biocides)

One of the legislative mechanisms that has been suggested to address this is to turn the medical device directives into a regulation. Although it would only be a change of form, therefore a decidedly lazy enterprise, it would have the effect of making it immediately binding on all member states. More substantively the Commission has discussed a range of suggestions; including extending the competence of the European Medicines Agency (EMA) to include certain key functions that now sit unclearly on the shoulders of working groups and competent authorities of the member states. This proposal has been opposed by both the industry and the member states. The industry fears that it would lead to adopting the pharmaceutical regulatory approaches and approximations.[41] The Competent Authorities have suggested that the RECAST should also focus attention on providing a firmer legal basis for the Central Management Committee or a similar body for allowing a process of regular (non-fundamental) updating of the regulatory regime.[42] Qualified or majority voting on MDEG product categorization and risk classification decisions have also been put forward in order to make it a binding decision.[43]

---

[38] IP/08/723, Commission launches public consultation on medical devices. Brussels, May 8, 2008.

[39] Available on the internet http://www.consilium.europa.eu/uedocs/cmsdata/docs/pressdata/en/lsa/122397.pdf (last accessed 28 November 2011).

[40] Available on the internet http://www.consilium.europa.eu/uedocs/cmsdata/docs/pressdata/en/lsa/122397.pdf (last accessed 28 November 2011). Page 4.

[41] Available on the internet http://whatsnew.eucomed.org/wp-content/uploads/2010/10/101006dppresentationrecast.pdf—EUCOMED has made the argument in support of better coordination and not more centralization (last accessed on 28 November 2011).

[42] Available on the internet; http://whatsnew.eucomed.org/wp-content/uploads/2010/10/1010062.MatthiasNeumannpresentation.pdf (last accessed on 28 November 2011).

[43] Although the proposal for making MDEG determinations obligatory, had been considered earlier as well, but had been rejected because it would dilute the flexibility, that allowed for technological innovation. See, European Commission, Impact Assessment, Annex to the proposal amending Council Directives 90/385/EEC and 93/42/EEC and Directive 98/8/EC of the European Parliament and the Council as regards the review of the medical device directives. SEC (2005) 1742, Brussels. Available on the internet, http://ec.europa.eu/health/medical-devices/files/revisiondocs/entrpedtsiamden.pdf (last accessed on 28 November 2011).

There also seems to some support in having a European determination of product categorization decisions via an independent supranational authority. The Dutch government representative has advocated the setting up of a supra-directive borderline committee, much like the FDA's Office for Combination Products.[44] A multidisciplinary team of experts could administrate an integrated consultation procedure for combination products based on the principle mode of action of the principle intended purpose of the product. To make this possible, the medicinal products directive would need to be adapted to include a consultation procedure for a medicinal product incorporating a medical device (because the medical devices directive already has a procedure in Annex I, point 7.4 for medical devices incorporating a medicinal product). The government will be pushing for the consultation procedure for medicinal products incorporating a medical device and the 'supra-directive borderline committee' as these are two points high on the wish list for the Netherlands to be included in the Recast.

Recently, Jacqueline Minor, Director of Consumer Affairs, European Commission DG SANCO, stated that the 'Recast' of the Medical Devices Directives would probably be a Regulation rather than a Directive.[45] Additionally, during a RAPS (Regulatory Affairs Professionals Society) meeting on 24 October 2011, Ms. Minor clarified that a 'recast' would not be the appropriate legal mechanism, with a 'revision' of the EU regulatory framework for medical devices. This underlines the substantive different nature of the initiative than what had begun in early 2008. On 23 November 2011, the EUCOMED (pre-eminent industry association for European medical device manufacturers), presented a position paper in response to this.[46] On the issue of borderline products; it supported the upgrading the European Commission's current MDEG from a voluntary committee to a formal Advisory Committee. This committee would then establish and oversee the guidance development process. Underlining this policy suggestion is the expectation that a firmer legal basis for the MDEG, would provide greater authority to its case-by-case pronouncements on borderline products.

Another very interesting proposal made by the EUCOMED, that underlined the importance of setting up a mechanism for impartial and high quality science advice, was their support for a joint mechanism that would include the DG SANCO acting with the Joint Research Centre to oversee critical aspects of the regulatory framework.[47] The EUCOMED proposal terms the JRC as independent and experienced in a number of different technologies and therefore a "natural ally" of the Commission in providing scientific advice on medical technologies to national member states,

---

[44] See http://medicaldeviceslegal.com/2011/03/30/update-on-eu-medical-devices-recast-regarding-combination-products/.

[45] See http://www.medtechforum.eu/conference-material/presentations (last accessed on 28 November 2011).

[46] EUCOMED (2011).

[47] EUCOMED; A new EU regulatory framework for medical devices: Six steps guaranteeing rapid access to safe medical technology while safeguarding innovation, Position Paper, November 2011.

commission, existing expert networks and also individual innovators. This proposal underlines that the dissatisfaction with the current system of consensual science that drives decision-making in the MDEG and that has proved to be unsuccessful in addressing the issue of borderline products.

8.6 Conclusion

An important policy formulation which I consider critical is the border area. A border-area construction (as opposed to borderline) products, allows a considerable number of advantages. First, it allows us to capture a larger number of products with multifunctionality and unclear modes of action. Second, it allows us to differentiate between neat borderline products and those which may display dual characteristics but clearly located towards a distinct product category—i.e. it will help locate medical devices with pharmaceutical characteristics and pharmaceutical products with medical device characteristics and thus providing for a finer and cleaner product categorization.

The legal effect or the authority of the MEDDEVs or for that matter all the guidance documents, interpretive statements that are issued regularly by the European Commission and other European level expert bodies like the MDEG in particular can be explored by briefly discussing the case law of the ECJ on the role of community soft law and how it should be considered by national courts.

Does this result in a duty of consideration of soft law instruments as mandatory interpretation aid, for the national courts? In other words do national courts have an obligation to take them into account while interpreting the legality of an action by the national authority which was in fulfilment of their obligation under a European directive? The short answer would be yes. Scholars have however rejected a broader reading of the judgment to include an obligation of consistent interpretation on the national courts. In this context MEDDEVs, are also soft law instruments that are regularly issued by the European Commission with reference to obligations under the MDD. There is therefore a case the national courts to take them into consideration.

Moreover, as discussed in Sect. 8.4, MEDDEVs unlike other soft law instruments are critical parts of the regulatory architecture itself—as defined by the New Approach directives. To reiterate, the regulatory architecture has been designed in keeping in mind three design features, first that it is a highly heterogeneous sector, second, it is driven by technological innovations; and, third, it operates in a multilevel context of Europe and its member states. The first two factors combine frequently to result in regulatory gaps that are best highlighted through the issue of borderline products. Borderline products are in that sense the natural outcome of the limitations of designing regulatory categories that are sufficiently broad to capture product development but also detailed enough to be effective. MEDDEVs and other interpretive consensus tools developed and updated regularly at the European level are designed to address this basic problem of regulatory design. The refusal of the national courts in the earlier cases, to consider MEDDEVs is therefore, not only ignores to the established jurisprudence of the ECJ, it also is contrary to the regulatory architecture as envisaged under the three directives.

The current discussion on the revision of the MDD is at an interesting point, wherein a wide variety of institutional options are being explored. The involvement of the Joint Research Centre is an important proposal and one which is worth considering and pursuing especially in the context of borderline products. As discussed earlier the JRC is in a position to provide impartial (and also of high quality) scientific advice and unlike the national competent authority is also not directly involved with regulatory enforcement. This allows it to not only provide regulatory support to existing expert networks but also intervene directly in legal cases of product categorizations of borderline products. As we are aware the scientific discipline itself could in some cases be unable to provide conclusive answers. Nevertheless having access to clear scientific advice on product determinations—provided under a firm legal basis would be an important institutional step in addressing this problem.

References

Chowdhury N (2012) Limits to the legal deliberation of science questions: a case study of borderline medical products in Europe. Pharm Policy Law 14:157–175

EUCOMED (2011) A new EU regulatory framework for medical devices, November 2011, Brussels. http://www.eucomed.org/uploads/Modules/Publications/111118_eu_mdd_positionpaper_eucomed_final_version.pdf. Last accessed 20 Nov 2011

Golub J (1995) Rethinking the role of national courts in European integration: a political study of British Judicial Discretion. Paper prepared for the Fourth Biennial International Conference of the European Community Studies Association, Charleston, 11–14 May 1995

Pollicino O (2010) The new relationship between national and the European Courts after the enlargement of Europe: towards a unitary theory of jurisprudential supranational law? Yearbook Eur Law 29(1):65–111

Chapter 9
Conclusion

9.1 Introduction

The basic premise of this book is that we are currently witnessing a series of changes that have undermined the idea of sovereign and territorially delimited national legal orders that lie at the foundation of the division between national and international law. These changes may be categorized as horizontal and vertical changes. The former alludes to the increasing participation of private actors in public rule-making. The latter alludes to the structure of rulemaking, rule application and rule adjudication that have been transformed from hierarchical modes to decentralized modes of governance. The two theoretical implications of these developments are the issue of legal certainty and the idea of legitimacy and accountability. As we have discussed in Chap. 1, it is evident that scholars have chosen to focus greater attention on the implications of these developments for legitimacy and accountability rather than for legal certainty. This book is an attempt to redress this imbalance. I study the idea of legal certainty through a sociological lens—in terms of perception and expectations of regulatees (manufacturers) in the context of two regulatory spaces in Europe—medical devices and pharmaceuticals. Thus the primary research question which this book addresses is:

How do regulatees pursue legal certainty in the context of the multilevel European medical product regulation?

The aim of this chapter is to collate the empirical findings of the two case studies in Chaps. 6 and 7 and to discuss the major theoretical implications of these findings. This chapter is divided into three parts. Section 9.2 provides a comprehensive response to the primary research question, drawing from the comparative responses of regulatees on their perception of multilevelness and their expectations of legal certainty in the two regulatory spaces. Section 9.3 considers the major theoretical contributions of this book specifically with reference to multilevel regulation and legal certainty. Finally, given that this is an exploratory study, Sect. 9.4 examines the issue of scalability and the limitations of this study. It further identifies a set of future research questions that may be interesting for researchers.

N. Chowdhury, *European Regulation of Medical Devices and Pharmaceuticals*, DOI 10.1007/978-3-319-04594-8_9,

9.2 Response to the Primary Research Question

The first step towards answering the primary research question was to differentiate between the two regulatory spaces as to where each of them stand in the continuum between multilevelness and a hierarchical legal order, since I was investigating if multilevel regulation has any impact on legal certainty. Therefore a formal review of the multilevelness of the two regulatory spaces was undertaken followed by an exercise to investigate whether the results of the formal review conformed to the perception of regulatees and finally their expectations with regard to legal certainty.

In case of the medical devices regulatory space, the formal review revealed that it would fall on the multilevel side of the continuum which has multilevel regulation and nationally delimited hierarchical legal order located at the two ends of the continuum. The regulatee perception of multilevelness agreed with the formal review. This was especially so in the case of rulemaking (specifically with reference to standardization), rule application (multiplicity of national mechanisms) and less in the case of rule adjudication (although despite the MDEG representing consensus of all principal stakeholders—it did not have the authority to issue legally binding decisions).

In this context, interestingly the regulatees chose to comment specifically on their relationships with notified bodies and regulators. They seem to consider this aspect critical in negotiating multilevelness—in other words operating in a regulatory space characterized by multilevelness. Regulatee relationship with notified bodies seems to be conducted with a degree of openness and negotiation. Apart from the obvious commercial relationship, shared disciplinary backgrounds have allowed for the evolution of a comfortable working relationship that ensures credible expectations on both sides. Regulatee relationship with regulators on the other hand is also undergoing change. Although regulatees generally regard it their duty to *appease* regulators, however they are increasingly challenging the basis of this regulatory authority on the strength of their superior domain knowledge. I use the term 'positional identity' to capture this growing stridency amongst regulatees, that is based on technical expertise—which has received privileged position in the context of regulatory spaces administered through the *New Approach*. Regulators may often be at a disadvantage because they are unable to keep pace with the product diversity and the standardization activities (owing to capacity constraints). Regulators therefore may benefit industry experience which allows them to gain technical expertise which is fast evolving. This result may compel us to rethink certain well established regulatory studies theories. For instance the risks of regulatory capture are often emphasized with reference to regulatory agencies where personnel closely interact with regulatees and wherein revolving door theory of joining industry and vice-versa is at play.[1] However a positive impact of the

[1] See for a good review of the academic literature on "regulatory capture", Dal Bó (2006), pp. 203–225.

revolving door theory may be that it would allow regulators to gain domain knowledge which is critical in enabling them to command regulatory authority.

Regulatee expectations with regard to legal certainty reveal that they find the current system to be predictable primarily by virtue that it is based on a clear classification of risk. This makes it relatively easy to identify products that fall within a specific risk category and therefore the regulatory obligations that are required to be implemented. Clarity in rule adjudication is a specific problem given that the MDEG decisions do not have legal basis and therefore cannot serve as precedent. This is a problem that particularly affects borderline products and is exacerbated by the lack of consideration shown to MDEG documents by national courts and the ECJ to in determining regulatory status of borderline products. Nevertheless at an overall level of this regulatory space, regulatees have been able to gain predictability, clarity and consistency by accessing rule-making via standardization activities. Further growing positional identity that is based on technical expertise has helped regulatees to leverage their position *vis-a-vis* regulators (and notified bodies in rule application) in emerging as partners in regulation (rule making rule application and rule adjudication) rather than passive receivers of rules. This also explains why there is a vociferous opposition by the regulatees (represented by the EUCOMED) to some of the proposals for fundamental change (pre-market authorization system for Class III—high risk category devices) that have been made by the European Commission and the rapporteur (Dagmar Roth-Behrendt)[2] as part of the ongoing review of the regulatory regime.

In the pharmaceuticals case study, the formal review revealed that rule-making, rule application and rule adjudication are administered through the European legislations and therefore there was reasonably clear division of responsibilities between regulators at the DG SANCO and the national regulators. The EMA is driven by the CHMP which controls decision-making on marketing authorization applications and it includes all the representatives of national regulators. Private actor involvement is limited to the ICH and in this regard as well it is the public actors who are in the driving seat. Accordingly the pharmaceutical regulatory space witnesses limited levels of multilevelness and is situated closer to hierarchical national delimited legal orders side of the continuum. Regulatee perception of multilevelness conformed to the findings of the formal review. Common membership of experts in the CHMP and the ICH has also contributed to consensus on substantive issues involved in rule making and rule adjudication and this helped avoid greater divergences amongst regulators and thus limiting multilevelness.

Clinical trials and pharmacovigilance were identified as specific parts that were experiencing uncertainty resulting from inconsistency in rule application by

[2] Dagmar Roth-Behrendt, 'Draft Report on the proposal for a regulation of the European Parliament and of the Council on medical devices, and amending Directive 2001/83/EC, Regulation (EC) No 178/2002 and Regulation (EC) No 1223/2009 [COM(2012)0542 – C7-0318/2012 – 2012/0266(COD)] Committee on Environment, Public Health and Food Safety, 12/04/2013, Brussels.

member states. Regulatees were however willing to tolerate regulatory uncertainty in certain pockets, because there is an appreciation that the project of European Single Market harmonization is incremental in nature. There have been instances in which regulatees have however proactively responded to address uncertainty—like in the case of the functioning of the pediatric committee (PDCO)—in which they set up a monitoring committee of the EFPIA to collate and examine decisions and to put forward a coordinated position to reform the decision-making criteria—which they perceived as impractical. This has been communicated to the EMA and talks are on to reach a suitable solution.

In terms of their perception of legal certainty, regulatees value consistency and predictability in rule application.[3] However they were of the opinion that absolute *ex ante* certainty in terms of the implications of rules is not possible. This was due to the very nature of the pharmaceutical regulatory space. This regulatory space is driven by scientific developments and technological innovation and this shapes product development. As long as they have access to a process by which they can clarify their doubts and thereby gain predictability, they are satisfied. Thus guaranteed access to the process is a pre-requisite for regulatees to gain legal certainty. Their enthusiastic response to the Scientific Advice Procedure introduced by the EMA is a reflection of such an expectation. Similarly, they cultivate greater participation in the DIA meetings which are neutral forums that allow interaction between regulators and regulatees. Regulatees contend that one of the primary means by which regulators have sought to ensure predictability and clarity in this regulatory space, is by producing copious amount of guidance documents. Given that these guidance documents are issued by regulators (and although they have no legal sanction) they carry an expectation of adherence and therefore contribute to the administrative burden. Thus for most regulators, legal certainty has come at the cost of greater administrative burden. The quantum of administrative burden has progressively arisen to current levels that makes it unsustainable for SMEs to function in this market.[4] The analogy of a Christmas tree overloaded with decorations (as shared by a national regulator) is an apt description of this phenomenon.

In terms of a comparative analysis, it is interesting to note that the formal review revealed two divergent findings in the two regulatory spaces. There is an expectation that in the case of the regulatory space of medical devices which is more

[3] This is also evident from the recent opinion of the Advocate General Sharpston in the *Laboratoires Lyocentre case* (Case C-109/12) in which he stated that "Council Directive 93/42/EEC of 14 June 1993 concerning medical devices, as amended, does not preclude a Member State from classifying a product, on the basis of its pharmacological, immunological or metabolic effects, as a medicinal product in accordance with Article 1(2)(b) of Directive 2001/83/EC of the European Parliament and of the Council of 6 November 2001 on the Community code relating to medicinal products for human use, as amended, even where another Member State considers that product to be a medical device within the meaning of Directive 93/42." This supports the view that within the internal market member states have taken divergent views on the interpretation of the Directive vis-s-vis the classification of the similar products.

[4] It is well documented that currently SMEs largely operate only in the ATMP product sector.

multilevel in nature—this will impact legal certainty. However as we have seen in the regulatee perception, uncertainty has been contained to a large extent by their participation in rule making, rule application and rule adjudication activities as equal parties. Thus for regulatees in the medical devices regulatory space legal certainty is a function of access and participation in rule making, rule application and rule adjudication. This is similar to my finding in the pharmaceutical space, wherein regulatees have accessed neutral venues like DIA meetings to interact with regulators in the hope of gaining greater clarity. Both these findings seem to underline that legal certainty for regulatees is contingent on access to a process (which involved interaction with regulators involved in rulemaking, rule application and rule adjudication) through which they can discuss their regulatory obligation in order to gain clarity and predictability. This seems to be especially critical in the case of sectors defined by high technology and product innovation—wherein it is difficult to provide *ex ante* clarity of legal rules by simple rule construction. This is a historical problem that defines the relationship between law and technology—wherein the latter will always outpace the former. In such regulatory spaces, access to forums wherein regulatees can interact with regulators—help in allowing the former to gain legal certainty.

In the case of borderline products the sector is plagued by regulatory gaps that have in a sense emerged not only as a structural problem—the limitations of designing regulatory categories that are sufficiently broad to capture rapid product development but also detailed enough to be effective. MEDDEVs and other interpretive consensus tools developed and updated regularly at the European level are designed to address this basic problem of regulatory design. However this structural problem has been exacerbated by the refusal of the national courts in many cases to consider MEDDEVs. This not only ignores the established jurisprudence of the ECJ, it is also contrary to the regulatory architecture as envisaged under the three directives. By embracing a strictly hard law interpretation of MEDDEVs as guidelines and therefore not 'law', they undermine the purposive role that these instruments have been designed to play—that of establishing an operating consensus amongst stakeholders on a variety of issues—including product categorization.

9.3 Theoretical Contributions

Development of the concept of multilevel regulation in terms of exploring its attributes and operationalizing the concept in the context of a regulatory space is an important advancement of this book, especially given the current debates on globalization and fragmentation of international law that have undermined domestic legal orders. Most regulatory spaces are increasingly aligned vertically crossing national and regional boundaries. Thus there is a trend towards regulatory spaces becoming characterized by multilevel regulation. The concept ensures three things; first, its descriptive function allows us to capture the current processes of regulation as they occur within specific regulatory spaces; and second, it allows us to assess whether significant aspects of this changing regulatory architecture itself results in legitimacy and effectiveness deficits that may arise from structural fragmentation and dispersion that is synonymous with multilevel regulation. And third, in addressing these deficits, it enables us to look beyond traditional constitutional mechanisms that are nationally embedded to heterarchically sensitive mechanisms that are more suited to address leakages in a system operating at various administrative levels—both above and below the nation state.

Legal certainty in terms of calculability of the law—from a regulatee perspective—has highlighted the novel ways in which regulatees have sought to limit regulatory uncertainty and pursue legal certainty.[5] Both the case studies therefore seem to suggest that legal certainty is not only a function of clarity in legislative texts and consistency of regulatory decision-making but also contingent on the regulatee' s ability to access forums in which they can interact with regulators and the quality of interaction between regulators and regulatees. This question of access and quality of interaction is shaped by the legal architecture. Thus in the case of medical devices the nature of the *New Approach* directives have facilitated a greater and growing role of manufacturers within the regulatory process (rulemaking, rule application and rule adjudication)—thus ensuring that manufacturers have been able to gain legal certainty. This provides credence to Habermas's discursive theory[6] that substantive legal certainty for all participants may be ensured if they have procedural rights that guarantee them access to the legal order. Thus in this case regulatee expectation of legal certainty seems to be ensured by way of access to forums in which they can interact with regulators or to actively participate in rule making, rule application and rule adjudication.

The emergence of an epistemic community of experts drawn from both regulators and regulatees, holding common membership of institutions participating in rule making and rule application—has ensured that there is *de facto* functional differentiation between them thus avoiding overlap and norm contestation between multiple institutional actors. Epistemic communities also play an important role in establishing shared meanings and harmonizing rule interpretations. The have had a positive impact on role differentiation. This is specifically relevant in the case of regulatory spaces like medical devices which is characterized by heterogeneity of products and high level of technological innovation. In such contexts where regulatory guidance documents may not be able to keep pace with technological developments—such communities ensure that guidance documents are regularly updated and remain applicable. Such epistemic communities therefore play a role

[5] See Sect. 2.1 page 29 of this book for my differentiation between regulatory uncertainty and legal certainty. However this remains a notional differentiation because it was beyond remit of this thesis to identify a threshold beyond which regulatory uncertainty may challenge legal certainty within a regulatory space. However this is definitely an area which should be explored in future research.

[6] Habermas (1985) at 220.

akin to the Court in legal orders—interpreting legal requirements to reflect social developments.

However it is important to underline the critical role played by these epistemic communities are dependent on ensuring continued membership of the primary stakeholders in these communities. So for instance, the specific *ex post formal* challenge mounted by European Commission against the harmonized standards—i.e. ISO 13485 and ISO 14971—both indispensable horizontal standards—may be viewed as a consequence to the decreasing participation of regulators in the membership of this epistemic community. Thus there is no ownership of these standards by the regulators—resulting in the formal challenge. Representativeness of this epistemic community is an important pre-requisite for it to be functioning effectively in reducing norm contestation in the context of multilevel regulation. In such cases, growth of positional identity amongst manufacturers has also contributed enormously in allowing them to circumvent and mitigate regulatory uncertainty. Development of this positional identity amongst manufacturers can be attributed to the architecture of the regulatory space. By privileging technical knowledge in rule making (through standardization) and rule application (conformity assessment) the legal regime has contributed to the growing authority of manufacturers (since they are the prime repositories of this technical knowledge). Multilevel regulation although has the potential to create regulatory uncertainty—in this case it does not lead to high levels of regulatory uncertainty—and therefore does not challenge legal certainty within this regulatory space. Thus for manufacturers calculability of the law is unaffected by multilevel regulation. Alex Faulkner's emphasis on the constitutive value of law[7] can be appreciated in this context, in terms the regulatory architecture creating spaces and opportunities for regulatees to pursue and access legal certainty.

In this context, empirical evidence from the two case studies seem to suggest that the Weberian proposition that specific formal structural characteristics of law like hierarchy, generality and coherence are critical in ensuring legal certainty, may not always capture the present reality. Causality—in terms of a hierarchic legal system delivers legal certainty—is therefore not as straightforward as was presumed by Weber.

9.4 Scalability, Limitations and Ideas for Future Research

The primary objective of this book was to explore the implications of the horizontal and vertical developments that have challenged the notion of a hierarchically structured nationally delimited legal orders, for legal certainty. Multilevel regulation as a concept was formed to better capture these developments in a regulatory space. And I explored legal certainty in terms of regulatee perceptions and

[7] See Faulkner et al. (2008), pp. 195–222; Faulkner (2009); and Faulkner (2012), pp. 389–408.

expectation, it must be reiterated that as an exploratory study of these two ideas—it was beyond the scope of this study to investigate whether there is any causal relationship between the two. This would necessarily have to be a second order question.

As an exploratory study the findings are indeed tentative. Results of the two case studies demonstrate that multilevel regulation may have an impact on legal certainty—like in the case of medical devices. However regulatees are in a position to negotiate that impact, because the regulatory architecture itself creates spaces and opportunities for regulatees—which they have exercised—that have enabled them to limit and circumvent regulatory uncertainty. On the other hand the pharmaceutical case study demonstrates that although less multilevelness may be concomitant with lower regulatory uncertainty—this has come at the cost of high levels of administrative burden that have meant that only regulatees with a certain financial threshold are able to function in the market.

One necessary implication of these findings is that different regulatory spaces may behave differently—and the difference is not only on how it is positioned along the continuum and the implications for legal certainty—but also specific architecture of the regulatory space may have a significant impact on regulatee perceptions and expectations of legal certainty. European regulatory spaces are presumably more multilevel than others—but even the formal review of regulatory spaces may be inadequate if not followed up by an exploration of regulatee perceptions which may reveal different aspects. Arguably a regulatory space which delivers legal certainty for the regulatees may not necessarily also be perceived as legitimate or accountable by other stakeholders. Thus this should not be seen as a *win win* scenario. Perceptions and expectations may differ across stakeholders—who may not be direct regulatees—but are indirectly affected by the regulations (e.g. patient groups). Limitations of this study are that it was conducted in the context of two regulatory spaces and only a specific group of regulatees (manufacturers). Perceptions and expectations of other regulatees may differ. Scaling up of such a study would entail closer and greater attention to different groups of regulatees.

The limitation of this study provides us with some ideas for future research. The framework of multilevel regulation is useful and may be applied to study other regulatory spaces. The present study focused on regulatory spaces that are characterized by science and technology innovation; it would be interesting to explore whether similar trends can be seen even in non-technology sectors. It may also be interesting to compare the perceptions of different groups of regulatees; between regulators and regulatees in the same regulatory space. There is also a need to explore the relationship between regulatory uncertainty and legal certainty—the possibility of a threshold—within which regulatees may tolerate regulatory uncertainty and beyond which it becomes intolerable thereby triggering demands for changes in the regulatory regime.

All of these issues are interesting for future research. These ideas have actually come out of this present investigation. The preceding discussion in fact highlights that although exploratory studies such as this book are a first step towards investigating novel developments and phenomenon, it is necessarily limited by its design in being able to address and explain a significant albeit only a very small part of reality. However this should not undermine the utility of such studies which in themselves are precarious ventures but with the accompanying promise of exploring an unknown or under researched phenomenon. This book has been shaped by this spirit and hopefully has been able to fulfil its destiny.

References

Dal Bó E (2006) Regulatory capture: a review. Oxford Rev Econ Policy 22:203–225

Faulkner A (2009) Medical technology into healthcare and society: a sociology of devices, innovation and governance. Palgrave Macmillan, Basingstoke

Faulkner A (2012) Tissue engineered technologies: regulatory pharmaceuticalisation in the European Union. Innov Eur J Soc Sci Res 25:389–408

Faulkner A, Geesink I, Kent J, FitzPatrick D (2008) Tissue-engineered technologies: scientific biomedicine, frames of risk and regulatory regime-building in Europe. Sci Cult 17:195–222

Habermas J (1985) The theory of communicative action, volume 1: reason and the rationalization of society, English translation by Thomas McCarthy. Beacon Press, Boston

Annexure I: Questionnaire for Medical Devices Case Study

N. Chowdhury, *European Regulation of Medical Devices and Pharmaceuticals*, DOI 10.1007/978-3-319-04594-8,

UNIVERSITY OF TWENTE.

MARKETING AUTHORIZATION OF MEDICAL DEVICES (COMPARISON BETWEEN GERMANY AND UK)

INTERVIEW QUESTIONNAIRE

For Further details contact:

Nupur Chowdhury
PhD Fellow in Law
Legal and Economic Governance Studies
School of Management and Governance
University of Twente

n.chowdhury@utwente.nl
T: +31 (0)53 489 5482 / 0031 630266054
Skypename: nupurchow

Version 09/6/2011

Part 1: Medical Devices Regulation: rules, stakeholders and important developments

S.No.	Question	Response
1.	What are the Main European/international regulations & guidelines that you follow/implement/apply (product safety and quality)? • Do you differentiate between directives and guidelines in terms of their applicability? • What are your reasons for choosing to follow a certain guideline – or what is your reference point for following a certain guideline – that they are MEDDEVs/national guidelines? • Is there a hierarchy between the guidelines issued by different authorities? • Has there been a case in which – there weren't any appropriate harmonized ISO product standard available – and you developed your own standards to prove conformity?	
2.	Are there additional national/regional requirements that you follow? (in addition to the above) • Are their requirements that are specific to Germany / UK – how can you compare it to other countries – points of difference and convergence? • Are there differences in registration/vigilance requirements between landers in Germany / Britain, Scotland and Northern Ireland?	

3.	Who are the other actors that you interact within Germany / UK and at the European level? • How do you engage with them – forums, consultative committees, expert bodies, etc.? • What has been your experience of GHTF – is it working fine – are there open discussions – how do you benefit from participating? • Have you been involved in standardization activities? What are your reasons for getting involved in standardization activities? • Are you member of any professional network or any other sectoral organization?	
4.	List three most changes (in law/ administrative policy) in this regulatory system – national and European (in the last 2 decades) • Germany Regulatory System: • Administrative rules? • Has your process of interaction changed? • DIMDI database – what is your opinion of the EUDAMED?	
5.	What has been the impact of these changes? (on the powers of regulators/administrative burden on manufacturers)	

Part 2: Perception of the Regulatory System and Strategies for Regulatory Compliance

S.No.	Question	Response
6.	Do you think that the regulatory system is clear? • In terms of what are your obligations under the law? • How often do you face a situation in which you had to consult external advice – from Notified Bodies /industry association/ BFarm/ MHRA? • Classification and demarcation of devices- done by the federal states – is that clear?	
	Do you find the regulatory system to be predictable? • Decisions of lander authorities /notified body assessments/BFarm/ MHRA? • Do you face any specific regulatory uncertainties vis-à-vis specific aspects of the regulatory system within Germany/ UK? • Have you been involved in any litigation – in the German/ UK Courts - regarding this – do they take into consideration interpretations by other German courts and other national Courts in Europe ?	

	Is there a problem with consistency of approach and interpretation of regulatory requirements? • Within Germany/ UK – is there a difference in interpretation and approach between lander authorities? • Between notified bodies – in terms of conformity assessments • European level – between competent authorities ? • What is your opinion of the formal objection system – have you been affected by such actions taken by member states and the commission? • What role has the MEDDEVs played in clarifying matters and in ensuring consistency of approach? Do national guidelines help in this regard?	
	How have you designed your compliance strategy to address these problems? - Internally: Dedicating more resources on regulatory affairs/ location of European Authorized Representative/regulatory intelligence? - Externally: Participation and lobbying through Industry association/specific networks/ choice of notified body/standardization activities?	
	Do you think the experience might be different in other member states / other kinds of companies – e.g. SMEs?	
7.	What are your demands from the regulatory system/ What do you expect from the regulatory system ? – (flexibility/clarity/consistency/ any other)	
	• What are main challenges that you face in the current regulatory system? • Can you rank them in order of priority?	

	• Give reasons for your ranking. • What are the most important cases on borderline products in Germany?	
8.	What is your opinion of the RECAST process initiated by the European Union ?	
	• What impact do you think the proposed changes will have? • How have you sought to engage with the process? • Do you think it will lead to an improvement?/will it have a negative impact?	

Supplementary questions:

- Would you like to share some reference documents on which you base your responses?
- Would you like to suggest other resource persons—who should be contacted for this study?

Annexure II: Questionnaire for Pharmaceuticals Case Study

N. Chowdhury, *European Regulation of Medical Devices and Pharmaceuticals*,
DOI 10.1007/978-3-319-04594-8, © Springer International Publishing Switzerland 2014

MARKETING AUTHORIZATION OF PHARMACEUTICAL

(comparison between the centralized and decentralized processes)

INTERVIEW QUESTIONNAIRE

For Further details contact:

Nupur Chowdhury
PhD Fellow in Law
Legal and Economic Governance Studies
School of Management and Governance
University of Twente

n.chowdhury@utwente.nl
T: +31 (0)53 489 5482 / 0031 630266054
Skypename: nupurchow

Version 05/10/2011

Part 1: Organization details

S.No.	Question	Response
1.	What kind of products does your company manufactures/markets?	
2.	Who are the other companies in this area ?	
3.	How would you describe your organization vis-à-vis other similar organizations? (e.g. is it an SME, or an MNC which is the biggest producer of dialysis machines,etc.)	
4.	How many of your products have got the marketing authorizations? • How many of which have been through central authorization? • Mandatory/optional procedure • How many through mutual recognition procedure?	
5.	Are you a member of any representative body/network that addresses the larger interest of similar organizations/is a forum for exchange of best practice?	
6.	What are the main functions that you perform?	

Part 2: Medicinal Product Regulation: rules, stakeholders and important developments

S.No.	Question	Response
9.	Which are the main European/National legislations (hard law) that you follow/ affect you/ you implement with reference to product safety and quality of your products?	
10.	Which are the national/European or international guidelines and recommendations (soft law) that are applicable to you / affect you/ you implement with reference to product safety and quality?	
11.	Who are the other actors that you interact with? • How do you engage with them	

	– forums, consultative committees, expert bodies, ICH? • Have you been involved in standardization activities? What are your reasons for getting involved in standardization activities? • Are you member of any professional network or any other sectoral organization?	
12.	List three most changes in this regulatory system? • Administrative rules? • Has the process of interaction changed?	
13.	What has been the impact of these changes? (on the powers of regulators/administrative burden on manufacturers)	

Part 3: Perception of the Regulatory System and Strategies for Regulatory Compliance

S.No.	Question	Response
14.	Do you think that the regulatory system is clear? • In terms of what are your obligations under the law? • How often do you face a situation in which you had to ask clarifications? • Do you ask for clarifications to the European Medicines Agency?	
	Which authorization process - central authorization/mutual recognition route to be more predictable?	

	Is there a problem with consistency of approach and interpretation of regulatory requirements? • Across expert bodies within the European Medicines Agency? • How do you cope with this problem?	
	Do you think the experience might be different in other member states / other kinds of companies – e.g. SMEs?	
15.	What are your demands from the regulatory system/ What do you expect from the regulatory system ? – (flexibility/clarity/consistency/ any other)	
	• What are main challenges that you face in the current regulatory system? • Can you rank them in order of priority? • Give reasons for your ranking.	
16.	What are the reasons for choosing a certain route for the marketing authorization of your products? Which system of marketing authorization do you prefer?	

Supplementary questions:

- Would you like to share some reference documents on which you base your responses?
- Would you like to suggest other resource persons—who should be contacted for this study?

MIX
Papier aus verantwortungsvollen Quellen
Paper from responsible sources
FSC® C105338

If you have any concerns about our products,
you can contact us on
ProductSafety@springernature.com

In case Publisher is established outside the EU,
the EU authorized representative is:
Springer Nature Customer Service Center GmbH
Europaplatz 3, 69115 Heidelberg, Germany

Printed by Libri Plureos GmbH
in Hamburg, Germany